Uncle John's
PRESENTS

MoM's
BATHTUB
READER

Uncle John's PRESENTS

MoM's BATHTUB READER

SUE STEINER

PORTABLE PRESS

SAN DIEGO, CALIFORNIA, AND ASHLAND, OREGON

Dedicated to All Moms Everywhere.

UNCLE JOHN'S PRESENTS
MOM'S BATHTUB READER

Copyright © 2004 by Portable Press.

"Uncle John's Presents" is a trademark of Portable Press.

For information, write
Portable Press
5880 Oberlin Drive, San Diego, CA 92121
e-mail: unclejohn@advmkt.com

Library of Congress Catalog-in-Publication Data
Steiner, Sue, 1947-
    Uncle John's presents mom's bathtub reader / Sue Steiner
        p. cm.
    ISBN 1-59223-159-4 (trade paper)
        1. American wit and humor. 2. Curiosities and wonders.
I. Title: Mom's bathtub reader. II. Title.

PN6162.S8264 2004
306.874'3--dc22

                                                    2004044481

Printed in the United States of America
First printing: March 2004
Second Printing: May 2004
Third Printing: July 2004

04 05 06 07 08   10 9 8 7 6 5 4 3

Project Team

Amy Briggs, Project Editor

Allen Orso, Publisher
JoAnn Padgett, Director, Editorial and Production
Victoria Bullman, Copy Editor
Dan Mansfield, Copy Editor
Mana Monzavi, Production Assistance
Lois Stanfield, Interior Design and Composition
Cover design by Michael Brunsfeld
(brunsfeldo@comcast.net)

THANK YOU HYSTERICAL SCHOLARS!

The author and the Bathroom Readers' Hysterical
Society sincerely thank the following people who contributed selections to this work.

Amy Briggs
Myles Callum
Jane Lott
Danielle Markson
Lea Markson
John Scalzi
Rebecca Steiner

Contents

Acknowledgments

I have lots of folks to thank, especially in my family. As a friend of mine so aptly put it after visiting with me while I was writing for the deadline: "Your husband is a saint!" It's true. Thank you, Saint Daniel Steiner and for the saintly puns you contributed too.

A big thanks to my daughters for their expertise. Rachel was a fine researcher. Rebecca wrote and co-wrote articles for the book, especially in the social sciences.

At Portable Press: Very special thanks to Amy Briggs, a wonderful editor who tirelessly—and always tactfully—improved my work and put the text into book form. And I'm very grateful to JoAnn Padgett and Allen Orso for encouragement and for making this book happen. They make the Uncle John series great to write for—and great to read.

Thanks to all the talented writers who contributed: Rebecca Steiner, Lea and Danielle Markson, John Scalzi, Myles Callum, and Jane Lott.

Thanks to agent Martha Casselman and also to Amy Rose.

And a thank you to all these talented folks who encouraged or helped me with this project. Alex Cohen, Sam Fisk, Brad Hennig, Marc Louria, Hannah and Dean Yurke, Kiki Goshay, Ted Andrews, Stephanie Spadaccini, Marty Markson, Silvia Landeros and Kathleen Glaubinger.

Last but not least, to Anne Berkowitz for her advice and patience through months of writing—thanks Mom.

Preface

Why an Uncle John book about mothers? In the immortal words of Shakespeare's *Hamlet:* "There are more things in a mom's world, Horatio than are dreamt of in your philosophy." Okay, maybe Hamlet didn't say that exactly . . . but he should have.

If we've learned anything from writing this book (aside from "Don't chew with your mouth open," and "If you can't say anything nice, don't say anything at all.") it's that the world of mothers is wider, richer, and wackier than even we ever suspected

Mothers really have the power to surprise. Did you know that cave moms were exceedingly fashionable? Or that ancient Egyptian ladies used a home pregnancy test kit that actually worked? How about that the food your mom ate when she was pregnant may have affected your genetic make-up? Certainly none of us ever figured that some moms-to-be would predict the sex of their babies— using Drano!

But if they're often doing the unexpected, mothers are also just what they're expected to be: loving, dedicated, inspired, and inspiring. Elvis Presley may be the King of Rock n' Roll, but Gladys Smith Presley is surely its Queen Mum. It was Gladys who saved up to buy Elvis his first guitar, who nurtured his talent and even helped to shape his sexy, side-burned 'do. Diki Tsering was a simple peasant mother who brought more kindness and compassion into our world simply by teaching those values to her son, the Dalai Lama.

Which brings me to a personal note and the most important lesson that I learned from creating this book. Mothers have an amazing ability to change the world for the better. Rich or poor, scholarly or illiterate, famous or unknown, mothers have achieved greatness simply by doing a good job of raising their kids.

So this book is a tribute from Uncle John to your mom, to mine, and to great mothers everywhere. I hope you enjoy reading it as much as I did writing for it.

Oh, and hi Mom!

Sue Steiner

Foreword

Moms. Where would we be without them? (Certainly not writing this foreward, that's for sure.)

Here at Portable Press, we're just bubbling with excitement and pride over the newest addition to the Uncle John's family.

MOM'S BATHTUB READER

Our new *Bathtub Reader* is a reader's delight, created for and dedicated to those wonderful people who mean so much to us all. Inside its covers, you'll find fun and fascinating facts about:

- Pioneering Mothers of Invention
- Heroic Mums from the Animal Kingdom
- Mothering Through the Ages
- Crying for Mama in Russian, Chinese, and Even Esperanto
- Rating Moms from the Movies—the Best and Worst!
- and much, much more!

Enough *about* the book, we want you to discover the delights for yourself . . . Please enjoy!

Uncle Al
Publisher

P.S. A very special thank-you to our moms from A.O., J.P., and A.B.

Mammismo!

That's-a-my-boy?

Have you heard of mammismo? No, it's not an ice cream flavor or a type of cappuccino, it's a way of life for guys and their devoted mamas. But is it the wave of the future?

"Mammismo," to get formal about it, usually refers to a relationship of privileged dependence on the maternal figure, who is seen as a symbol of protection and safety. To get less formal: When the moon hits your eye like a big pizza pie, that's *amoré*. But when your son stays at home and doesn't go out on his own? That's mammismo.

LIVING IT UP IN THE HOTEL MAMA

In mammismo households, a mama nurtures (some would say "spoils") her sons to the point where they completely rely on her to take care of them—even when they're all grown up. In Italy these days, everybody knows about the problem of mammismo. Especially wives and girlfriends.

Why would a thirtysomething successful businessman still live at home? Why not? Mama has a home-cooked supper ready when he comes in from work. She gets his laundry done, irons his designer shirts, and she doesn't question him when he goes out. Oh, and some mamas even serve coffee in bed every morning. That's classic mammismo.

As for the son who has such a bad case of can't-leave-mom-itis, he has a name too. He's a "mammoni."

Mammismo and mammoni. They're a phenomenon that's on the rise.

CAN YOU ANSWER THIS SURVEY OR DO YOU NEED MOM'S HELP?

In 2000, the Italian National Statistics Institute took a survey that revealed what a lot of frustrated single Italian women already knew. Seventy percent of unmarried Italian men reached the age of 30 while still living at home with mama. That percentage rose sharply in the 1990s and shows no signs of falling.

Over 30 percent of unmarried Italian men between 30 and 34 still live at home, and even when they marry, many still find it hard to say *ciao* to mom. The Institute's survey also found that 43 percent of all married children live within a half-mile of their mama's house. Some guys even stayed with their mama after they were hitched. Oh, and 70 percent call their moms every day.

INVESTIGATING MAMMISMO

So why are Italian sons and mothers so inseparable? Since ancient times the bond between an Italian man and his mother has been strong. A mammoni will often say that his mother is happiest when she's waiting on him, and he'll be right. Italian mothers have been known to equate devotion with coddling, and many would feel mortified if sonny had to make his own lasagna. When mama is reluctant to cut the cord and her boy is reluctant to give up home-cooked pasta, mammismo is the result. But other factors contribute to it as well. Factors like euros.

Italians are better educated than ever, attending universities in large numbers. But scholarships and financial aid are hard to come by. Many students are dependent on their parents while in school and may remain so after graduation. When stiff job competition meets long periods of unemployment, lack of funds can force children of both sexes back to their mothers' homes.

Since many Italian homes are not as authoritarian as they once were, most adult children report that they can come and go as they please. For an Italian man, this combination of economic benefits and individual freedom is sweetened with the strong traditional tie between himself and his mother. It all adds up to a down-home life with mama. And, say many Italians, if it makes both mother and son happy . . . hey, what's-a so bad?

MAMA-IN-LAW-MISMO

More and more Italian guys vote for mammismo with their seats (they sit down at their mom's dinner table and don't leave), but not everyone is happy with the cultural phenomenon. Psychologists warn that mammismo encourages a long adolescence, postponing a man's ability to become independent and meet life's challenges. Indeed, some mama's boys will never break away, choose a partner, and create a family of their own.

Italian women often complain that they must impress their sweetie's mother to get anywhere with him. Some say they hold second place in their man's heart, with first place reserved for mama. And since so many guys refuse to move far from their devoted mothers, daughters-in-law can find themselves competing over who should feed, clothe, and spoil their man.

When both husband and mother-in-law agree that mama should still have the pleasure of doing hubby's laundry and cooking his dinner, new wives get frustrated. When he takes mama along on vacation—well, sometimes that's the last straw . . . or noodle.

Since extreme mammismo can put a stress on marriage, in 2003 the Italian courts weighed in on the side of wives. They ruled that an overbearing and interfering mother-in-law could be considered grounds for divorce.

THE WAVE OF THE FUTURE?

But will the court ruling put a dent in the trend toward more mammismo? Hard to say. Mama continues as a force to be reckoned with—and not just in Italy. Belgium is experiencing a trend of adult children staying closer to their parents. In the 1980s, 50 percent of Belgian 18-year-olds left home. These days the figure is closer to 20 percent. In Spain, half of the male 28-year-olds are still *viviendo con* mama. Even more traditionally independent-minded British and American kids are residing longer at *chez* you-know-who. We'll be watching and waiting to see if mammismo truly goes global or if mamas eventually go crazy from all those darn grown kids in the house!

"A man loves his sweetheart the most, his wife the best, but his mother the longest." —Irish proverb

Goddesses, Saints, and Moms

*On Mother's Day, get in the spirit of ancient times
and treat mom like a goddess!*

In ancient times mothers were greatly honored—sort of. In many ancient religions, the "Great Mother" was the dominant figure, worshipped under many names: Isis in Egypt, Ishtar in Babylonia, Rhea in Greece, and Cybele in Rome. And that's just to mention a few. She was the creative force in nature, a symbol of fertility, and the mother of all things.

But if there was great reverence for the Great Mother, then what about the ordinary mom? The one who spent all day cooking and cleaning and taking care of the kids—not to mention working in the fields or at a loom or spinning wheel? Did she get any respect?

A TASTE OF HONEY

The first known celebrations that honored mom (more or less) were held in ancient Greece. Individual mothers got glory—even if it was just reflected glory. Ancient Greeks honored their divine mother goddess, Rhea, every spring. They held celebrations at dawn, replete with flowers, wine, and honey cakes. It was the beginning of traditions that eventually resurfaced in modern times. Moms who get flowers and breakfast in bed can thank the ancient Greeks.

WHEN IN ROME, PARTY LIKE THE MOMS DO

By 250 BC the Romans decided that if the Greeks could honor Rhea as the mother goddess, Rome would darn well honor Cybele, their mother of the Roman pantheon (after all, why should the Greeks have all the wine and honey cakes?). Then, when the citizens of Rome began honoring Cybele, they acted with typical Roman restraint, which is to say no restraint at all. They threw a huge party for her.

Rites to honor Cybele lasted a wild three days, from March 22 to March 25. On the 25th, there was a *hilaria*, or "celebration." The hilaria featured parades and games dedicated to Cybele. In the evening, Romans indulged in feasts, disguised themselves for masquerades, and in general partied very hearty.

FROM SINNING TO SAINTS

Scholars believe that when Christianity came to Rome, Cybele's spring romp formed the basis of a new religious holiday. In an attempt to woo pagan followers, the church adapted Christian celebrations to resemble the pagan ones. In place of celebrating Cybele, Christians devoted a day to Mary, the mother of Christ. So in the spring, instead of racy fertility rites and masquerades, people honored Mary by bringing offerings to church one day during Lent.

As Christianity spread to the British Isles, Brigit, a Celtic mother goddess, began to fade from public memory when people began to honor St. Brigid, the patron saint of students, milkmaids, blacksmiths, and healers. Among her miracles was the ability to make her cows produce milk three times a day! It's no wonder that her symbol is the cow. St. Brigid put a very different spin on the day, since she'd turned down many good offers of marriage to become a monastic nun.

MUM FINALLY GETS A VISIT

Despite all this reverence and revelry for the Western mother, it wasn't until the 1600s that a day actually focused on ordinary mothers. (And about time too!) In England, Mothering Sunday was the first holiday that really resembled our modern Mother's Day. On Mothering Sunday, the fourth Sunday in Lent, hardworking folks like domestic servants were given a special day off so they could go home to visit their mum.

On Mothering Sunday, children would also "go a-mothering," which meant they returned home carrying small gifts to thank their mums. These gifts might include a small bouquet of flowers or a "mothering cake." This was usually a fruitcake known as a "simnel cake" (the word "simnel" came from a type of flour and had nothing to do with mum).

Special dinners also played a part in the family reunion. In 17th-century England, mum might serve frumety, a kind of wheat pudding made with wheat grains boiled in sweet milk and flavored with sugar and spices. In Scotland, dinners featured "carlings," a type of pancake. Eventually the name "Carling Sunday" became the Scottish name for Mothering Sunday.

But no matter what they called her day, very likely Mom was glad to finally get a visit.

TV Moms I: The Perfect Years

Get ready for those 1950s moms—with perfect hair, aprons, and pearls!

Nobody claims that watching TV is the best way to study history. But then again, you can just about track the changing attitudes toward motherhood by tracking the changing roles of moms on television. In tribute to all those TV moms, we're happy to recall some of our favorites, beginning with the batch that started it all!

HARRIET NELSON: REALLY PERFECT

The Show: *The Adventures of Ozzie & Harriet* (1952–1966) It may surprise you that the first TV mom married to an Ozzie was Harriet (not Sharon!). Harriet was the eminently sensible mother and housewife of *The Adventures of Ozzie & Harriet*, a long-running sitcom about the Nelson family. The show was one of the first sitcoms and a forerunner of the reality TV shows of today. Even though the episodes were fictional, they featured the real-life Nelson family starring as themselves. Even the house the TV family lived in was modeled on the Nelsons' real-life home.

Of course the TV show wasn't exactly realistic when it came to the portrayal of Harriet Nelson. On TV, Harriet was a housewife who never seemed to stray far from the kitchen, but the real Harriet was a working mom who spent long days at the studio.

Fun Fact: *The Adventures of Ozzie & Harriet* actually started out as a radio show in 1944.

JUNE CLEAVER: PERFECTLY DRESSED

The Show: *Leave It to Beaver* (1957–1963)

June Cleaver (played by Barbara Billingsley) was the stylish mom married to Ward Cleaver in *Leave It to Beaver*. Most of the stories in the series revealed how June and Ward and their older son, Wally, coped with the misadventures of young Theodore, a.k.a. the Beaver.

Whenever June appeared (whether she was handing Beaver his lunch box, tucking him into bed, or vacuuming the living room rug) she was dressed to the nines, sporting a fancy string of pearls and usually wearing heels. Mrs. Cleaver never had a bad hair day and never lost her temper.

The Cleavers were the ideal family, and to this day, when you say nuclear family, many people immediately envision the Cleavers—two kids, a dad who works, and a mom who stays home to take care of the kids and the house. (Though the pearls are optional.)

Fun Fact: *Leave It to Beaver* aired its very first episode on October 4, 1957, the same day that the Soviet Union launched *Sputnik I*.

DONNA REED: PERFECTLY WHOLESOME

The Show: *The Donna Reed Show* (1958–1966)

On *The Donna Reed Show*, Donna Stone (played by Donna Reed) adopted a daughter after her oldest girl went off to college. Living in the appealing small town of Hillsdale,

Donna was another stay-at-home mom with three kids and a pediatrician husband, Dr. Alex Stone. Her wholesome family relied on her to help them out with family misunderstandings, as well as school and dating woes.

Like her counterparts Harriet and June, Donna was a stay-at-home mom, but she was more involved in the lives of her friends and those in her community—even in her husband's problems. Viewers liked Donna's friendly, warmhearted ways and considered her a perfect wife and mother.

Fun Fact: Few series fans realized that the actress was actually one of the first female TV executives; Donna Reed was an uncredited director and coproducer of her own show.

In March 2003, a huge snowstorm shut down the Front Range along the eastern slope of the Rockies. Forced to stay at home, people huddled very close together for warmth! The Colorado blizzard yielded a lot more than snow and snowboard rentals. The result? A baby surge 9 months later! Lynne Snyder of the Avista Adventist Hospital in suburban Louisville, Colorado, said it was not unusual, since an up-tick in births often followed major events, like when the Denver Broncos win the Super Bowl.

Saving Kitty's Litter

*The brave feline mother who nearly died—not once,
but five times—to save her kittens demonstrates
the true meaning of mother's love.*

A NEAR CAT-ASTROPHE

The scrawny calico cat was living the hardscrabble existence of a stray in a gritty neighborhood in Brooklyn, New York. She would have remained one of the thousands of nameless stray cats had it not been for her heroic actions on March 29, 1996. On that fateful date, the calico had been tending her five kittens, born just four weeks before, when the abandoned garage she had made her home in suddenly burst into flames.

As the fire raged, firefighters were shocked to observe the plucky mom, though seriously burned herself, repeatedly brave the inferno—emerging each time with another of her kittens. She carefully placed each kitten just outside the door before going back for the next. When all five were safely outdoors, she began taking them, one by one, across the street, farther away from danger.

At four weeks old, the kittens could never have survived the blaze had it not been for their mother's loving attention. But the mother cat was severely injured. Her eyes were blistered shut and she could not see. The pads of her paws were scorched and her ears and nose were singed. There were bare patches on her face and body where the fur had been burned off.

RESCUING THE RESCUER

David Gianelli was one of the firefighters on duty the night of the garage fire. An animal lover, he was touched by the little cat's courage and determination. As soon as the fire was contained, he found a cardboard box and gently transported the mother and her kittens to the North Shore Animal League in Port Washington on Long Island. During the trip, the calico cat kept touching each of the kittens in turn. Even though she couldn't see them, it seemed as though she were counting them to make sure they were all right.

By the time they reached their destination, the mother cat was barely alive and two of her kittens were in bad shape. The doctors at the Animal League worked feverishly to save them. League workers named the brave little mother Scarlett after the red patches of skin showing where the fur had burned away.

Scarlett needed oxygen to breathe, intravenous antibiotics to fight infection, drugs to combat shock, and antibiotic ointments for her skin. Despite the odds, she began to improve within a couple of days of constant care. When the swelling around her face dissipated, she was able to open her eyes; to everyone's surprise, she was able to see again. Eventually the tips of her ears had to be amputated, but her recovery from her ordeal was deemed miraculous.

Only one of the kittens succumbed to pneumonia as a result of smoke inhalation. The others made a full recovery.

A FAMOUS FELINE

News of Scarlett and her exploit spread quickly as tales of her bravery were featured on numerous news broadcasts and television talk shows. North Shore Animal League was deluged not only with local requests for news and offers to adopt her and her kittens but also those from around the world, from as far away as South Africa and Japan. With over 1,500 adoption offers, Marge Stein, manager of public relations at the Animal League, held a contest to find Scarlett and the kittens the best home.

A PURR-FECT ENDING

From the thousands of entries they received, the Animal League selected Karen Wellen to be Scarlett's proud owner. Wellen had written of her great empathy with the cat. Having survived a car accident, which left her with a slight disability, Wellen felt that she and Scarlett had much in common.

Today Scarlett is living a life of ease at the Wellen residence in Brooklyn, a far cry from the Brooklyn she used to know. Her life couldn't be more different from her existence on the streets. She is healthy, has gained weight, and only occasionally appears somewhat distressed at the sound of fire sirens. Scarlett's four surviving kittens have also found good adoptive homes with families in New York.

SCARLETT'S HONORS

Even after adoption, Scarlett continued to be honored for her exemplary motherhood. In 1999, the IAMS pet food company named Scarlett "the Top Cat of the Century," after she won 29 percent of the vote online. On September 19, 2000, she won the first Scarlett Award for Animal Heroism, which was named after her. The award-winning cat has even had two books written about her.

Perhaps the most touching tribute of all came on May 12, 1996. The New York *Daily News* printed part of a poem composed by one of Scarlett's many admirers. The poem is titled, "The Heroine," and reads in part:

Why is everyone so surprised that I saved my furry five
That in spite of pain and danger, I brought them out alive...
Every trip was a burdened choice but I could make no other
The rescuers have called me cat, but I am also mother.

"I looked on child-rearing not only as a work of love and duty but as a profession that was fully as interesting and challenging as any honorable profession in the world and one that demanded the best that I could bring it." —Rose Kennedy

"God could not be everywhere and therefore he made mothers." —Jewish proverb

Bringing Up Baby

*A trip around the world shows that there's
more than one way to be a great mom to your baby.*

Any new mom will tell you that everyone from grandma to a stranger in a grocery store has an opinion on the best way to care for babies. From the moment of conception to the utterance of a first word, everyone is quick to offer advice.

But are there any right answers? A quick look at the traditions of the world's moms shows that different cultures have very different ideas on what makes a good mother.

DINNER FOR TWO, PLEASE!

Pregnant moms in England and the United States know about eating right when there is a baby on the way. They avoid alcohol, eat a balanced diet, include plenty of protein, and take supplements like folic acid and iron. In India, cautious moms may avoid foods traditionally believed to cause miscarriage or premature delivery, such as meat, eggs, fish, onions, garlic, pineapple, mangoes, and blackberries.

In the West, pregnant mothers are urged to stay active, advice that is taken by moms worldwide. In Vietnam, a pregnant woman is careful not to sleep too much because that is believed to prolong the labor. Instead, to stay strong she will continue to do her housework to keep those labor pains as short as possible.

EDUCATION BEGINS AT CONCEPTION

Many Vietnamese mothers believe in prenatal awareness and try to teach their children even before they are out of the womb. Ideally, a mother listens to sweet music to help enhance her baby's artistic and musical skills. They'll also stay away from horror stories and scary films or pictures, as they can affect the mind of her baby-to-be. Even etiquette can be learned as an embryo; moms are careful to avoid bad attitudes and practice good manners so that their kids will be positively polite too.

In the United States, some pregnant mothers are going after the "Mozart Effect." Two scientists from the University of California-Irvine found that a group of college students had a temporary increase in spatial-temporal reasoning after listening to Mozart. Their current research has shown that listening to Mozart heightens brain function in preschoolers. Anxious to get in on the action, pregnant mothers are listening to Mozart and hoping their unborn babies reap the benefits in the womb. So if toddlers start humming along to *The Magic Flute*, those moms may be on to something.

SMOKING IS BAD FOR BABIES—OR IS IT?

Smoking cigarettes while pregnant is a big no-no. But what about smoking your baby after it's born? Don't worry, "smoking" a baby means exposing him or her to smoke from a smoldering fire so that he or she can be purified by it. In Australia, Warlpiri women purify a newborn baby with smoke from buring acacia leaves. Held high above the fire so as not to burn him or her, the baby is exposed to smoke—first the backside, then the front. In India babies are also "smoked" but benzoin is added to a fire so that the smoke contains antibiotic properties.

BABY, RELIEVE THYSELF!

For those predisposed to diapers, in the West moms can choose between cloth diapers or disposable paper and plastic. Nepalese babies have diapers made of soft yak hair. The Inuit might use lichen or rabbit skin.

Some moms forgo diapers altogether. Many African mothers who carry their babies much of the day are quick to sense when a baby needs to relieve him- or herself. Mom is even quicker to move baby from her chest or back and place him or her in a squat on the ground

When it comes to more developed bathroom behavior, has anyone ever agreed? The American Pediatric Society states flatly that children younger than 12 months have no control over bladder or bowel movements and little control for six months or so after that. In the United States, moms are urged not to begin toilet training until 18 months at the very earliest. Some Beng mothers from the Ivory Coast of Africa begin toilet training their children when they're as young as 3 or 4 months! Apparently they're not listening to the American Pediatric Society much!

RUB-A-DUB

Keeping babies clean, soft, and smelling good is a common aim among moms. How they go about it can be quite different. Mothers in Africa and Asia put herbs in the babies' bathwater to keep them smelling good. And if you think you keep your baby clean, tell it to a Beng mother. She scrubs her baby at least twice a day, believing it's as important as feeding him. In India, some mothers don't consider a baby's bath complete until they've blown water into the ears, nose, eyes, and mouth to clear them.

Western mothers often smooth a lotion on a baby after a bath. But not all moms have access to running water or baby lotion, so they resort to homemade remedies. In Africa, a Masai mother will warm water in her mouth before spitting it in a strong stream to shower over her infant. New Caledonian mothers chew herbs into a lotion and then spit them out to rub on a young infant's skull.

Some Western moms are going to classes to learn a skill that Dogon mothers in Mali have developed over centuries—baby massage. Western moms are often encouraged to give their babies a massage before bedtime. Dogon mothers finish each baby bath with a massage. Indian mothers will also massage a baby all over its body after a bath.

GO, BABY, GO!

Because moms are on the go, baby often comes along for the ride. When they go out on errands, Western moms often hop into the car and baby goes along in a car seat. If mom is on foot, baby still may be on wheels—in the stroller.

Nepalese mothers take their little ones to the field in portable cradles. When the mothers of the Ache tribe in Paraguay need to work, they carry their baby in a sling until he or she is about 18 months old, at which time the baby graduates to riding in baskets. Because they live in dangerous terrain, busy Ache moms carry their children until they're five years of age. Other moms, like those of the Arapesh of New Guinea, get their babies off their backs earlier—at about three years.

LULLABY AND GOOD NIGHT!

In many industrialized nations, moms train their infants to sleep in a crib. In Holland, Dutch moms emphasize quiet routines for their babies during the day so that they'll be able to follow a nighttime schedule. But in industrialized Japan, moms and dads share their bedrooms with the babies and kids too. Kung San mothers sleep with their babies. In South America, Yanomamo babies sleep with their mothers until they are weaned and then graduate to hammocks of their own. In Russia, Scotland, Australia, Africa, South America, Polynesia, and other cultures all around the world, moms are softly singing lullabies to urge baby to sleep.

ANY RIGHT ANSWERS?

So what have we learned? It seems there aren't any hard and fast rules when it comes to baby care. Try everything and settle on what works for you and your baby—no matter where your family comes from!

"The lullaby is the spell whereby the mother attempts to transform herself back from an ogre to a saint."
—James Fenton

You Know, That Song Called "Mother"?

Know how many songs are titled "Mother"? A lot. We listened to some of them, both famous and obscure, to see if you'd want to play any of them for your own mother. Here's what we've got.

"Mother" by Tori Amos (album: *Little Earthquakes*, 1992) **What it sounds like:** A piano line nicked from a Charlie Brown special, while the red-haired one begs her mother to leave a light on before Tori goes out into the big bad world.
Play for mom? Sure, it's a great song for letting mom know you'll always need her. Perfect for the night before your wedding. At the very least, the tinkly piano will mellow both you and mom out.

"Mother" by Burning Spear (album: *Man in the Hills*, 1976)
What it sounds like: A vast reggae groove sweeping over the land, as Burning Spear relates the wisdom his mother passed down to him.
Play for mom? You bet. Everyone can use some reggae —even moms.

"Mother" by Danzig (album: *Danzig*, 1988)
What it sounds like: Goth metal rocker warns mothers of the world not to let their kids be like him (which is to say, short, hairy, and shirtless), while the band apes Deep Purple.
Play for mom? Does your mom ride Harleys, hang out with outlaws, and pick hard-rock songs on the jukeboxes to start bar fights by? No? Then, no.

"Mother" by E-Trance
(album: *E-Trance*, 1995)
What it sounds like: Like this Japanese art-rock group is playing guitars with kitchen sinks and armadillos. There are lyrics—in English, even—but they're too distorted to make out.
Play for mom? Only if you're testing to see how long she can politely listen to white noise before telling you to turn it off.

"Mother" by Cyndi Lauper
(album: *Sisters of Avalon*, 1997)
What it sounds like: Surprisingly atmospheric, with a world-beat vibe (including pipes and talking drums). It's a long way from "Girls Just Wanna Have Fun."
Play for mom? Heck, yeah. Your mom probably already likes Cyndi. What could possibly go wrong?

"Mother" by Mission Man
(album: *Into My Mind*, 1998)
What it sounds like: A guy standing in front of a karaoke machine, rapping out his memories of his deceased

mother in a sludge-paced rap. Both sad and bad.
Play for mom? Not even if your mom is a hip-hop queen. Really. No.

"Mother" by Anika Moa
(album: *Thinking Room*, 2002)
What it sounds like: Just lovely. Moa has a sweet, evocative voice, and this lilting appreciation of mother would be perfect for a very special episode of the *Gilmore Girls*.
Play for mom? Oh yeah. It's a total parent-child four-minute bonding experience. She'll get teary and everything.

"Mother" by Pink Floyd
(album: *The Wall*, 1979)
What it sounds like: Years of therapy imploding over the course of just one song! But also nicely melodic and pretty to the extent any song about an overbearing mother smothering her son can be.
Play for mom? If she's a prog-rock gal, yes (and you know, a surprising number of moms are). Otherwise, you're going to have to explain why you're suggesting she's suffocating you. Have fun with *that*.

"Mother" by Sally Rogers (album: *Generations*, 1989) **What it sounds like:** Broadway musical–like tune about putting stars on strings and saving various mementos to share with dear ole mom. Lots of piano. Inoffensively pretty. **Play for mom?** Sure. Especially if she digs Sondheim.

"Mother" by Barbra Streisand (album: *Barbra Joan Streisand*, 1972) **What it sounds like:** Are you kidding? It sounds like *Barbra*. Only Barbra could make this song about parental disappointment sound like a glorious anthem of freedom. **Play for mom?** Yup. It's not a "happy mom" song, but that will get ignored because of The Voice.

"Nobody loves me but my mother, and she could be jivin' too." —B.B. King

"My mother told me I was blessed and I have always taken her word for it." —Duke Ellington

"Mama was my greatest teacher, a teacher of compassion, love and, fearlessness. If love is sweet as a flower then my mother is that sweet flower of love." —Stevie Wonder

The Classic Moms

Classic Athenian and Spartan moms were
different from each other as night and day

Four thousand years ago, the Greeks may have been speaking the same language, but they weren't ruled by one king or queen. They lived in city-states, all with their own politics, traditions, and customs. For moms and their kids, life was very different in the city-state of Athens than it was in the city-state of Sparta.

ALIENATED ATHENIANS

Athens is famous as the "cradle of civilization." The Athenians gave the classical world cultural gifts: great art, architecture, and theater. They also began our most valued political traditions—big stuff like trial by jury and democracy. But when it came to women, those advanced Greek leaders were a little backward.

An Athenian woman was expected to submit to her husband's "wisdom," which was problematic if he didn't have any. She couldn't eat, sleep, or drink in the same room as men or make financial decisions. She wasn't allowed to vote, go to political meetings, or attend the theater. She couldn't even go to the market without a chaperone. And a famous Athenian quote went like this: "Teaching a woman to read and write? What a terrible thing to do! Like feeding a vile snake on more poison." It seems that the prevailing attitude was that women were dangerous enough already; if one went and gave them ideas and started them thinking, they would become even more perilous to men. So when it came to women's rights, it was all Greek to the Athenians.

Why all this female bashing? Blame it on the brilliant Athenian philosopher Aristotle, who figured out that if a wife decided to fool around she might bear her lover's child without anyone being the wiser. (Well, duh.) Aristotle also knew that if a woman was uneducated and powerless it was easier to control her and limit any possibility of hanky-panky. That way when a husband died, he wouldn't have some other man's kid inheriting his stuff.

SPARSELY COVERED SPARTANS

But now for something completely different—Sparta. Most Greek city-states were like Athens in their attitude toward women and children. Not Sparta. Instead of being kept at home, Spartan gals went to their own schools, just like the guys did.

The Spartan women were tougher and freer than other Greek women. Like their brothers, Sparta's young women were trained to be fine athletes and to hand the enemy his head in battle. Since Greek sporting games were often conducted in the nude, girls practiced running races without a stitch on, even when men were around. (Athenians considered it shocking!) Spartan ladies were as "exposed" as Athenian women were hidden away. The Spartan women's athletic prowess was respected and admired by the Spartan guys, who believed that strong women meant a strong state.

But the Spartans were hardly feminists or even democrats. There was no great art or theater. Sparta was a tough warrior culture where men and women served the state. (The word "spartan" doesn't mean "austere" and "self-denying" for nothing!) Still, unlike Athenian young ladies, the tough chicks in Sparta were encouraged to develop their abilities. They were expected to be educated, fit, and courageous so that they could defend their homes when their men were away and produce great warriors for the state.

GETTING HITCHED

These differences between the homebound Athenians and the warrior Spartans showed up in their marriage plans. The short list of what Athenian women *could* do included attending religious functions, funerals, and, of course, weddings. Perhaps because it was one of their few nights out, Athenian girls had wedding ceremonies that fans of *Modern Bride* could probably relate to.

On a night with a full moon, the veiled bride, dressed in her best, would meet her bridegroom as guests looked on. There would be an animal sacrifice (OK, maybe *Modern Bride* readers would pass on that part) in the bride's honor and feasting that included cakes made with honey before the groom led the bride to his chariot to take her home. Unfortunately, the romance could be superficial since it was often a ritual where a very young bride was transferred from being the property of her father to the property of another older man whom she barely knew.

A wedding in Sparta was a heck of a lot cheaper than in Athens. No caterers, no bands, no bridesmaids, no fuss. Instead, the groom showed his strength to his bride by abducting her and carrying her off into the night for a quickie honeymoon that usually didn't include hotel reservations. But a Spartan woman did marry someone who was young and strong, and often there was mutual attraction.

PITTER-PATTER OF LITTLE GREEK FEET

As for motherhood, when a child was born in Athens, friends and relatives sent gifts. Mom decorated the doorway with an olive branch or a wreath of olive branches for a boy and a wreath of wool for a girl. Athenian women were encouraged—or should we say allowed?—to enjoy motherhood.

But the birth of a child in Athens wasn't always a happy occasion. Sometimes a husband decided not to keep the baby. It might be too great a financial burden or partially deformed or the wrong sex—female, of course; little girls got bigger every day and then eventually required a dowry from their dads when they got married. In that case, the baby was put outside the gates of the city and left to die or adopted and raised as a slave.

Meanwhile back in tough Sparta, mothers weren't having a terrific time either. Soon after a baby was born, soldiers arrived to make sure the infant was physically perfect. Otherwise it was removed to die or become a slave. Being a society devoted to military might, an imperfect child could grow up to be an imperfect soldier, which was viewed as a threat to the state. Spartans were not known for their sentimentality.

A Spartan mother was trained to have one emotion: pride in her child's courage, honor, and prowess as a soldier. As legend has it, before battle a Spartan mother told her son to "Come back with your shield or on it!" This not-so-sweet advice meant her sonny boy had better either win (come home *with* his shield) or die in battle (be carried home *on* his shield). Capture or surrender were clearly not options, so you can bet that running home to mom wasn't exactly smiled upon either.

IT'S ALL GREEK TO MOM

Despite their differences, when it came to motherhood both Spartan and Athenian moms had something in common. A quote from Lycurgus, the lawgiver of Sparta (who wanted females to care only for duty and honor), summed it up when he complained, "All women are by nature fond of children."

Greek Mom Streaks

Back in ancient Greece, women couldn't attend the Olympic games because guys competed in the buff. But one brave mom, Kallipateira, had trained her son to be a great boxer and was desperate to see him compete. She disguised herself as a male trainer to watch the match. When he won, she jumped over the barrier and lost her clothes! Mom was fortunately pardoned, since not only her son, but also practically all of her male relatives were Olympic victors. After Kallipateira's unsuccessful masquerade, trainers had to be as naked (though not as buff) as the athletes.

Meeting Mom
on the Road

A traveler's guide to statues of outstanding mothers.

You've surely heard of some of these women, and others may be unfamiliar to you. But each of them has a statue dedicated to her somewhere in the United States. One, in fact, has eight statues. So hop in your car and take a road trip to visit these statues of outstanding women and devoted mothers.

Joan Benoit (b. 1957) won a gold medal in the 1984 Los Angeles Olympics. No small accomplishment. But did you know that she is the only American woman to have won a gold medal in the Olympic marathon—and one of the few living women to have a statue devoted to her? Take a look at her statue if you happen to be driving through Cape Elizabeth, Maine—a summer resort on the coast, seven miles south of Portland. The full-length bronze statue by sculptor Edward Materson is located at the Thomas Memorial Library at 6 Scott Dyer Road in Cape Elizabeth. Benoit, a native of Cape Elizabeth, married Scott Samuelson; they have two children, Abby and Anders.

Harriet Beecher Stowe (1811–1896) was the author of the antislavery novel *Uncle Tom's Cabin*, which sold 300,000 copies within the first year and influenced the advent of the Civil War. She was also the mother of seven children. Her bronze bust by the famed architect Stanford White is at the Hall of Fame for Great Americans at

University Avenue and West 181st Street, The Bronx, New York. The bust has a dress with a round collar, a pin, and a shawl around the shoulders. Quite a prim look for such a dynamic lady!

Ella Fitzgerald (1918–1996) "practically invented scat," said her obituary in the *New York Times*. Her first record, made at age 17, was "Love and Kisses." In 1938 her "A-tisket, A-tasket" was a huge novelty hit. Her full-length bronze statue shows her standing, wearing a dress and high-heeled shoes, and in the act of singing. The statue, by sculptor Vinnie Bagwell, is at the Trolley Barn Plaza in Yonkers, New York, where Fitzgerald lived for 13 years. The woman who was called the "First Lady of Song" married twice, the second time to jazz musician Ray Brown. They adopted a son, Ray Jr.

Elizabeth Patton Crockett (c. 1788–1860) was the second wife and widow of famed frontiersman Davy Crockett, who was killed at the Alamo. Elizabeth's statue, sculpted in Italy in 1913, is a larger-than-life figure of Italian marble, located at Farm Road 167 at Acton State Historic Site in Texas. This site is something of a curiosity—it's the smallest state park in Texas, occupying all of .01 of an acre! The statue is dedicated to "all pioneer wives and mothers."

Mary Martin (1913–1990), the American singer and actress, was best known for her award-winning Broadway performances in *South Pacific*, *Peter Pan*, and *The Sound of Music*. A 1976 life-size bronze statue by Ronald Thomason stands outside the Weatherford Public Library in Martin's hometown of Weatherford, Texas. Martin was the mother of actor Larry Hagman, *Dallas*'s J. R. Ewing of "Who shot J.R.?" fame.

Sacajawea (c. 1787–1812), the famed Shoshone guide and interpreter for the Lewis and Clark Expedition of 1805, carried her infant son on her back during the journey. She has no fewer than eight statues dedicated to her in the United States. The most famous is the heroic bronze monument by the sculptor Alice Cooper at the Portland, Oregon, Washington Park, erected in 1905. You can also find statues of her on the grounds of:

- The North Dakota State Capitol in Bismarck, North Dakota;

- The Bozeman Tourist Information Bureau in Bozeman, Montana;

- Pioneer Park in Lewiston, Idaho;

- Central Wyoming College in Riverton, Wyoming;

- Breaker's Point in Cannon Beach, Oregon;

- Sacajawea Interpretive Center, Sacajawea State Park, in Pasco, Washington; and

- On Sacajawea Street in Portland, Oregon.

So many honors for such an important lady! Sounds like a Sacajawea road trip is in order!

Sacajawea Becomes a Mother

"One of the women . . . halted at a little run about a mile behind us . . . I inquired of Cameahwait the cause of her detention, and was informed by him in an unconcerned manner that she had halted to bring forth a child and would soon overtake us; in about an hour the woman arrived with her newborn babe and passed us on her way to camp apparently as well as she ever was."
—Meriwether Lewis, *The Journals of Lewis and Clark*

Mrs. Brown, You've Got a Lovely Daughter

Mrs. Brown changes the way women have babies.

In 1977, Lesley Brown was a frustrated young woman in Bristol, England. For nine years, she and her husband, John, had been unsuccessfully trying to have a baby. They had gone from doctor to doctor, searching for help, but had found none. Lesley (like about 20 percent of infertile women) had blocked fallopian tubes, which in those days meant that there was no hope of her ever conceiving a child. Luckily, she was referred to a special gynecologist, Dr. Patrick Steptoe.

FALLOPIAN TUBE 101

Conception occurs when an egg cell (ovum) is released from a woman's ovary and travels through a fallopian tube, where it is fertilized by male sperm, becomes an embryo, and travels into the uterus, to which it attaches and where it grows into a baby. When the fallopian tube is blocked, the eggs can't travel through the tube to be fertilized.

Still, hopeless as her situation seemed, after talking to Dr. Steptoe at Oldham General Hospital, Lesley felt a surge of hope. Steptoe, along with Dr. Robert Edwards of Cambridge University, had been experimenting with a way to fertilize the egg in a lab's glass petri dish, a process called *in vitro* (in glass) fertilization, or IVF. So far, the process had yet to make a woman pregnant, but the doctors hoped that Lesley would be the first success.

She knew it might be painful and could easily end in failure, but Lesley felt she had to grasp at what she saw as her last hope. On November 10, 1977, Lesley Brown took the first step in the process. Using a laparoscope, Dr. Steptoe removed an egg from one of Lesley's ovaries. Dr. Edwards put Lesley's egg in a laboratory dish that already contained John's sperm. After the egg was fertilized, it was placed in a special solution created to nurture it while it divided. Two and a half days later, the newly fertilized egg was placed into Lesley's uterus.

FICTION BECOMES SCIENCE

Lesley was overjoyed as she began to experience what seemed to be a perfectly ordinary pregnancy. But as each month passed without incident, controversy swirled around the woman from Bristol. The fears concerning Lesley's pregnancy and the process of in vitro fertilization became more and more sensational. People feared that science had overstepped its bounds.

Many pundits considered it immoral to create "test-tube babies." The doctors were condemned for tampering with nature. There were worries about monster babies or the government creating breeding farms like those in Aldous Huxley's novel Brave New World.

Then, nine days before her due date, Lesley developed toxemia, and Dr. Steptoe decided to deliver the baby via cesarean section. On July 25, 1978, Lesley and John had blonde-haired, blue-eyed Louise Joy Brown. Her birth was so special that it made the cover of Time magazine. If every baby is a miracle, Louise was a bit of an extra miracle—

after all the dire warnings, she was healthy and normal—not a monster baby at all.

HAPPY 25th

Lesley's famous pregnancy brought new hope to hundreds of thousands of infertile mothers. Since 1978, proud parents have had more than one million babies through the use of *in vitro* fertilization. About 1 percent of babies are born with the aid of IVF and doctors think that the numbers will go higher as the technology continues to improve.

In 2003 Louise Joy Brown had her 25th birthday. Despite all the publicity that surrounded her birth—and still surrounds her birthdays—Louise has confounded critics by brushing off celebrity and remaining as ordinary as the day she was born.

"I just get on with my life," Louise has said. "Just normal—I just plod along." Engaged to be married, she is a Bristol postal worker who, as the press likes to pun, now makes "deliveries" of her own.

Louise also has a younger sister, Natalie. Their proud mum showed her faith in technology by once again relying on IVF for Natalie's conception.

"I'm proud of being the first test-tube baby. But I don't know if I could go through what Mum did. I hate hospitals."
—Louise Brown

Lit 101:
The Play's the Thing

Remember all those classic plays with all those classic moms who did all those classic things? Test your knowledge with our little Literature 101 multiple-choice test. No fair peeking at the answers either.

1. The Play: *Medea* by Euripides, 431 BC

The Plot: Medea is a sorceress and the daughter of a king. She betrays her father and kills her brother to help Jason, the man she loves, steal the Golden Fleece. The two settle down together in Corinth and have two sons. All is well until Jason abandons his family to take up with the Corinthian king's daughter.

What's a mom to do?

__ A. Kill everybody. Kill Jason's new bride, the Corinthian king, and your two sons.
__ B. Get liquored up and crash the wedding.

__ C. Knit sweaters for your sons from the Golden Fleece.
__ D. Have your grandfather provide a chariot drawn by dragons and hightail it outta there.
__ E. Both A & D.

2. The Play: *Oedipus Rex* by Sophocles, c. 424 BC

The Plot: Jocasta, the queen of Thebes, is upset because the Delphic Oracle has prophesied that her husband, King Laius, will be murdered by their own son.

What's a mom to do?

__ A. Go on the pill.
__ B. See a midwife about herbs that will ensure the birth of a girl.

__ C. Hand your son over to a shepherd who will take him away and kill him.

__ D. Declare the oracle a fraud and have the king pass a decree that outlaws it.

__ E. Get a second opinion from the Psychic Hotline.

3. The Play: *Hamlet* by William Shakespeare, 1603

The Plot: After the death of her husband, the king of Denmark, Gertrude marries Claudius, her late husband's brother, who becomes the new king. Her son, Hamlet begins acting oddly, claiming he's seeing ghosts and insisting that Claudius had a hand in his father's murder and that his mother's quick remarriage is unseemly. Is Hamlet crazy or is there a method to his madness? Gertrude can't tell if he's faking or not.

What's a mom to do?

__ A. Kill your son and new husband. Rule Denmark by yourself.

__ B. Consult an elderly windbag for advice.

__ C. Hold a séance to consult your dead husband.

__ D. All of the above

__ E. None of the above.

4. The Play: *Titus Andronicus* by William Shakespeare, 1587

The Plot: Tamora, queen of the Goths, has been taken prisoner by Roman general Titus Andronicus, along with three of her sons and her lover, Aaron. Once in Rome, Titus has Tamora's eldest son sacrificed to avenge the deaths of some of his own sons during the bloody war against the Goths.

What's a mom to do?

__ A. Trick Titus's surviving sons into falling into a pit and be blamed for the murder of the emperor's brother.

__ B. Have your lover trick Titus into chopping off his own hand.

__ C. Arrange for the heads of Titus's sons to be brought to him on a platter, along with his own hand.

__ D. Enjoy the pastry served at a party hosted by Titus.

__ E. All of the above.

Answers on page 299.

Mom's Got You Under Her Skin

Feel like mom's always getting under your skin?
That's because she never left!

Thomas Wolfe once wrote that you can't go home again. Well, it turns out that it might be just as tough to leave home and mom too. It's true—at least on a cellular level.

CELL MATES

Even if you're all grown up, you can still have blood and tissue cells that you picked up during your time in the womb. Meanwhile, there's a good chance that mom can't part with parts of you either. Decades after a woman gives birth, she can still have cells in her body that came from the babies she carried during her pregnancies. The cells are actually descendants of stem cells that have transplanted themselves, taken root, and begun reproducing in both mom and baby.

In fact, women who've had sons have been known to have male cells in their bloodstream for up to 27 years. A woman who has been pregnant can have both her mother's cells and her kids' cells floating around—no wonder moms sometimes say they have trouble keeping their own identity straight.

HAS MOM INVADED YOUR INNER SPACE?

This foreign-cell phenomenon is called microchimerism. Foreign cells are few (up to 61 fetal blood cells per tablespoon of blood translates to less than one in a million). Medical researchers using genetic tools to identify foreign cells believe they are a common phenomenon in both sick and healthy people.

The impact of mom's cells staying in your body is still a mystery. While there's evidence that foreign cells might encourage autoimmune diseases (where the body mistakenly attacks its own tissues), some scientists believe that a mom's cells will be shown to benefit her offspring. The jury is still out.

Meanwhile, if you feel an inexplicable urge to wear clean underwear or close the door because you weren't born in the barn . . . you know the reason. Seems there's a bit of mom in all of us.

"Motherhood is the strangest thing, it can be like being one's own Trojan horse." —Rebecca West

"And so our mothers and grandmothers have, more often than not anonymously, handed on the creative spark, the seed of the flower they themselves never hoped to see—or like a sealed letter they could not plainly read."
—Alice Walker

Mom Makes the World Go 'Round

In the ancient world, mom could explain the mysteries of life.

We all know motherhood is a powerful thing. But did you know it could make the seasons change, bring stormy weather, and turn night to day?

THE MOTHER OF ALL WINTERS

For a time, the earth knew no winter. It was always warm, always sunny, and always growing season! People owed this eternal summer to the Greek goddess Demeter, who was in charge of agriculture and vegetation. Demeter had a beautiful daughter, Persephone, who was the apple of her mom's eye.

But everything changed when Hades, god of the under-world, noticed Persephone and realized she was a total babe. He doubted that mom would consent to let her daughter marry him and live underground to preside with him over the souls of the dead. So when Persephone was out picking flowers, Hades split open the earth below her and took her underground to rule as his queen.

Meanwhile, a worried Demeter searched the lands and seas for her beloved daughter. When she finally found out about the kidnapping, Demeter fell into a funk. She let the world turn dark and cold.

Hungry and frostbitten, the unhappy gods came down from Mount Olympus. They tried to reason with Demeter and reassure her that empty-nest syndrome was completely normal, but the kid did have to marry someday. They brought Demeter gifts and begged her to restore the fruits and blossoms of summer. The mourning mom told the gods, more or less, to go to Hades. The earth remained cursed, cold, and barren.

Finally, realizing that even tackling the lord of death was easier than arguing with a grieving mom, the gods went down to see Hades. "Enough!" they cried. "We're freezing! Let that kid go home!" Hades reluctantly returned Persephone to her joyful mother, who immediately caused the dead earth to bloom again.

Life seemed to be headed back toward eternal fruits and veggies, but alas, it was not meant to be. Persephone overlooked the first rule of visiting the underworld—don't eat anything or else you will not be able to return to the land of the living. In her misery, Persephone had turned to food. (Hey, who hasn't?) She tasted the seeds of a pomegranate, so by celestial laws she had to return to Hades for at least a third of the year. Now when Persephone dwells underground, her mother sadly lets the earth go cold and dark, a phenomenon otherwise known as winter. It's only when Demeter is reunited with her daughter that spring and summer can return and you can pack away your long underwear.

THE MOTHER OF ALL SUNRISES

The Aztec warriors in ancient Mexico believed in the fierce mother goddess called Coatlicue, "the Lady of the Skirt of Snakes." In addition to her unique fashions, Coatlicue was known for her many, many children. One hundred and one, to be exact. She gave birth to a daughter, Coyolxauhqui, and a hundred sons, who became the stars.

One day Coatlicue found a ball of hummingbird feathers, a bit of an oddity that she tucked into her bosom. Suddenly she got that old queasy feeling and realized that oops, she was pregnant again. But her feather-pregnancy story was so strange that her sons and daughter just didn't believe her. (Can you blame them?) The kids wanted to know who the father *really* was. They decided their mother had dishonored them, so they decided to kill her. Seems that even goddesses can have dysfunctional families.

But just as they were about to attack her, Coatlicue gave birth to Huitzilopochtli, the warrior sun god and son of hummingbird feathers. He came into the world ready to protect his mother with the help of a fire serpent and his strong sun rays. The fierce Huitzilopochtli destroyed his brothers and beheaded his sister, throwing her head up in the sky to become the moon.

This murderous family squabble was the way the ancient Aztecs explained the sunrise. Every sunset launched a battle between day and night. When the sun came up, it symbolized the victory of Huitzilopochtli and his fertile mother over the forces of darkness.

"A little child born yesterday
A thing on mother's milk and kisses fed"
—Homer, "Hymn to Hermes"

The Mother of All Mothering Advice

When he advised American families on how to raise their children,
Dr. Spock rebelled against the legacy of his own mother.

"**T**rust yourself," Dr. Benjamin Spock wrote. "You know more than you think you do."

With those calming and now famous words, the New England pediatrician revolutionized the way American moms bring up babies. His book, *Baby and Child Care*, was an immediate best seller in 1945 (selling for 25 cents) and went on to become one of the best-selling books of all time. Though there was no dedication to Spock's mother on the cover, in a strange way you could say she'd been his inspiration.

GOOD-BYE, DR. WATSON

As mothers thumbed through Dr. Spock's book for advice on everything from family dinners to diaper changes, they also learned that hugs and kisses wouldn't spoil their babies. They were encouraged to ignore rigid feeding and toilet-training schedules in favor of flexibility with the individual needs of their baby.

Hugs, kisses, and flexibility were revolutionary ideas for the 1940s. Prior to Spock's book, the most influential baby-care expert was John B. Watson, who gave stern orders. "Never, never kiss your child," Watson insisted. "Never hold it in your lap. Never rock its carriage."

Watson's antiaffection theory was that mother love was dangerous; it was smothering and kept a child from developing into a strong adult. It left a "never-healing wound" that damaged the chances for a successful future.

With Watson demanding that mothers tie their child's arm to the crib if a toddler sucked his thumb, imagine the relief when Dr. Spock advised mothers that both they and their babies could enjoy the experience of child rearing. But if the moms who sought advice from Dr. Spock knew he was opposing the standard ideas of his day, they probably didn't know that his advice also directly contradicted the views of his own mother.

MEET THE NOT-SO-MELLOW MILDRED

In 1903 Mildred Louise Stoughton and Benjamin Ives Spock gave birth to the first of their six children, Benjamin McLane Spock. Well-to-do Mildred had her share of maids, but she hired no governesses or nannies that might interfere with her child management. Papa Benjamin quietly watched from the sidelines while Mildred ran a strict home with the goal of raising perfect children.

Ben's mother took some of her child-raising ideas from Dr. Luther Emmett Holt and his book, *The Care and Feeding of Children*, a popular baby-care tome of the day. Other ideas were her own (how she came about them is anyone's guess). But all of them were promoted with an eccentricity that made Ben feel peculiar when he longed to feel like a regular kid.

Spock's mother believed that children under 12 should have a special diet, constant exposure to fresh air, and a very early bedtime. Mildred rigidly enforced her ideas. No matter how Ben protested, his diet was *always* mainly vegetables, fruits, and eggs—and absolutely no bananas. (Odd, but true. Mildred wanted bananas nowhere near her children!) For a time, instead of going to a local school, Ben was educated in a tent school organized by his mother so that he would be outside in the fresh air while he was learning. Bedtime was *exactly* 6:45 p.m., even if other kids were still playing.

MOM COULD BE COLD

Mildred's rules were so rigid that she was unwittingly cruel. The young Spocks slept out on the sleeping porch (in the fresh air, of course). Always. They were warmly dressed, with warm blankets, but they were also outside in the frigid winters of New Haven, Connecticut. Nights were so cold that after little Ben used a chamber pot, the urine froze. But rules were rules and there was no hope of getting back into the warm house after 6:45 until morning.

Ben always knew his mother loved her children. In fact, the arrival of a baby in the Spock household was a celebration, and Mildred's joy in her infants would later inspire Spock's own career as a pediatrician. But Mildred was so stern and moralistic that it was almost impossible to win her approval. And when she thought herself in the right, she never hesitated to punish her children—though usually with deprivation or withering scorn rather than with spankings.

If physical punishment was rare, hugs were even rarer. Ben found his mother intimidating and he wrote late in his life that, thanks to Mildred, "All my life, up to this day, I've felt guilty until proven innocent."

TAKING THE FIRST BOAT OUT

As Ben grew into his teens, his relationship with his mother only got worse. Mildred continued to control Ben's life, but now she also showed a strong puritanical streak. To get him away from girls, she sent him to a boarding school for boys. There the teenager experienced all the usual emotions of a young man trying to fit in—except homesickness (can you blame him?).

Successful in his education, Ben went on to Yale University, but lived at home. His mother continued to dominate and frustrate him until 1924, when he competed in Paris on the U.S. Olympic rowing team. The United States won a gold medal, but Ben's real victory was the joy of being so far from Mildred and emerging from under her thumb.

THERE'S A DOCTOR IN THE HOUSE

After graduating from Yale, Spock went on to attend medical school at Columbia University. He married and settled down in New York City—a sophisticated location far from mom. He opened a pediatric practice and fathered children of his own. But Mildred's legacy remained, so much so that Ben felt it hurt his ability to be a loving father to his own boys. He decided that "there must be pleasanter ways to raise children."

A FLEXIBLE APPROACH

Spock began formulating his own ideas on child raising and wrote them into a book. From the beginning of his work until the end, he had differences with Mom. Instead of putting an emphasis on raising the perfect child as

Mildred had, he believed in supporting and loving every child as an individual. "Every baby needs to be smiled at," Spock advised, "talked to, played with, fondled—gently and lovingly."

The pediatrician turned his back on Mildred's harsh control of her children to make them better people. "Positive traits in children," said Spock, "emerge naturally when they are given love and nurturing." And where Mildred was stern and rigid, Spock was flexible. "You may hear people say that you have to get your baby strictly regulated in his feeding, sleeping, bowel movements, and other habits—but don't believe this. He doesn't have to be sternly trained." (Translation: if the sleeping porch is too cold, you can bring your child indoors, and if he likes bananas—no problem!)

The good doctor didn't always disagree with Mildred. He found it "absolutely fair to expect children to go to bed at a designated hour." Late in his life, he credited vegetarianism with helping to restore his health. Also like his mother, he recommended less meat for children and even mentioned the benefits of fresh air! "Cool or cold air improves appetite, puts color in the cheeks, and gives more pep to humans of all ages." But his recommendation was for playing in fresh cold air, not sleeping in it. Spock warned against putting babies and children to sleep in too cold a spot because "that could lower their body temperature to dangerous levels."

THE MILDRED EFFECT

Spock denied that he wrote his book to rebel against his mother. And though Dr. Spock's book was widely acclaimed, he wasn't comfortable until he found out what

Mildred thought of it. "[A] young man's book on child-bearing might be thought of as a possible criticism of his mother," he later admitted. But when Spock asked her opinion, Mildred, 70 years old and widowed, looked at her son and gave him the answer he least expected. "Why Bennie, I think it's quite sensible," she said.

Mom Pops Her Cork

When you pop open a bottle of champagne, it's a cool, clear, fizzy delight. This wasn't always the case, and we have a French mom to thank for setting things right. Nicole-Barbe Ponsardin married a French winemaker, Francois Clicquot, in 1799. The two had a child before Francois's untimely death three years later. Madame Clicquot took over the business and turned it into a champagne dynasty.

Nicole is rumored to have invented pink champagne, but her most valuable contribution to the wine industry came in 1816 when Madame devised a way to rid champagne of the troublesome sediment that accumulates in a bottle as wine ages. Her *table de remuage* allows bottles to be rotated so that sediment gathers in the neck of the bottle and can be easily disgorged once the champagne is mature. No sediment equals nice, crisp, and clear bubbly!

You can still enjoy wines from Madame Clicquot's vineyards today. Just look for the yellow Veuve-Clicquot-Ponsardin label to experience some *trés magnifique* wine!

Good Moms
Movie Festival

It's the maternal instinct—at 24 frames a second!
Herewith a sampling of films featuring some of
the best moms the cinema has to offer.

Aliens—Wait a minute, you say? Sigourney Weaver's Ellen Ripley may be a xenomorph-killin' action heroine in this classic 1986 sci-fi film and she even saves a little girl, but she's not a *mother*. Ah, just go to your local video store and rent the director's-cut version on DVD and you'll discover that Ripley is indeed a mother, who learns to her grief that she was 57 years late to her daughter's 11th birthday party because she was floating in space for all those years. This maternal grief and guilt provides an extra dimension of depth to her subsequent bonding with pre-teen alien-attack survivor Newt (Carrie Henn) and illuminates the lengths she'll go to in order to protect her, including fighting hand to hand (well, claw to mechanical claw) with the 20-foot-high queen alien in the film's climactic scenes. It's a "good mom/bad mom" kind of thing. Shame that *Alien 3* came along and ruined everything. But forget about that and just enjoy Ripley's fierce maternal instinct, backed up by guns. Lots and lots of guns.

Bambi—The world's most selfless mother. First she raises the child of the ruler of the forest as a single mother, with no help at all from the dad. She teaches her child the ways of the forest, explains about evil ("Man was in the forest"), and then, when that evil threatens her child, sacrifices herself so her child can live. Only then does Dad show up (yeah, nice absentee parenting there, *pops*). Bambi's mom is so selfless that she doesn't even *get her own name*. Go on, see if you can think of it. The death of Bambi's mother famously traumatized generations of tiny filmgoers into an aversion to killing deer so pronounced that it actually has a term in wildlife management circles: "the Bambi effect."

Dolores Claiborne—In a slightly different take on the definition of "good mom," Kathy Bates plays a hardscrabble Yankee suspected of murdering the woman for whom she works. As the film goes on, we find out that this isn't the first time she's been suspected of killing someone—and that the previous suspected murder has to do with Dolores's now-estranged daughter, played by Jennifer Jason Leigh. The movie is based on the Stephen King novel of the same name, but the film both elaborates and centers on the contentious relationship between mother and daughter and just how far a mother will go to protect the innocent child in her care. Not cheerful, but certainly gripping.

Stella Dallas—The world's most selfless mother, human division. Ironically the film shares some plot points with *Bambi*. There's a mom raising the child of a powerful man as a single mother, teaching the kid the ways of the world, and then sacrificing herself for the good of her offspring. In this case, however, mom doesn't take a bullet, she just sends her kid to go live with the rich and powerful dad. The story is not unfairly described as a politically incorrect melodrama by critics, who are legion, but as film historian scholar Leslie Halliwell noted: "Audiences came to sneer and stayed to weep." If you're interested, this film comes in three flavors: the hard-to-find 1925 silent version; the classic 1937 *Stella Dallas*, which features Barbara Stanwyck as the selfless mom in question, and the more recent 1990 version *Stella*, which features Bette Midler. Whichever one you choose, keep the tissue box nearby.

Almost Famous—Frances McDormand plays a mother who lets her 15-year-old son, a budding journalist, tour with a rock band in the hedonistic days of the early 1970s. Normally this would probably qualify someone as a *bad* mom. But McDormand's character is neither stupid nor clueless, and shows how a good mom is not only the mother to a child, but the midwife to the man that the boy will become. She understands and trusts her son enough to let him have the adventure—one which does ultimately open his eyes to the world. Which is not to say mom passively waves good-bye to her kid as he goes on the road. One of the film's best scenes has one of the rockers picking up the phone to charm McDormand and getting slapped down by her no-nonsense awareness of what's really going on out there on tour. Anyone who can humble a rock star deserves your respect.

"You have this myth you're sharing the birth experience. Unless you're passing a bowling ball, I don't think so."
—Robin Williams

You Say Mama, I Say Mada...

Can you match the language to the mom?

How do you say mother around the world? Surprisingly, most countries have remarkably similar words for "mother," which is defined as "a woman who conceives, gives birth to, or raises and nurtures a child." Some linguists theorize that the sound comes from the baby-talk sound "ma." Whatever the reason, a mother can be called "mama" in countries that are as far flung as Lithuania, Hungary, Indonesia, and Turkey. Despite these similarities, cultures have still come up with distinctive ways to cry for mommy.

MAKING A MOM MATCH

Match these words for "mother" to the proper language or country of origin. For you experts, we've thrown in a couple nontraditional examples. See if you can root them all out!

_____ 1. mada	_____ 6. madre
_____ 2. mamangu	_____ 7. ne'ni
_____ 3. anne	_____ 8. mitera
_____ 4. mutter	_____ 9. matka
_____ 5. ngambaa	_____ 10. e tsi

_____ 11. janani

_____ 12. moeder

_____ 13. moder

_____ 14. ma'

_____ 15. haha

_____ 16. mama or
makuahine

_____ 17. mami

_____ 18. yum

_____ 19. mere

_____ 20. maht

_____ 21. patrino

_____ 22. sosoy

A. Cherokee

B. Chinese (phonetic)

C. Polish

D. Dutch

E. Esperanto

F. French

G. German

H. Greek

I. Hawaiian

J. Jamaican patois

K. Japanese (Romaji)

L. Kamilaroi
(Aboriginal Australian)

M. Klingon
(yes, as in *Star Trek*)

N. Potawatomi

O. Russian

P. Sanskrit

Q. Spanish

R. Swahili

S. Swedish

T. Tibetan

U. Turkish

V. Vietnamese

Mama, You Puzzle Me

We all know the fear of not being able to find our mamas. Put those fears aside and locate mama in the puzzle. As always, she is the key to success.

Across
1 Dogpatch creator
5 Scarlett of Tara
10 "Born Free" lion
14 Another, in Andalusia
15 Fit for a king
16 Hefty regular at Cheers
17 Graf ___ (German warship)
18 Blow one's top
19 "___ that barge..."
20 He gets paid for doing nothing
23 "Twelfth Night" count
24 Highlands tongue
25 "Three Days of the _____" (Redford film)
28 MIT and RPI
32 "... _____ will!" (threatening words)
35 What the three long entries each have two of
36 Dog cousin
37 Nutty
41 Reveal all
42 Floored
43 Newsman Koppel
44 Nebraskan natives
45 Accepting willingly
48 Spiced Indian tea
50 Vamps

54 2002 Jennifer Lopez romantic comedy
59 Opposite of ecto-
60 Sound of amusement
61 Blood: Prefix
62 Laugh-a-minute type
63 Fudd who bugs Bugs
64 "___ soft, gentle, and low," like Cordelia's voice
65 Besides
66 Some leather workers
67 Sit a spell

Down
1 "That ___ Girl" (one who reads a certain mag)
2 How some bonds are sold
3 Targets, with "on"
4 Like a Browning line
5 It shows the way to Salem
6 Munich Mister
7 Chills and fever
8 Busta Rhymes, for one
9 Hitching post
10 Dig in
11 Weaver's apparatus
12 Mexican miss: Abbr.
13 Prayer ender
21 "It's ___-win situation" (2 words)

22 Hoop star Thomas
26 Leave it to beavers
27 Hideo Nomo's birthplace
29 Three-handed card game
30 Container weight
31 What Rosebud was
32 Melville novel set in Tahiti
33 All ears
34 Logical start?
36 Dagwood Bumstead's boss
38 Short, amusing account
39 Rice-and-fish fare
40 Soldier of the '50s

45 Appropriate
46 Arts-supporting gp.
47 Get together
49 Chipped in chips
51 Martin or Garvey
52 Chair designer Charles
53 Horse's sound, at times
54 No more than
55 Blue dye
56 Some vows
57 "Alas!"
58 Not e'en once

Answers on page 302.

Koko Kares for Kitten

A kitten and an ape change how we think about gorillas.

Scientists are still debating whether animals can reason the way humans do. It's an age-old debate, with recent evidence indicating that intelligence and the ability to feel emotions aren't limited to humans. Weighing in heavily (about 300 pounds) on the side of animals is Koko, the famous signing gorilla.

LEARNING TO SPEAK HUMAN

In 1972, Francine "Penny" Patterson was a young graduate student in psychology at Stanford University when she met Hani-ko, a year-old gorilla at the San Francisco Zoo, and began teaching him sign language. Within two weeks the little gorilla, nicknamed "Koko," was signing for food and juice. Project Koko became the longest continuous attempt to teach language to another species.

Today Patterson states that Koko has a vocabulary of more than 1,000 signs in American Sign Language and can understand 2,000 words. The gorilla has participated in (with human help) a live e-mail chat on AOL and conversations with famous folks like presidential speechwriter Peter Forbes, Apple CEO John Scully, and celebrities like William Shatner and Robin Williams. Other animals have since learned to sign, but few are celebs like Koko, whose initial rise to fame was linked with mothering a little kitten named All Ball.

KOKO'S KITTEN

Among young Koko's favorite toys were books with pictures of cats. In 1984, Koko signed to Patterson that she wanted a cat. As an experiment, abandoned kittens were brought to the gorilla compound, and Patterson let Koko chose one for a pet. The gorilla picked out a round, gray male kitten with no tail and named him All Ball.

Koko mothered All Ball in devoted gorilla fashion. She tried to nurse him and carried him on her back, imitating the way gorilla mothers carry their babies in the wild. When she wanted to play with All Ball, Koko often signed the word "tickle," and she would gently tickle the cat.

The Ron Cohen photo, "Koko and Kitten," showed Koko cradling All Ball. Though her large arms could crush the seemingly helpless kitten, she cuddled it carefully and gazed at it fondly. That now-famous photo surprised the public, who were fascinated by the gentleness of a supposedly ferocious animal. Koko's good mothering of All Ball won her millions of admirers.

KOKO IN MOURNING

Tragedy struck when All Ball died suddenly. In December of 1984, he escaped from his enclosure and was struck by a car. Koko seemed distraught and signed words like "cry," "sad," and "frown" when shown a picture of a kitten that looked like hers. Disagreement raged in the scientific community over whether or not Koko could actually grieve for her lost kitten and feel emotions in the same way that people do. Despite the arguments, the public had no trouble believing that Koko could feel a mother's pain and loss. Expressions of sympathy and offers to replace All Ball with another kitten poured into Woodside from around the world.

ALL BALL'S LEGACY

Koko's reaction to All Ball's death and her ability to communicate those emotions sparked more research and heated debate about behaviors once considered exclusively human. Today she stands as a diplomat for the gorilla community, once believed to be bloodthirsty. Koko's mothering and sadness at the loss of her kitten made many people rethink traditional ideas of what it is to be human and what it is to be animal. Perhaps there is more going on than we think.

Today the famous Koko cares for a gray pet cat, Smoky. Now she wants a gorilla baby to mother and love.

The Joke's on Mom

What's the difference between a Rottweiler and a mother?
Eventually a Rottweiler will let go.

Did you hear about the cannibal mom?
She had a husband and ate kids.

What's the difference between an Italian mother, an Irish mother, a Chinese mother, and a Jewish mother?
The accent.

Mom's Brave Brain

Science has discovered that a mom's brain
isn't only smarter—it's braver too!

onfronted by the myriad problems of raising kids, moms can feel a bit better about themselves. Research done by Dr. Craig Kinsley, a neuroscientist at the University of Richmond, has given moms a much-needed boost of self-esteem by showing that being a mom can make you smarter. Kinsley has found that moms' brains do change (for the better!) because of pregnancy and child rearing.

FOLLOW HER NOSE, IT ALWAYS KNOWS

Kinsley did studies with rats, believing these studies also apply to people. He found that female rats with offspring were smarter. And they stayed smarter even after their pups had grown.

Motherhood doesn't only change mom from the neck down. It also changes the brain with what Kinsley describes as "dramatic alterations." Pregnancy and breast-feeding hormones seem to nurture the brain cells involved in learning, memory, and spatial skills. Kinsley measured these effects by setting up a maze with a Fruit Loop reward at the end. When Kinsley sent female rats through a challenging maze, he found it was always the moms who were best at finding the Fruit Loops at the end of the day. They learned faster and remembered more than the control rats who'd never mothered. Rats who were lactating (the equivalent of breast-feeding human moms) did best of all.

"Reproduction shapes and alters a female's brain in significant ways," Kinsley has said. The rats who were best had actual physical changes in their brains. In nursing mama rats, the hippocampi (the part of the brain used for learning and memory) contained twice as many neural connections as those of their childless sisters. The more neural connections, the faster and better the brain works. And the good news is that the brainy improvements from motherhood continue throughout a woman's life and may help ward off senility as she ages.

WHY YOU CAN'T RAT-TLE MOM

And what about a mom being cool when stressed and brave in adversity? Lab challenges with female rats showed that superheroes have nothin' on supermoms.

To stress the female rats, they were put in scary conditions. While humans might be scared by dark, creepy places, rodents are terrified of open, lighted spaces because they cannot hide and become vulnerable to predators. The rats found themselves inside clear Plexiglas tubes placed in a brightly lighted room in an open space. The childless rats often froze with fear, while the mother rats methodically explored their surroundings, looking for an escape route. If those little whiskered moms could talk, they'd probably give motherly advice: when you're stuck in a bad place, instead of dwelling in fear, look for a way out. The mama rats were more interested in escape, perhaps because they needed to get home to protect their young.

"Pregnancy and offspring create a more adaptive brain, one that's generally less susceptible to fear and stress," according to Kinsley. And in the area of fearlessness, just as in the area of intelligence, there were physical differences in the brains of moms and nonmoms. Mother rat brains showed less activation in those regions of the brain that regulate fear.

BUT WHAT IF I DON'T HAVE KIDS?

Want to get smart, calm, and fearless too? Not interested in a babe of your own and can't afford a tutor in physics and karate? Maybe babysitting could work for you. "Foster rats," who'd never given birth but who cared for other rat pups, performed well on the maze tests. Male rats who were exposed to infants also improved their mental functions—though not to the same degree as the females.

A RAT IS TO A HUMAN, AS . . .

Kinsley's work does give a mom some bragging rights. But do mother rats running mazes really have that much in common with human moms driving kids to school through a maze of traffic?

Kinsley, whose research was inspired by watching his wife conquer challenges as a new mother, feels sure that there's enough of a connection to make studies about rodents useful across species. Pregnancy hormones are similar in every species, and early MRI scans of pregnant individuals (of both lab rats and humans) show similar brain patterns. Plus, many genes are similar in rats and humans. As Kinsley says, "I like to think of humans as rats with two legs."

The Flying Dutchwoman

Mom Fanny Blankers-Koen took the Olympics in stride

The year was 1948, the place, London. Fanny Blankers-Koen was 30 years old and a mother of two. What in the world was she doing competing in the Olympics?

HITLER STEALS THE GOLD

Born in Amsterdam, the Netherlands, Francina Elsje Koen began competing in track and field when she was 17, a relatively late age. She made it to the 1936 Olympics, where she finished with a respectable sixth place in the high jump and fifth with the Dutch 4 x 100-meter relay team.

Jan Blankers, a former Olympian—who became both Fanny's coach and her loving hubby—believed the tall, lanky blonde could be a gold medal athlete. But time wasn't on Fanny's side. Hitler's rise to power and the outbreak of World War II nearly ruined her chances of being an Olympic athlete.

Throughout the war years, most Dutch citizens struggled just to survive. They were busier tracking the progress of the Allied forces through Europe than the progress of athletics. If they had, they might have noticed that Fanny, who was now a mother, continued to train—and to set new world records in the high jump, the long jump, and the pentathlon.

TOO LATE FOR MOM?

Finally the war was over and in 1948 the London Olympics began. The war-weary world celebrated the chance to watch javelins being hurled instead of bombs. Fanny Blankers-Koen celebrated by entering the 100 and 200 meter races, the 80 meter hurdles, and as the anchor for the 4 x 100-meter team relay. But most experts thought Fanny's prime competitive years were behind her, and many thought that as a mother she shouldn't even be there.

Back in Holland there were grumbles that Fanny should be home taking care of her house and two children. Then a British newspaper article noted that she was not only a mother but also 30 years old and the writers dismissed her as too old to be competitive. Fanny made up her mind to show everyone that a good mom can't be beat.

THIS MOM IS GOLD

The blonde streaked her way through the 100 meters in 11.9 seconds and won the gold! After a shaky start in the 80 meter hurdles, she set a new Olympic record of 11.2 seconds in a photo finish to win the gold medal. But as the finals of the 200 meter race approached, far from being excited about her triumphs, the lonely mother was in tears because she missed her kids terribly. Her husband had to remind her that she could quit at any time she wanted but that she would be sorry for it afterward.

His words turned Fanny around. She'd always wanted to do her best, so after a good cry, she set about winning the 200 meters in 24.4 seconds. In her last event, Fanny won gold as anchor in the 4 x 100-meter team relay. A spectacular achievement, she had the honor of being the first woman to win four gold medals in a single Olympic games.

Now her former detractors lauded Fanny as the flying housewife, even daring to call her "the Flying Dutchwoman"! There was no more grumbling about Fanny staying home; now all the grumbling was about Olympic rules limiting her to three individual events. Though she held the world records in the broad jump and the high jump, Fanny hadn't been allowed to compete in those events. Many fans thought she could have won those as well.

Fanny returned to Holland as a national hero and found well-wishers crowding the streets of Amsterdam. The city presented her with a new bicycle in honor of her achievements. After her Olympic triumph, Fanny continued her career with some success, winning European titles in 1950 and setting a world record in 1951. In 1999, she was an 80-year-old grandmother when the International Association of Athletic Federations named her the "Female Athlete of the Century." You just can't beat a great mom.

"At work, you think of the children you have left at home. At home, you think of the work you've left unfinished. Such a struggle is unleashed within yourself. Your heart is rent." —Golda Meir

Kiddin' Around the World

Need some quick tips? Here's how moms around the world cope with the challenges of raising kids.

Kids can be a handful no matter where you live. And even though a baby has successfully made it to kiddom, that doesn't mean that mom's job is done. What's best for kids? Around the world, the question has different answers. In different societies, devoted mothers meet their children's needs in ways that might shock or inspire you.

DO YOUR CHORES, OR NOT?

In Africa, you probably won't hear a Central Bantu yelling at a child to clean up his or her room, much less help out around the house. Dwellers in thatched huts, the Bantu mom might even pull out a piece of the roof to start a campfire at night. The Bantu periodically move and build new homes, so keeping everything in its place takes a backseat. Also big fans of temporary housing, the Inuit, who live in igloos in North America, have been known to simply leave an old igloo when it's dirty and move into a new one. (Now there's a way to cut down on chores!)

But in Western cultures with more permanent residences, parents are keen to have kids pitch in to keep the house tidy. In the United States, parents even tie their kids' allowances to how well they do their chores. "Chores and jobs are important steps on the road to independence," according to drspock.com. They teach children "responsibility, diligence, and new skills."

Chores on the other side of the world can be put off in some cultures. Australian children raised in a traditional Aboriginal manner are indulged as much as possible and don't take on many serious responsibilities until they reach puberty. In Thailand and Kahalapur, India, many mothers believe in letting their children be free from chores so they can play—life will be hard enough later.

SHARE AND SHARE ALIKE, OR NOT?

American pediatricians recognize a child's need to keep his or her own toys and believe that sharing should be encouraged—but not forced—in a child after she is two. Other cultures don't see it that way. Sharing can be crucial to survival to a culture, especially those with limited food resources. West African tribes place a premium on learning to share. Mothers who are usually very permissive with their children can suddenly become quite strict as they teach their children to share all objects and their food from an early age.

SEEN AND NOT HEARD, OR NOT?

Some cultures believe that allowing children to speak enhances their expressive abilities, while others feel that shushing your child won't squash his creativity. Traditionally raised Australian Aborigine kids are free to speak their minds and express their feelings. Even a child who swears at his elders might not be punished—he's more likely to be laughed at or ignored.

The Hopi, in the southwestern United States, have a much different view. In the Hopi tradition, a young person is considered inexperienced in life; his elders expect him to be quiet until he knows what he's talking about. Mothers in Japan expect their children to master early the skills of self-control and politeness with adults, and kids are expected to listen to their parents and not talk back.

SPARE THE ROD, OR NOT?

As everybody knows, all kids are not angels. They do get out of line from time to time, and parents have to become the enforcers. How they enforce their rules and punish misbehavior varies from culture to culture.

In the West, the jury has long been out on the benefits or detriments of corporal punishment. About a third of U.S. parents will give a pop on the behind when a child acts up, but many pediatricians advise other forms of discipline—like time-outs or deprivations such as taking away a favorite toy. In Mexico, kids are rarely spanked if they are under seven years old. Up north, the Inuit see their children as treasures and rarely rebuke them—certainly they never spank them. In farming societies where children are expected to be obedient and work hard, punishment may be physical, as with the Ngandu in the forests of the Central African Republic.

Discipline isn't always for parents of some cultures. Sometimes the messages are mixed. In Okinawa a Tairan mom might scold her small child, then relent and apologize if her child cries. In India, a Rajput mother might nag her kid to do chores—then let the matter drop. In the United States, Dr. Spock noted that a mother might tell a child to turn off the TV set and go to bed, then back down when the child protests that none of her friends have to go to bed so early. He advised moms to make simple rules and stick to them, no matter what the other kids are doing. Consistency is key.

SUCCESSFUL STRATEGIES OR NOT?

In all cultures, moms work to raise their children to be healthy, wealthy, and wise. It seems there are as many routes for success as there are children. No matter what the maternal strategy, moms around the world seem to be doing just fine.

My Sainted Mom

Saint Monica (c. 331–387)
The mother of St. Augustine, Monica is the patron saint of mothers, especially those with undisciplined sons. She is also sacred to recovering alcoholics, as her son's *Confessions* indicate that she too overcame addiction.

Saint Paula (347–404)
Paula's husband died when she was 32 and had five kids. It's no wonder that she is the patron saint of widows. Paula was taken in by Saint Jerome and followed his teachings and eventually him to the holy land. She founded a monastery and hostel for pilgrims.

Moms Rally for Peace? And Howe!

Julia Ward Howe, the author of "Battle Hymn of the Republic," motivates moms for peace.

J ulia Ward Howe (1819–1910) was the founder of Mother's Day for Peace, a predecessor of modern Mother's Day. Only her day wasn't devoted to gifts and breakfast in bed. Julia's day was rooted in mothers' political unity for international peace.

MOTHER'S DAZE

Actually, when it came to motherhood, Julia herself had a tough time adjusting to it. She grew up the daughter of a wealthy New England banker, had an excellent education, and was used to enjoying exclusive parties and plenty of male attention. But after she married educator Samuel Howe, life changed drastically. The couple had six children (five of whom lived) in twelve years.

Though Julia came to treasure her brood, in her first years as a mom she was depressed and miserable. Why, she wondered, had she "traded in a life of easy circumstances and brilliant surroundings" to become a harassed mother of five, isolated from fashionable society and intellectual stimulation? Samuel unintentionally made her more miserable. As a traditional husband, he wanted Julia to remain at home.

Finally, Julia decided to take a few moments every day to read and do some writing. She discovered (as the world soon would) that she had talent, and she published a volume of poetry. Samuel tried to get her to give up writing because he thought it too revealing of their marriage problems. He is said to have even become violent, but Julia refused to give up her work. She began a lifelong battle for liberty: first for herself as a writer, then to abolish slavery, next to establish rights for women, and finally to free the world from war.

JULIA'S BATTLE HYMN

During the Civil War, Julia "gave birth" to a poem that would become a rallying cry for the Union. Unable to sleep one night in 1861, she was humming a popular tune of her day, "John Brown's Body." New lyrics began to come to mind, inspired by the gravity and sadness of the war. Julia sent the poem to the Atlantic Monthly and received five dollars—along with eternal fame. Julia's poem was the fierce and rousing "Battle Hymn of the Republic": "Mine eyes have seen the glory of the coming of the Lord / He is trampling out the vintage where the grapes of wrath are stored / He hath loosed the fateful lightening of his terrible swift sword. His truth is marching on."

Set to music, the poem swept the Union. The last verse inspired Northerners ("As He died to make men holy / Let us die to make men free") with the call to end slavery. Union troops sang the "Battle Hymn" with a vengeance as they marched to battle. When Abraham Lincoln heard the song, he gave an opinion in his usual succinct fashion. "Sing that again," the president said. Lincoln would later claim he knew only two songs, "Listen to the Mocking Bird" and "Battle Hymn of the Republic."

MOTHER'S DAY FOR PEACE

Julia became so famous and sought after as a public speaker that even Samuel's opposition turned to grudging admiration. But though her success came from a song of battle, Julia soon changed her tune. After volunteering to work with soldiers, widows, and orphans (both Yankee and Confederate), she saw enough misery to convince her that there had to be a better way than warfare to solve grievances.

After the Civil War ended, Julia turned her eyes to international relations. In 1870 Julia became concerned by the Franco-Prussian War, which she found "cruel and unnecessary." Julia began to envision a worldwide mother's rally for peace. She issued a proclamation calling for mothers to arise and speak out against war. In Boston she held her first rally in 1872 and called it the Mother's Day for Peace. "Who knows the cost of violence better than mothers who've lost their children on account of it?" Julia asked. Mother's Day for Peace was an annual event for many years, and although it was never officially recognized, the idea of a special mothers' day had taken hold in the public mind.

HER TRUTH IS MARCHING ON

Although Mother's Day for Peace never became an official holiday, the importance of Julia's rally cannot be underestimated. Following Julia's example, mothers saw how they could harness their numbers to make their voices heard. Groups like Mothers Against Drunk Driving and events like the Million Mom March can trace their roots back to Julia, the mom of activist moms!

Your Mother
Should Know...

Music to Moms' Ears

Mom, Mama, Momma, Mother . . . the lovely words
for the maternal have worked their way into a lot
of songs. Think you can match the mama-lyric with the
title and artist?

___ 1. Oh, Mama, can this really be the end?

___ 2. And no one's gettin' fat, except Mama Cass.

___ 3. Your momma's waiting for you
. Wearing her high-heeled shoes and
her low-necked sweater

___ 4. Cause your mama told you that love ain't right
But don't you know good lovin' is the spice of life

___ 5. "Kids are different today," I hear ev'ry mother say
Mother needs something today to calm her down

___ 6. My daddy was the family bassman,
My momma was an engineer

___ 7. Don't let 'em pick guitars and drive them old trucks
Make 'em be doctors and lawyers and such

___ 8. I love you, Mamaaaaaa
More than golf with Arnold Palmmmaaaa

___ 9. I come home in the morning light
. My mother says "When you gonna live your life right?"

___ 10. I said, "Mom, what are you doing, you're ruining my rep"
She said, "You're only sixteen, you don't have a rep yet"

___ 11. When I was just a baby, My mama told me, "Son
Always be a good boy, Don't ever play with guns"

Your Face Will Freeze Like That!

Was mom's advice right?

"Don't suck your thumb" to "Don't be a bum," mothers doled out quite a few pearls of wisdom. guys in white coats with PhDs after their names to verify mothers' advice in the lab. Was mom ?

. It's brain food.
d mom know?
tty acids in fish,
nportant com-
r little gray
ds your brain's
mmunication
duction. In
ors who ate
k had a better
d Alzheimer's.

**ide without
r you'll**

ds are con-
is usually
s. They aren't
veather or
germs you

pick up when you don't wash your hands.

Wash your hands!
True. See above, silly.

Eating carrots will help you see in the dark.
True. The vitamins in carrots help improve your night vision.

Breakfast is the most important meal of the day.
Right on, mom. Studies found that kids who eat breakfast do better academically than those who don't. In one study, breakfast eaters often averaged nearly a whole grade higher

___ 12. Mama, life had just beg
But now I've gone and

___ 13. Hey, Hey, Mama the
Gonna make you swe

___ 14. You say your mother
was a reputation
Awww, she never car
prayer for me?

___ 15. Oh, Mama, I'm in fe
of the law
Lawman has put an
from my home

A. "Mama, Don't Let Your
Willie Nelson

B. "Parents Just Don't Un
Fresh Prince

C. "Stuck Inside of Mobi
Bob Dylan

D. "Renegade," Styx

E. "Mother's Little Help

F. "Mother's Day Song,'

G. "Only the Good Die

H. "Black Dog," Led Ze

I. "Bohemian Rhapsod

J. "Creeque Alley," Th

K. "Folsom Prison Blue

L. "Girls Just Wanna

M. "Get Back," The B

N. "Baby Driver," Sim

O. "Mama's Pearl," Th

. F; 9, L; 10, B; 11, K; 12,

F
rom "
our m
Now the g
are trying t
always right

Eat your fish
True. How di
One of the fa
DHA, is an i
ponent of you
cells; DHA ai
cell-to-cell co
and nerve con
one study, sen
fish once a we
chance to avoi

Don't go outs
your coat on
catch a cold.
Sorry, mom. Co
tagious infection
caused by viruse
caused by cold
dampness but by

than those who went to school on an empty stomach!

If you keep making that face, your face will freeze like that!

Sorry, mom. Our faces really do "freeze" into a pattern of creases, or wrinkles, we create whenever we smile or frown, but making a silly face for a few minutes won't affect anything—except your mother's blood pressure.

It's important to get a good night's sleep.

True. Experiments at Harvard Medical School showed that college students who slept after they learned a new task remembered more about it the next day than students who stayed up all night after learning that same task.

If you can't say anything nice about someone, don't say anything at all.

True. Experiments show that when someone gossips about the personality traits of another person, the listener will transfer those personality traits to the speaker. So if you tell Harry that Jim is a liar, Harry might think you are dishonest. When you only say positive things about other people, you'll always be perceived in a positive light.

Too much TV is bad for you.

True. Too much TV and too little exercise combine to increase body fat and obesity. And to avoid Alzheimer's, researchers suggest that you turn off the TV and exercise your brain by reading, doing crossword puzzles, playing music, and even gardening.

Don't swallow your chewing gum or your stomach walls will stick together.

Sorry, mom. What were you thinking with this one? A popular variation on this one is that gum takes seven years to digest. Please. Stomach acid is as strong as toilet bowl cleaner and can liquefy chewing gum in no time.

If you crack your knuckles, you'll get arthritis.

Yes. No. Maybe So. Clinicians have found that cracking your knuckles pushes joints past their normal range of motion and puts stress on the ligaments and tendons that hold the joint together. Cracking your knuckles for a period of years could result in inflamed, arthritic knuckle joints.

Eat slowly and chew your food.
True. Eating too fast can lead to painful acid reflux disease. People can die choking on a piece of food. Plus chewing more slowly really allows you to *taste* your food.

If you cross your eyes, they might stay that way.
Nah, give up, mom. Keeping your eyes crossed for a while may cause a temporary spasm of the eye muscles, but this condition usually passes shortly. The condition called "cross-eye" often begins at birth. It isn't related to voluntarily crossing your eyes.

Nobody likes a smart mouth.
Oh please, mom! Why do millions love to watch Leno and Letterman? Sorry, mom, you're wrong. But then, as you'd be the first to advise us—nobody's perfect!

"I love my mother for all the times she said absolutely nothing. . . . Thinking back on it all, it must have been the most difficult part of mothering she ever had to do: knowing the outcome, yet feeling she had no right to keep me from charting my own path. I thank her for all her virtues, but mostly for never once having said, 'I told you so.'" —Erma Bombeck, *Motherhood, the Second Oldest Profession*

Lucky or Lethal Livia?

Did Livia really poison her son's rivals to the throne?

Oh, the glory that was Rome! Those ancient marble palaces, statues, arches, and baths; the feasts and festivities—they were to die for! Unfortunately, plenty of people did—die, that is. Especially if they crossed the ambitions of regal first lady Livia. Did Livia kill off her husband and her step-grandchildren so that her son Tiberius would rule the Roman Empire? Was she one of history's most murderous and manipulative moms? Or was powerful Livia the victim of bad press?

POWER GRABBY

Born in 58 BC into a noble Roman family, beautiful Livia Drusilla was married with one son, Tiberius, and another on the way. She was fortunate enough to strike the fancy of a very powerful but unhappily married man, Octavian, the adopted son and heir of Julius Caesar, who wanted her for his bride. Livia's husband was "persuaded" to divorce her. Once Octavian divorced his first wife, the scandalous pair was married in 38 BC. Livia later gave birth to her second son, Drusus, after her marriage to Octavian.

PROMOTING FAMILY VALUES

Octavian took power and became emperor in 27 BC when the Roman senate proclaimed him Augustus Caesar, ruler of the empire and a divine descendant of the gods of

Rome. Augustus's reign lasted 45 years and Livia was his first lady throughout. Unfortunately, their marriage never produced any children, but the union survived.

Livia was an ideal politician's wife. She sponsored charities, dedicated buildings, and presented a public image of the humble wife and mother. Actually, Augustus relied on Livia to help him in affairs of state. She even wielded his personal seal, signing orders for him when he was away. Livia had so much power at home, some said that although Augustus ruled Rome, Livia ruled Augustus.

MURD'HEIRS?

Though Livia publicly helped Augustus promote family values, privately she may have been poisoning the family—her husband's family, that is. Livia wanted to put her son Tiberius on the throne, but Augustus kept picking males from his own line to rule when he was gone. Augustus may have listened to Livia's advice, but when it came to succession, he certainly had his own ideas.

First, Augustus picked his nephew and stepson, Marcellus, to succeed him. Then, Marcellus mysteriously died. So his widow Julia married again, this time to Agrippa. The pair had two sons, Gaius and Lucius, that Augustus then named as his heirs. But strangely enough, each of those young men fell ill and died too. It seemed that being first in line for the throne was a dangerous place to be, especially if you stood in front of Livia's son. Every time Augustus named an heir who was not Tiberius, he seemed to keel over prematurely. Was Livia lucky or what?

Seems that Rome was no different from modern times when it comes to conspiracy theories. Romans and other historians from classic times onward declared that Livia poisoned off Augustus's heirs until he was forced to tap

Tiberius to be the next emperor. They even go so far as to claim that after Tiberius's appointment as heir, Livia killed Augustus himself with poisoned figs. Augustus did mysteriously become ill and was called to that great marble palace in the sky.

Everyone seemed to bite the Roman dust except Livia and her son. Hmm. Mighty suspicious.

Only lately have some historians said that Livia got a bum rap and was no murderess. They say that the biographers in ancient times blamed Livia for all those deaths because she was such a powerful woman and much resented by all those men, especially her own son Tiberius.

THIS IS THE THANKS SHE GOT?

However she got it, Livia enjoyed the authority that came her way when Tiberius came to power, but her son didn't necessarily enjoy it. Tiberius, who by this time was 46, resented her interference and did not welcome her help in the way Augustus had. Rumor has it that he left Rome and moved to Capri to get away from her. He visited her once in the last three years of her life, and only for an hour or two then. Tiberius's resentment even lasted beyond the grave. After Livia's death, he refused to honor her will or attend her funeral.

But not everyone had as bad an opinion of Livia as her son. When she died at age 86, the Roman senate dedicated an arch to her, honoring her "acts of kindness and generosity." It was the first and last time ancient Rome gave that honor to a woman.

Honor Thy Stepmom

It's only natural. Just ask Honest Abe.

Thanks to fairy tales, we've all heard of the wicked stepmother. But how about the wonderful stepmother or blessed stepmother? Unfamiliar as those phrases sound, they made perfect sense to Abraham Lincoln. Few people realize that as far as mothers of presidents go, one of the most important First Mothers in American history was in fact First Stepmother Sarah Bush Lincoln. Without her loving assistance, one of the country's greatest presidents might never have made it into politics—he might not have even survived.

A celebrity in life and death, Lincoln's life has been thoroughly examined by historians. Scholars have worked harder than the *National Enquirer* to dig up Honest Abe's secrets and scandals. There are wrangles over Abe's true parentage, whether or not he was faithful to his wife, and even whether or not he had a boyfriend! But no one argues about one vital fact in Lincoln's bio. The future president adored his stepmother, Sarah Bush Lincoln, and she was a huge factor in his success.

LIFE WITHOUT MAMA AIN'T NO LIFE AT ALL

In 1818, when Abe was nine years old and his sister Sarah was 11, the Lincoln family lived in tough frontier conditions in a log cabin in the southern Indiana woods near a community called Pigeon Creek. The Lincolns' windowless cabin had a dirt floor and no door so the winter wind could whistle right on through. But a tough life turned unbearable when Abe's hardworking mother, Nancy, fell ill and died.

While young Abe and his sister, Sarah, grieved for their mother, they labored harder than ever. The family struggled to put food on the table and keep the cabin warm. But Thomas knew that his motherless family was floundering, so he returned to Kentucky to find a wife and left the children under the care of their 18-year-old cousin, Dennis— hardly the best supervision.

GETTING MARRIED IS GOOD BUSINESS

On his quest for a wife, Thomas Lincoln sought out an old flame, the widow Sarah "Sally" Bush Johnston. Lincoln and Sarah had known each other in Elizabethtown, Kentucky, but Sarah had married another man. Now Thomas found her a widow, free to marry her old beau.

There was no time for holding hands or candlelight dinners. In a quick, businesslike arrangement, Thomas paid Sarah's debts and they were married the following day. Thomas, Sarah, and her three children packed up and headed for Indiana.

THE WAY TO A BOY'S HEART

Meanwhile, back in the cabin, it had been nearly six months since Thomas left. Ragged, filthy, and hungry, his abandoned children were sure they were orphans. Abe struggled to comfort his sister with presents like a baby raccoon and a turtle, but secretly he feared they would soon die. Imagine his feelings when his father returned with a wagon full of people, including three playmates, Elizabeth, Matilda, and John, and a stepmother who hugged Abe lovingly, then energetically set about making sure he was well cared for.

Sarah immediately bathed the Lincoln children. She mended their clothes and as their cousin Dennis later said, made them "look human." Once the children were clean and fed, she got to work on the house, eventually insisting that the Lincoln cabin be fitted up with a wooden floor, a window, and a real door that opened and, most importantly, shut. A loft bedroom was made for Abe, Dennis, and John, while the girls and their parents slept downstairs.

Abe's new stepmother brought treasures with her. A table and chairs replaced the tree stumps that had provided seating. Abe and little Sarah learned to use real knives and forks and spoons. Best of all, their lumpy cornhusk mattresses were replaced with feather beds.

A MIND IS A TERRIBLE THING TO WASTE

But most important of all, Sarah brought books to Pigeon Creek—biographies of Ben Franklin and George Washington and fiction such as *Robinson Crusoe*, *The Pilgrim's Progress*, and *Aesop's Fables*. Abe had always had a hunger for learning and he read the books eagerly. Sarah's books, along with the Bible, provided his curriculum, since formal schooling on the frontier was unpredictable.

Abe much preferred reading and studying to splitting logs or working in the fields. This strained his relationship with his father. Thomas didn't see much value in book learning when there were so many farm chores that needed doing just to survive. It was Sarah who valued Abe's sensitivity and intelligence and who encouraged the boy to read, do arithmetic, and write poetry. Her stepson, starved for affection and understanding, blossomed under the attentions of the woman he called "mother."

With Sarah's help, a lonely, unhappy boy grew into a clever, self-confident man, determined to become a success in the greater world. To the Lincoln children, Sarah brought comfort and stability. More important, she gave them love and support. Neighbors said that she managed her blended family well, treating all the children impartially. But years later, Sarah admitted to an interviewer that she secretly had a favorite. "Abe was a good boy," she said, "the best boy I ever saw. I never gave him a cross word in all my life. His mind and mine . . . seemed to move in the same channel."

WITH MALICE TOWARD NONE AND CHARITY FOR ALL

Abraham Lincoln always revered Sarah. He made sure that after his father's death she received 40 acres to live on as long as she lived. Proud Sarah lived to see her "good boy" become the president who held the Union together and ended slavery.

Today a grateful nation still honors the president, who, despite the hatreds formed in a raging civil war, called for "malice toward none and charity for all." Along with his eloquence and courage, Abraham Lincoln is beloved for qualities of kindness, tolerance, and forgiveness—qualities he learned at the knee of his stepmother.

Dear Uncle John

Straight answers for Mother's Day dilemmas

Perplexed as to how to show your mom that you care? Just ask Uncle John. He has the answers to all your Mother's Day questions.

HOW MUCH TO SPEND?

Dear Uncle John,
Help! I need you to settle a spat among my siblings. We can't agree on how much to spend on mom for this Mother's Day. I won't say who's the cheap one, but it's not me!
*   Sign me,*
*   Grateful One*

Dear GO,
It doesn't really matter what you spend, as long as you show your mom you love her. But for the numerically inclined, we did some research and found that a 2002 National Retail Federation survey showed that consumers planned to spend an average of $97 per household on Mother's Day gifts. That was 36 percent more than the previous year's average of $62! Men get the honors for generosity to mom—$118 versus $79 for the ladies.

Curious as to how we are spending these bucks on mom? About 80 percent of us will buy cards, sending about 144 million of them. More than half will give flowers, with mixed bouquets, roses, or tulips as the most popular choices.

And we'll eat too. Mother's Day is the second-most-popular occasion to dine out (the first is birthdays), with 30 percent trooping to a restaurant to give mom a break.

HOW TO CHOOSE?

Dear Uncle John,

I admit I'm not the best gift giver, but I thought I hit a home run last Mother's Day, only it turns out I struck out big time. Who knew she wouldn't like that new baseball mitt? I'd like to hit it out of the park this year, so do you have any help for picking the perfect present?

Sincerely,

Cleanup Hitter

Dear CH,

The best advice that I can give you is to do your research. What does mom like? A Yahoo survey showed that despite our good intentions, we have bad info when we go to get mom a gift. Eighty-eight percent wanted to give their mothers a gift this Mother's Day but didn't know the basics.

For example:

- 50% of respondents couldn't name their mother's dress size.
- 35% didn't know their mother's favorite perfume and an additional 15% weren't even sure if their mother wore perfume.
- 25% didn't know their mother's favorite color.
- 25% didn't know which flower was mom's favorite.

So what can help Mother's Day go well? Experts simply advise talking to mom and asking her what type of day she'd prefer. Treat her like the individual she is and tailor your gift to her individual preferences, not yours. Experts also suggest that honoring mother all year will help all to relax and enjoy Mother's Day, since there will be less pressure on you to make this one day perfect.

WHAT NOT TO GIVE?

Dear Uncle John,
I often read advice about what to give my mom for Mother's Day, but I never see advice on what NOT to give. What are the worst things you can give?
Sign me,
Not Wanting to Be the Worst

Dear NWBW,
An interesting question! Several online polls gave moms the chance to sound off about the worst Mother's Day gifts they've ever received. Odds are the best things to avoid are:

• *Nothing.* Mom will always remember when you do nothing, so do something, anything, lest you run the risk of forever being reminded of that Mother's Day when you did nothing.
• *Kitchen and cooking supplies.* If mom loves to cook, this isn't a bad idea. But if she dreads time in the kitchen, pots and pans are not the way to go.
• *Gardening tools and housecleaning supplies.* Avoid gifts that create more work or summon up images of drudgery! So no vacuums, toilet brushes, or rakes unless they're specifically asked for. It's just too risky.

- *Socks*. If they don't work as kids' presents—surprise!—they don't work for moms either.
- *Clothes*. It's tough to buy clothing for other people, especially if you're trying to surprise them. Best to give mom a gift certificate to her favorite store if fashion is her thing.

GIFT IDEAS, PLEASE

Dear Uncle John,
Help! I've asked my mother many times what she would like for Mother's Day. She just smiles and says that she'll love whatever I give her. Since I'm not a little kid anymore, I'm not sure that answer really applies to me. Can you help?

Sign me,
Damage Control

Dear DC,
What a pickle! You've tried to do your homework and you've been thwarted. So we did some digging and found some great ideas for Mother's Day gifts that fit all kinds of budgets. For the kind of present you can tie a bow on, here's what we found moms liked:

- *Flowers* (her favorite blossoms can be so sweet)
- *Perfume* (just be sure to get the kind she actually wears)
- *Electronics* (seems DVD players and digital cameras are hot tickets!)
- *Jewelry* (an option for the husbands in the crowd)
- *Homemade cards* (probably best for the grammar school set)

Other moms prefer gifts of events or outings. Here are just a few:

- *Breakfast in bed* (tried and true)
- *Sunday brunch* (a nice option for the culinarily challenged)

- *Dinner* (at her favorite restaurant, not yours)
- *Quality family time* (her definition, not yours)
- *Spa trip* (massages and wraps and facials, oh my!)
- *Help with chores* (a classic)

Whatever you do, you'll be sure to make mom feel special!

Ghostly Highway

Have you heard this oft-told urban highway legend? As the story goes, a visibly injured woman flags down a couple driving on the highway. She tells them that there has been a terrible car accident. She fears that her husband is dead, but begs them to save her baby who's still alive. Leaving the hurt woman with his wife, the husband rushes to wreckage and pulls the baby from the car.

When he returns to his car, the injured woman is gone. His wife tells him that she saw the mother follow him back to the ditch. Only then does the man recall that he saw two adults slumped in the front seats of the car. He gives the baby to his wife and runs back to the scene, but finds a dead man and woman, buckled into their seats with seatbelts. The dead woman is the same one who had enlisted his help to save her baby. This popular legend illustrates the belief in the power of a mother's love—which can reach from beyond the grave.

Lights! Camera! Action Moms!

Five maternally fueled action films that say:
Don't make mom angry. You wouldn't like her when she's angry.

The Mom: Sarah Connor
The Movie: *Terminator 2: Judgment Day* (1991)
The Story: In this sci-fi/action classic, Sarah Connor (Linda Hamilton), the hard-bodied mother of John Connor, a 10-year-old kid who will one day save the world from the evil machine empire, must keep her son from being killed by a time-traveling, shape-shifting robot. Luckily, the robot played by Arnold Schwarzenegger is on her side in this movie! Aside from being a lean, mean, fighting machine, Sarah is actually an interesting exploration of parental responsibility—she loves her kid but comes off as incredibly cold because she must give him the military skills he needs to survive. Leave it to writer/director James Cameron to skillfully take the most masculine of film genres and turn it into a study of maternal duties and failings—right under the nose of the teenage boys in the audience. Shhhh. Don't tell.

The Mom: Samantha Caine, a.k.a. Charly Baltimore
The Movie: *The Long Kiss Good Night* (1996)
The Story: Just your average mom, Samantha Caine (Geena Davis) bakes cookies, teaches school . . . oh, and suffers from amnesia. She discovers little by little that in her past life—the one she doesn't remember—she was Charly Baltimore, a pistol-packin', cigarette-smokin' badass for one of the more disreputable parts of the U.S. government. Once she gets

her memory back, it's only a matter of time before some old nemeses track her down and use her sweet little daughter as bait to draw her out in the open. Now, if you knew a woman was a super-assassin, would *you* threaten her kid? Yeah, neither would we. Don't let that scare you away: a bit bloody and violent, but probably a little better than you expect, even if it was directed by Renny Harlin, Davis's then-husband, of *Cutthroat Island* infamy.

The Mom: Evelyn O'Connell
The Movie: *The Mummy Returns* (2001)
The Story: This light-hearted sequel to 1999's *The Mummy* finds librarian turned tomb-raider Evelyn (Rachel Weisz) happily married to adventurer Rick O'Connell (Brendan Fraser) and raising a precocious little boy. Then that awful mummy from the first film rises from the dead yet again, and this time he needs a bracelet to reveal the location of a secret undead army —a bracelet strapped to the arm of Evelyn's kid. Kids. They're always getting into

something. The boy's kidnapped (of course), and Evelyn and Rick work as a team to bring their boy back home. Maternal action highlights include Evelyn picking off bad guys with a rifle as Rick rescues their kid and duking it out with the Mummy's reincarnated girlfriend both in the 20th century and ancient Egypt. That's right, she kicks butt across four millennia!

The Mom: The Bride
The Movie: *Kill Bill* (2003)
The Story: In this bloody Quentin Tarantino–directed flick, Uma Thurman stars as "the Bride," a pregnant woman whose name we never learn and who also happens to belong to an elite team of assassins. The Bride is, quite naturally, getting married when the film opens. Unluckily for her, her workplace isn't so family friendly, and her former coworkers crash the wedding to bump her and her guests off. They don't quite do it . . . and the Bride wakes up several years later, widowed, without her child, and thirsting for revenge. And boy, does she wreak havoc. Despite

the violence, interesting threads of maternity and family wind their way through the film. Aside from Uma's character, another assassin turns out to be a mother, which has future consequences as the two women battle to the death. Another character's backstory has her avenging the death of her mother and father at the hands of the Japanese "Yakuza" crime gangs. *Kill Bill* is only part one of the story, so be on the lookout for part two to find out what happens to the Bride.

The Mom: Heather Langenkamp
The Movie: *Wes Craven's New Nightmare* (1994)
The Story: If you prefer your maternal action with a horror edge, this twist on the *Nightmare on Elm Street* series may float your boat. Actress Heather Langenkamp (who played the teenage heroine in the very first film) is living the happy life of a B-list actress and mom, when suddenly Freddy, the monstrous villain from the film series, is loosed into the real world. Seems that when the movie studio killed off the film series (presumably with 1991's *Freddy's Dead*), it allowed Freddy's evil energy out into reality, where it could invade the dreams of the filmmakers. And since Freddy famously feeds on the children of those who killed him, well, that's bad news for Langenkamp's little boy. But it's not as if our heroine is going to meekly offer up her kid. This leads to her and Freddy going at it in a confrontation that twists reality and Hollywood horror fantasy. Considered one of the better *Nightmare* films by horror fans, it's doubly spooky for moms.

The Single Mother of Invention

It sounds like an urban legend, but it's not.
A Monkees' mother invented Liquid Paper!

Bette Nesmith never was a whiz at typing. Not that she cared much. She was going to be an artist just like her mother, not a secretary. Unfortunately, Bette's plans fell through in 1946, when she found herself divorced and supporting her young son, Robert Michael, otherwise known as Mike. She desperately needed a good job.

TOUGH PRECOMPUTER TIMES

Opportunities were limited for women in the late 1940s. Bette took up typing and shorthand and became a secretary. To earn extra cash, she worked as a freelance artist. But Bette was the family's sole provider and found it tough to make ends meet. As Mike later said bluntly, "We were dirt poor . . . just miserable."

When Bette became executive secretary to the chairman of the board of Texas Bank and Trust, she was determined to keep her job—despite those darned electric typewriters. Back in the dark ages, before desktop computers existed, the only way to type a letter was on an actual typewriter. Electric typewriters powered keys that flew quickly with a light touch, but they also had carbon ribbons that made typos tough to erase. Bette often made typing errors, and when she erased them the paper would get smudged.

MISTAKES CAN BE ARTISTIC

Bette wished she could cover up secretarial mistakes the way artists did. They simply painted over their errors and no one was the wiser. One evening she had a brainstorm, and using her artist's skills, she mixed tempera paint (an opaque water-based paint) to a shade that perfectly matched her boss's business stationery. She put her solution in a small bottle and brought it to work, along with her watercolor brush. Now when Bette made a typing mistake, she simply painted it out with her new correcting fluid, which she called "Mistake Out."

Bette's boss didn't notice her corrected mistakes, but other secretaries did. They wanted some of that correction paint for themselves! Eventually Bette began selling her concoction and founded the Mistake Out Company. After work she turned her kitchen into a laboratory and used her electric mixer to whip up new batches of paints and chemicals until she had her product perfected. In the garage, her son Mike and his friends used ketchup squeeze bottles to fill little bottles of Mistake Out and supply the ever-increasing orders.

LIQUID PAPER? I'M A BELIEVER

Bette tried to sell her idea to IBM, but they turned her down. Realizing she'd have to manufacture and market her product herself, Bette went back to work after work. Now, along with learning about paint and paper, she read up and sought advice on marketing. In a flash of inspiration, Bette renamed her product "Liquid Paper." A trade magazine published the story of her little business and she received her first big order. General Electric wanted 400 bottles in three colors!

Bette took the plunge and devoted all her time to Liquid Paper—a risky move, as her business still wasn't profitable. But Mike was a big boy now and could support himself, so Bette was really able to focus on the business. Luckily, she had help. In 1962 she married Robert Graham, who helped her run the company.

Mike also married, then went off to California to try his luck in the music business. And boy, did he make mom proud! He rose to fame in *The Monkees*, a sitcom about four young musicians in a pop band. The tall Monkee in the goofy wool hat, Mike was an instant star, known for his dry humor and quick wit. The show was a huge hit and so were the group's albums and singles, like "I'm a Believer."

Meanwhile, back in Dallas, Bette's hard work was finally paying off. As word spread that Liquid Paper could correct typing mistakes, business skyrocketed. Eventually Bette was selling so many millions of bottles of Liquid Paper that she moved her operation into an automated plant. Next, the company built an international headquarters and produced 500 bottles of correcting fluid a minute.

While Liquid Paper brought in wealth, generous Bette set up foundations to help other women. She never forgot the hard times she and Mike once faced. And as a single mom, it was no accident that her company was one of the first to offer on-site child care. Said Bette, "Most people in my income bracket build estates. I can't understand why. My estate will be what I can do for others. I want to see my money working, causing progress for people."

STILL SAVING SECRETARIES

In 1979 Bette Nesmith Graham sold her corporation to Gillette for over $47 million, allowing her to continue her charitable work. Meanwhile, her invention continues to save the jobs of the world's secretaries—one little bottle at a time.

TV Moms II:
Groovy Gals

*Take a short broom ride, put on some polyester duds,
and crank up the pop tunes!*

In the 1960s and 1970s, moms began to loosen up a bit on the small screen. Witches, mixed families, and rockin' road trips all made the scene!

SAMANTHA STEPHENS: WITCHY MAMA

The Show: *Bewitched* (1964–1972)
Mere mortal Darrin Stephens married his beautiful wife, Samantha (played by Elizabeth Montgomery), only to discover that she was a witch who could cast a spell with just a twitch of her snub nose. Samantha tried to please him by giving up witchcraft to be a normal wife and mother, but her mother, Endora, was hell-bent on getting Darrin out of the picture so Sam could stay supernatural. Every week, Samantha's twitching nose would cause all witchcraft to break loose in the Stephens's household—usually saving Darrin and their children, Tabitha and Adam. Throughout the series, Sam remained true to herself—keeping both her powers and her husband. A powerful statement for the times!
Fun Fact: Agnes Moorehead, the actress who played Sam's meddling mom, also played a mother on the big screen in *Citizen Kane*. She played Charles Foster Kane's mother.

CAROL BRADY: LOVELY LADY

The Show: *The Brady Bunch* (1969–1974)

Carol Brady (played by Florence Henderson) mothered the Brady Bunch, of course! As the famous theme song explains, Carol was a "lovely lady who was bringing up three very lovely girls" when she married a widower, Mike Brady, who "was busy with three boys of his own." The series and its theme song were much loved, but the portrayal of a mixed family endeared it to kids whose own families were a bit more "blended" than the traditional nuclear family.

A stay-at-home mom, Carol was a busy lady nonetheless. She had Alice, the maid, to help with cooking and cleaning, so she could spend time promoting local political causes, singing in church, and indulging her creative side through needlepoint and sculpture. Carol was a mom who liked to use her brain. (Though some would argue that the scriptwriters didn't.)

Fun Fact: While we know that Mike Brady is a widower, it is never revealed in the TV series how Mrs. Brady's first marriage ended. What ever happened to the father of those three very lovely girls?

SHIRLEY PARTRIDGE: ROCKIN' MOM

The Show: *The Partridge Family* (1970–1974)

TV moms could be pop stars too, as *The Partridge Family* showed us in 1970. Widowed Shirley Partridge (played by Shirley Jones) needed money and so she formed a band with her five kids and got into the music biz. In an old painted school bus with a sign that read: "Caution: Nervous Mother Driving," Shirley took her kids on tour and into music success with only a few sour notes.

With hits like "I Think I Love You" and "I Woke Up in Love This Morning," mom and the kids were one of the TV families who didn't rely on mom's husband to provide for the family. Though Shirley didn't behave too much differently than other sitcom moms, her financial independence signaled that changes were coming.

Fun Fact: Shirley Jones was a real-life stepmom to David Cassidy, who played her on-screen son Keith Partridge.

"A mother is the truest friend we have, when trials, heavy and sudden, fall upon us; when adversity takes the place of prosperity; when friends who rejoice with us in our sunshine, desert us when troubles thicken around us, still will she cling to us, and endeavor by her kind precepts and counsels to dissipate the clouds of darkness, and cause peace to return to our hearts."
—Washington Irving

She Had a Dream

*When you celebrate Martin Luther King Jr. Day, don't forget
the gentle lady who helped create his dream.*

A t first glance, Alberta Christine Williams seemed an
unlikely candidate to raise one of the United States'
most important social activists. Fashionable Alberta was
born into a life of comfort. She always had access to the
best schools, clubs, and social functions in black Atlanta.
She was also so shy and quiet that not many people realized how strong she could be. And it didn't seem likely
that someone so elegant and refined would ever teach her
son to rock the boat—let alone shake up an entire nation.

But when Martin Luther King, Jr., led the battle to end
segregation in the Jim Crow South, his mother backed
him. Meticulous, reserved Alberta became beloved
"Mama King," not only to her family but also to King's
followers throughout the country. Many people knew that
she was a devoted warrior for the cause of justice. Only
family and close friends knew that her loving nature
started Martin Luther King, Jr., on his famous path of
nonviolence.

GROWING UP WITH EBENEZER

In the early 1900s, the prosperous African American
community in Atlanta thrived. The South might have
been segregated, but in Atlanta the black middle-class
and professionals were respected. They formed a tight

society that outsiders found hard to penetrate. In Ebenezer Baptist Church, many of the best and brightest of black Atlanta attended Sunday services. Reverend Williams, Alberta's father, was an influential preacher and he made Ebenezer Baptist into one of the strongest black churches in the South.

In 1924 Alberta received her teaching certificate from Hampton Institute, but she taught school only briefly. Most of her life centered on Ebenezer. For 12 years she ran its Women's Council, and for more than 40 years she was its musical director and organ player. When Alberta fell in love, she and minister Mike King (who later changed his name to Martin Luther) announced their engagement at Sunday services. On Thanksgiving Day 1926, the couple married in the old and venerable brick church. And when her father passed on, Alberta's husband took over as the head minister of Ebenezer Baptist Church.

MOTHER DEAR IS A SWEET BUNCH

The new Mrs. King, also known by her nickname "Bunch," had a strong sense of fashion, a great sense of humor, and a determination to practice Christian goodness, not just preach it—all qualities later remarked on in her famous son. Alberta loved music and fancy dancing, though what with being daughter, then wife, and finally mother of conservative Baptist ministers (the Baptists frowned on dancing), she didn't often get the chance to strut her stuff.

It took some effort to get to know the soft-spoken, reserved young woman, but those who did often commented on her sweet nature. Her son Martin found her warmth and gentleness unfailing. To him, she was always "Mother Dear."

Martin, his older sister, Christine, and his younger brother, Alfred Daniel, were all born in the Queen Anne home on 510 Auburn Street. Church became a second home to the children and Mama King echoed weekly sermons by encouraging high moral purpose.

Despite her high standards, Alberta told at least one fib. Sure that her eldest son was precocious, she lied about his age and put him in school a year early. When little Martin innocently bragged about his birthday cake with five candles on it, he was promptly expelled until he was six. That fib aside, Martin always praised his mother's character and claimed that his own optimism about human nature had a lot to do with the love and goodness he'd experienced as her child.

While her children were young, Alberta was happy, but never secure. She constantly feared for her husband's safety. Daddy King had grown up in the poverty of a sharecropper's shack and worked his way through high school and college. He was a strong, proud man, too proud to accept the humiliation of Jim Crow.

When a police officer stopped Daddy King for missing a stop sign and ordered, "All right, boy, pull over and let me see your license," the elder King pointed out in no uncertain terms that he was a man and wasn't about to talk to anyone who couldn't figure that out. Rattled, the officer hastily wrote out the ticket and sped off. But Alberta knew the confrontation could have led to a beating, imprisonment, or worse for her husband. Lynching was a very real threat.

Alberta also grieved at the hurts inflicted on her children by the unfairness of segregation. When six-year-old Martin came home in tears, announcing that his white friends wouldn't play with him anymore because of his race, Alberta tried to help him understand the unthinkable. "She told me about slavery," Martin later wrote. "She tried to explain the divided system of the South—the segregated schools, restaurants, theaters, housing; the white and colored signs on drinking fountains, waiting rooms, lavatories—as a social condition rather than a natural order. She made it clear that she opposed this system and that I must never allow it to make me feel inferior. Then she said the words that almost every Negro hears before he can yet understand the injustice that makes them necessary: 'You are as good as anyone.'"

JUNIOR MOVES TO THE FRONT

Most days, Alberta's kids had few worries; they enjoyed good clothes, good schools, and good times. When in trouble they relied on the strength of their parents. The future was bright, especially for Martin, who married Coretta Scott, a beautiful outsider from Alabama, and took over the pastorship of a church in Montgomery, Alabama.

Not long after Martin moved to Alabama, Rosa Parks famously refused to give up her bus seat. She was arrested and taken to the Montgomery courthouse. At a rally to protest Parks's arrest, Martin gave a stirring speech to an overflowing black crowd, urging a boycott of the bus line. His fellow ministers were stunned at the power of his oratory, while the inspired crowd responded with cheers. Martin's life as America's most powerful civil rights advocate had begun, and his mother prayed for his safety now.

Alberta had feared for Daddy King, but she agonized over Junior, who took far greater risks on a much larger scale. Even so, through years of dangerous sit-ins and mass rallies, arrests, beatings, stabbings, and bombings, Mama King forced herself to be a source of strength for her crusading son. She was there when, to the young man's own surprise, his work awakened the conscience of a nation and the world.

In 1964 Martin told his mother about going to the White House for the signing of the Civil Rights Act. Later that year, along with Daddy King and Coretta, Mama King accompanied Martin to Oslo, where he became, at 35, the youngest man ever to receive the Nobel Peace Prize.

A ROCK OF AGES, A GENTLE LEGACY

Encouraged to retire and enjoy his accomplishments, Martin instead went back to righting wrongs. One afternoon in Memphis he had some rare relaxation, enjoying a long phone conversation with "Mother Dear"—laughing and talking about family instead of politics. Hours later on April 4, 1968, he was assassinated while standing on a motel balcony.

As the nation grieved for her son, Alberta rallied herself for the sake of her family and especially her grandchildren. Those who'd known only the sweet side of Mama King discovered that (yet again like her son) she was tougher than they knew. Many turned to her for strength.

Though she was always too reserved to speak out like her son did, Alberta gave her own legacy to history. Her husband said of his wife's lessons to his children: "She taught them the sense of kindness, the sense of forgiveness, the sense of love." With those teachings, Mama King raised a hero who never stopped fighting for the oppressed but always practiced nonviolence and forgiveness toward the oppressors.

Martin explained himself this way: "I think that my strong determination for justice comes from the very strong, dynamic personality of my father, and I would hope that the gentle aspect comes from a mother who is very gentle and sweet."

Mom Is a Stand-Up Gal

Why is it that when a comic mouths off,
Mom always gets into the act?

FAMILY SECRETS

"My mom told us how she learned to swim. Someone took her out in the lake and threw her off the boat. That's how she learned how to swim. I said, 'Mom, they weren't trying to teach you how to swim.'"
Paula Poundstone

"My mother had so much work to do that when one of us was being born she never used to go to the hospital until the last possible second. In fact, three of us were born on a bus . . . and after each one, Dad would go up and ask for a transfer."
Bob Hope

"My mother buried three husbands, and two of them were just napping."
Rita Rudner

"My mother's menu consisted of two choices: take it or leave it."
Buddy Hackett

"My mother could make anyone feel guilty. She used to get letters of apology from people she didn't even know."
Joan Rivers

"My grandmother started walking five miles a day when she was sixty. She's ninety-seven now, and we don't know where the hell she is."
Ellen DeGeneres

"My mother treated us all equally . . . with contempt."
Groucho Marx

"My mother taught me to think of myself as a sex symbol for the men who don't give a damn."
Phyllis Diller

POSITIVE THINKING

"My mother talks to herself and complains of hearing voices."
Phyllis Diller

"Changing a diaper is a lot like getting a present from your grandmother—you're not sure what you've got but you're pretty sure you're not going to like it."
Jeff Foxworthy

"Mother never stops complaining. She hired a nursing aide recently, so that she could complain someone was stealing from her."
Judith Gold

"Mother always said that honesty was the best policy and money isn't everything. She was wrong about other things, too."
Gerald Bazan

"My mother thought the doctor had left the stork and taken the baby."
Bob Hope

"I was so ugly when I was born, the doctor slapped my mother."
Henny Youngman

OBSERVATIN' MOM

"The hand that rocks the cradle usually is attached to someone who isn't getting enough sleep."
John Fiebig

"It is said that life begins when the fetus can exist apart from its mother. By this definition, many people in Hollywood are legally dead."
Jay Leno

"What's a home without a mother? Dirty."
Soupy Sales

"Don't forget Mother's Day. Or as they call it in Beverly Hills, Dad's Third Wife's Day."
Jay Leno

"If evolution really works, how come mothers only have two hands?"
Milton Berle

MOM'S-I VIEW

"Never lend your car to anyone to whom you have given birth."
Erma Bombeck

"There's a lot more to being a woman than being a mother,

but there's a hell of a lot more to being a mother than most people suspect."
Roseanne

"I lost everything in the postnatal depression."
Erma Bombeck

"Having a baby can be a scream."
Joan Rivers

"My husband and I are either going to buy a dog or have a child. We can't decide whether to ruin our carpet or ruin our lives."
Rita Rudner

"When my husband comes home, if the kids are still alive, I figure I've done my job."
Roseanne

"Ask your child what he wants for dinner only if he's buying."
Fran Lebowitz

"Always be nice to your children because they are the ones who will choose your rest home."
Phyllis Diller

THE LAST WORD

"You're not famous until my mother has heard of you."
Jay Leno

Did You Know?

Believed to be the world's oldest mother, retired schoolteacher Satyabhama Mahapatra lives in India and gave birth at age 65. Her son (6 lb. 8 oz) was born on April 8, 2003. The baby was conceived using an egg from the woman's niece and the sperm of her husband. The Mahapatras had been married fifty years and this is their first child.

Giving Charity
Her Due

This former Harvard grad student is teaching us all a lesson.

There's a lot less crying in the hallowed halls of Harvard lately. Not the crying that comes from students with tough exams or homesickness. No, what's missing are the crying sounds of an infant wrapped in a swaddling blanket and attending class in the arms of Charity Bell.

Charity, 30, recently graduated with a master's in public policy from the John F. Kennedy School of Government (part of the university), where she was a dedicated student and a dedicated foster mom. Charity became well-known as the mom who took babies with her to Harvard.

HARVARD BABES

Since 1997, Charity has been caring for foster children, most often the babies of drug-addicted mothers. Bell is one of the youngest moms in the Massachusetts foster-care system, taking on a demanding job. These babies often come into the world with symptoms of drug withdrawal. They can have trouble sleeping, eating, and even breathing. They're often irritable, jittery, and hard to comfort. Charity's methods of coping with foster babies' problems are simple. She gives her disadvantaged charges good physical care, combined with lots of snuggling and calm, soothing attention. Her babies go everywhere with her—which is how they wound up at Harvard.

With little fuss but lots of fortitude, Charity managed to juggle the demands of getting an education with giving a good start in life to at-risk babies. Harvard's professors and fellow students grew used to the sights—and sounds—of an infant cradled in one arm while Bell busily took notes in class or at the library. But rather than complaining about these (sometimes noisy) visitors to academia, hip grads and dignified professors were more likely to be found cooing over a cute baby or even combining a bit of babysitting with peek-a-boo.

WHO IS MA BELL?

Not everyone can charm Harvard grads and profs into child care, but Charity Bell was never the usual student. She told Harvard's Kennedy School *Bulletin*, "I'm not supposed to be here . . . I was supposed to be a statistic."

Charity's father left her family and she grew up on welfare, along with her sister, Faith. (Her mom thought those names sounded nice.) Their mom, though loving and supportive, had an alcohol problem, and getting by was never certain. Charity beat the odds that she'd be a "statistic" with a scholarship to the New England Conservatory of Music, where she planned to become an opera singer. Then Bell became a volunteer at the New England Medical Center. It changed her life.

At the hospital Charity found a little girl—alone with no attention or visitors—crying in her crib. The girl hugged and clung to Bell in desperate need of loving contact, sobbing when Charity had to leave. This sweet little girl, Bell learned, had been abused and was kept alone in a crib because there was no available foster family. Charity began her foster parent–training program, intending to temporarily care for the lonely little girl. Today she's still caring for children in trouble.

HOW DOES SHE DO IT?

Now that she's graduated from Harvard, Charity works full-time as the regional director for a Massachusetts foster-parenting program. She oversees two programs, one that helps foster parents find affordable day care and a second that gives support to grandparents raising their grandchildren.

And just like in her grad school days, Charity is nearly always comforting a baby snuggled in her lap or resting on her arm. She's admitted that juggling care for troubled newborns with a job isn't easy and that it's put other things she wants on hold. She's joked about the need for a husband, a new stove, and a washing machine—in that order.

But the hardest part of Charity's mission isn't the workload, the effect on her social life, or the low pay—less than $15 a day. Charity enjoys her kids too much for that. She gets "payback" from receiving their love and watching them grow and thrive. No, the toughest part is when it's time for her kids to go on to the next step . . . a stable home or perhaps an adoption. Saying good-bye to a beloved child is always a wrenching loss. For devoted foster moms like Charity, it's part of the job.

"I become deeply attached to every child I care for," Bell says, "even if it is only for a few weeks." But she also says, "I am proud to have been one of the people in each of my kids' lives who have loved them. I hope that I have helped them learn how to accept love and give it to someone else."

CHARITY'S CHARITY

Because she's so familiar with the difficulties—as well as the joys—of foster parenting, Charity has founded Foster the Future (www.fosterthefuture.org), a nonprofit organization to improve foster care. Foster the Future works to recruit nurturing families and healing homes for kids in need of foster care and raises money for the extras that foster parents need—anything from a double stroller to linens for a child's bed.

With interviews in magazines and newspapers and after being featured on NBC and MSNBC as an everyday hero, Charity is getting her message out. There are children in desperate need of parenting, and foster parenting is the toughest job you'll ever love.

"The heart of a mother is a deep abyss at the bottom of which you will always find forgiveness."
—Honore de Balzac

"Mothers are the most instinctive philosophers."
—Harriet Beecher Stowe

"I find, by close observation, that the mothers are the levers which move in education. The men talk about it, but the women work most for it."
—Frances Watkins Harper

"It is not what you do for your children but what you have taught them to do for themselves that will make them successful human beings." —Ann Landers

Are You What Mom Ate?

Laboratory mice are proving that what a pregnant mom puts through her lips may wind up on your hips.

What makes a brown mouse brown and a yellow mouse yellow? Does it have to do with the color of the mama mouse's fur? Or the color of the papa mouse's fur? Well . . . not exactly. When biologists at Duke University Medical Center began adding vitamin supplements to the diets of pregnant yellow mice, the vitamins changed the fur color of the babies!

WERE THEY ALL YELLOW?

The scientists fed yellow mother mice vitamin B_{12}, folic acid, choline, and betaine before and during their pregnancies. These mothers gave birth to offspring with brown fur. Not so for yellow mother mice that ate a normal diet with no added vitamins—their babies were yellow. Yet both the pregnant mice and their litters were the same genetically. The only difference between the litters was that some mice had moms who ate vitamins and some did not.

What happened? How could baby mice with the same exact set of genes look so very different? Could diet alone produce such a colorful difference? Scientists have long known that even if a gene is present in the body, it may not have much effect. Everyone inherits two sets of genes—one from each parent. Usually one set of genes is dominant (active) and one set is recessive (inactive). That's why two brown-eyed parents can have a child with blue eyes. Both mom and dad had blue-eye genes that they passed on and that became active in their offspring.

WHAT A TURNOFF!

In these experiments, scientists worked with a strain of mice that have an extra piece of DNA in their agouti gene. This deviation makes them obese and yellow. When this gene is active, it turns their fur yellow. When the agouti gene is turned off or silenced, i.e., when it isn't having an effect on the mouse's body, their fur should be brown. When those mama mice at Duke took their vitamins, chemicals in the vitamin supplements turned off the expression of the agouti gene.

Inside the vitamin-supplemented mama mice, molecules containing carbon and hydrogen became attached to the gene and switched it off—a process called DNA methylation. Basically what that process did was cause the fat, yellow mother mice to produce slim, brown babies.

The agouti gene doesn't only change fur color in mice, it also impacts health. This gene plays a role in controlling brain signals for appetite. Mice with a highly active agouti gene tend to eat more and get . . . well . . . fat. Turning off the agouti gene produced brown mice that ate less, were not obese, and were also less susceptible to diabetes and cancer than their fair-furred brethren.

TAKING CARE OF MOM

So what does this mean to human moms? More studies will have to be done on human DNA methylation (just pronouncing it is hard enough!). But many studies have already shown that pregnant women who eat a poor diet have children who are more susceptible to diabetes and heart disease. Those brown baby mice at Duke suggest that human genes—like those in mice—are being influenced by prenatal nutrition and chemicals.

Looks like what a pregnant mom eats and the vitamins she takes can have a permanent influence on the physical characteristics and the health of her baby—and maybe even her grandchildren! So when a pregnant lady says she's eating for two, she's not kidding. The only other question is—what do all those cravings for ice cream and pickles mean?

"A mother is a person who seeing there are only four pieces of pie for five people, promptly announces she never did care for pie." —Tenneva Jordan

"My mother was a good recreational cook, but what she basically believed about cooking was that if you worked hard and prospered, someone else would do it for you." —Nora Ephron

"When my mother had to get dinner for 8 she'd just make enough for 16 and only serve half."
—Gracie Allen

Snugl Up!

Ann Moore made the world better for babies
with a lesson she learned from African mothers.

In the 1960s, newlyweds Ann and Mike Moore went to Togo in West Africa as Peace Corps volunteers. Ann was a pediatric nurse who had taught at Columbia University and worked with refugees in East Germany and earthquake victims in Morocco. Well-educated and experienced, she was eager to share her information and expertise with mothers from a developing, poverty-stricken nation.

OUT OF AFRICA

While Ann fulfilled her assignment teaching nutrition classes in Togo, she was surprised to find that Africans could teach the industrialized world a thing or two when it came to raising children. African children and their mothers had a closer bond than most mothers and children did back in America.

Ann knew that back in the States when a sick child had to go to the hospital, mother and child were separated and the medical staff took over, leaving the traumatized child alone with strangers. In Africa, mothers stayed at the hospital to be with their sick babies. Ann saw how comforting it was for suffering children to be able to rely on the presence of their mothers. She saw that the closeness between mother and baby was of benefit to both.

Outside the hospital Ann saw more of African mothers and babies practicing togetherness. What most impressed

Ann was the African mothers' custom of carrying their babies in fabric slings tied to their backs. Togo babies rarely cried and seemed remarkably contented compared to Western infants. Moore came to the conclusion that the babies were calm because being so close to their mothers made them feel secure.

OOPS, IT'S NOT AS EASY AS IT LOOKS

Soon after their Peace Corps assignment was over and Ann and Mike returned to the United States, their daughter was born. Wanting the very best for little Mande (Mande's full name is Mandela, after South African freedom fighter Nelson Mandela) and remembering those contented Togo babies, Ann decided to carry her own daughter in a fabric sling. Unfortunately it wasn't as easy as African mothers make it look. Mande kept slipping out of the sling.

Luckily, Ann's own mom was an excellent seamstress. She sewed a sling for her granddaughter according to Ann's design. With Mande safely swaddled on her back, Ann (or Mike) could clean, cook, run errands, or enjoy a walk or bike ride while keeping Mande close, comfortable, and secure. The Moores' baby carrier may have been based on ancient ideas, but it was totally new to Americans, and the soft carrier turned heads wherever they went.

Some observers warned the Moores that they were spoiling their daughter by allowing her to be constantly close to them. Mike and Ann explained that making infants feel secure and loved helped create self-confident and independent children. Many loved the whole concept and wanted to know how to get a backpack of their own or for a gift. As they began to produce more and more baby carriers for envious mothers, Mike and Ann began to feel they had a mission and a business.

AMERICA STARTS SNUGLING

Soon Mande's grandma was hiring friends to help her keep up with orders. Ann worked to improve the carrier with adjustable straps and a pouch to hold up the baby's head. Many moms wanted to be able to carry their babies on their chests, so Ann adapted the carrier for "front loading." By 1969 Ann had a patent on the Snugli carriers and by 1984 the company had sales of more than $6 million.

Ann's successful innovation and enterprise has brought her recognition—the *Wall Street Journal* named her one of the most influential inventors of the millennium. But Ann has been quick to stress that she adapted a centuries-old technique developed by African mothers. "There have been so many times that I've been thankful in my prayers to the African mothers," Ann has said. "They were really our inspiration and it is so wonderful to think that we in America can have the same closeness with our babies."

The Moores sold their company in 1985, but in the late 1990s, when their grandchildren were born, Ann went back to the drawing table and devised another soft carrier called the Weego. Once again the Moores were in a booming baby business, but this time they had the help of their three grown daughters: Mande in charge of marketing, Hopi in charge of sales, and Nicole running purchasing. The Moores may also have a ready-made market, since many new moms and dads were, themselves, once contentedly viewing the world from inside a soft Snugli.

Oh, Mama!

*There are even more songs named "Mama"
than named "Mother." We listened to them all because
we love mama just that much. Here's a sampling.*

"Mama" by Half Pint
(album: *Victory*, 1987)
What it sounds like:
Standard-issue pop reggae
vibe with Half Pint ladling
out standard-issue praises to
his single parent. He's a good
son, sure, but this is mediocre.
Play for mama? Nah. Why
settle for so-so reggae when
Ziggy Marley & the Melody
Makers have a song called
"Mama," which has more zest,
vibe, and groove? It's on the
Joy and Blues album.

**"Mama" by Dream City
Film Club** (album: *Dream
City Film Club*, 1997)
What it sounds like: Music
for a particularly morose scene
from a David Lynch movie,
with out-of-key guitars and
accordions, and lyrics sung as
if through a cardboard tube.
Play for mama? If you do,

mama will probably wonder
what's wrong with your head
to make you think she'd enjoy
this art-punk mishmash mess.

**"Mama" by Chubby
Carrier & the Bayou
Swamp Band** (album: *Boogie
Woogie Zydeco*, 1991)
What it sounds like: Like
you're sitting on the porch
of a Louisiana swamp shack,
dipping your toes in the water
and sucking the meat out of
the head of a crayfish.
Play for mama? Hoo-eeee!
You bet! Clearly the most fun
you can have with an accor-
dion. Put it on and stomp
merrily through the kitchen.

"Mama" by the Spice Girls
(album: *Spice*, 1997)
What it sounds like: Pop
drivel about how the various
Spice Girls, like, totally *hated*

their moms, but now they realize they only did good things for them! They love their mamas!

Play for your mama? She probably won't *hate* it. But if this sort of sugary, brainless pop appeals to your mom, maybe you could take her to the record store and broaden her horizons.

"Mama" by Connie Francis (album: *The Return Concert*, 1996)
What it sounds like: Big, sweeping orchestral, with just enough mandolin and ear-busting emoting from Francis to make a New Jersey mobster sob like a baby.
Play for your mama? Of course you should. Especially if she's from the old country, the "old country" understood to be either Italy or the 1950s.

"Mama" by the Katinas (album: *The Katinas*, 1999)
What it sounds like: Exactly what they are: a boy band proclaiming their love for their passed-on mother (all the Katinas are brothers), who now resides in heaven with Jesus.

Play for your mama? If your mama loves boy bands and religious pop, sure.

"Mama" by Max Roach (album: *Percussion Bitter Sweet*, 1961)
What it sounds like: Like one of the best jazz percussionists whacking away merrily while a hot jazz combo swirls and pulses around him. Driving, mad beats and licks.
Play for your mama? If your mama's a cool cat who digs her jazz hot, daddy-o (snap, snap), you know it.

"Mama" by Oingo Boingo (album: *Boingo Alive: Celebration of a Decade 1979–1988*, 1988)
What it sounds like: Like the raving homeless guy you saw on the subway if only he had mucho musical ability and the belief that mama could save his soul.
Play for your mama? Okay, but its claustrophobic and sinister feel will likely inspire mom to schedule a psychiatric examination for you afterward. Fair warning.

"Mama" by Yo-Yo Ma, Edgar Meyer, and Mark O'Connor (album: *Appalachia Waltz*, 1996)
What it sounds like: Like three of the best players of classical string instruments getting warmly down home right in your living room, sending notes ascending and descending through the entire house.
Play for your mama? Yes, if she's a classical buff and thought you'd never get past that whole "mullet rock" stage in your life. (You don't have to get past it, you know. Just pretend.)

"Mama" by the Sugarcubes (album: *Life's Too Good*, 1988)
What it sounds like: Several musical citizens of one of the coldest countries in the world (Iceland) going completely nuts, especially freakish pixie singer Björk. Yet, very tuneful.
Play for your mama? For fans of angular, brainy pop and those moms with a quirky streak.

Uncle John's "Spiff" Notes

Need a juicy read about the Hollywood lifestyle and its effects on a mother and daughter? Look no further than Carrie Fisher's *Postcards from the Edge*, which tells the story of one woman's struggles with being the daughter of a movie star mom. You'll wonder if mom and daughter will ever work it out, but you won't question how much these flawed characters really do love and need each other.

The Gold(a) Standard

*She was Israel's favorite mother—but that
doesn't mean the job was a cinch.*

In the 1970s, when the Israeli prime minister visited the
United States, Washington's hard-bitten journalists
shot tough questions. Did the prime minister believe Israel
could have peace with its neighbors? Would Israel employ
nuclear weapons if its survival were in jeopardy? Then
came the real stumper: what was the best way to make
gefilte (stuffed) fish?

Probably one of the few world leaders who could make
a mean gefilte fish or chicken soup, Golda Meir was one of
the first elected officials in the Western world who was also
a mother and grandmother. She was proud of her maternal
status (as well as her gefilte fish recipe), and her caring personality won international friends for her beleaguered
nation. But while the world saw Golda as the ultimate
devoted Jewish mother, the truth was that of all the problems this great prime minister ever faced—from the need
to improve economic and employment conditions to a
fight for her country's life—the one problem she never felt
she conquered was being a successful working mother.

DEDICATION VS. KIDS

Though she came to the United States when she was eight,
Golda was born in 1898 in Kiev, Ukraine, which was part of
Russia at that time. Her family was poor and Jewish—not

the best combination in the Ukraine in those days—and Golda knew persecution firsthand. Encounters with anti-Semitism scared the young Golda, who remembered the Cossacks, mounted soldiers, riding through her village and persecuting Jewish people. Golda never forgot Kiev; she dedicated her life to building a Jewish homeland where her people would be safe from persecution. She got involved in the cause early and joined the Milwaukee Labor Zionist Party after earning her degree at the Milwaukee Normal School (now the University of Wisconsin–Milwaukee). She later married but continued to hope for a Zionist state in the Middle East.

In 1921, Golda and her husband Morris emigrated from the United States to Palestine, where the British government had encouraged Jews to settle. Golda was thrilled to be a pioneer for a future Jewish nation, but the birth of two children, Menachem and Sarah, soon complicated things for their family. In Jerusalem at that time, conditions were primitive and jobs were almost nonexistent, so Golda took in laundry to try to make ends meet. The young mother hadn't realized so much of her life with young children would be bound up in "poverty, worry, and drudgery."

GUILT! GUILT! GUILT!

Finally, Golda found a job in Tel Aviv and wanted to move there with her two children. Not wanting to leave his job, Morris agreed to stay in Jerusalem and would visit the family on the weekends. Golda would be working as the secretary of the Women's Labour Council, a political position that could lead to great things. Talented Golda was soon a rising political star, leading the nation-building that would become her life's work.

But Golda's success came with the burden of guilt. Few women of her day worked outside the home. Morris criticized her time-consuming political work, as did her mother and sister. Golda herself worried that her children needed more mothering. She tried to solve the problem by working as energetically at cooking, cleaning, and raising her children as she did at her political work. But it sometimes seemed impossible to do both jobs well.

MOM'S WILL OF IRON

In 1932, motherhood finally forced Golda to leave Palestine and temporarily focus exclusively on her duties as a parent. Six-year-old Sarah was dying from a kidney disease. Once again Golda went against the advice of others. Her parents and the local doctors admonished her not to travel with Sarah to a hospital in New York. But Golda's decision proved the right one and her daughter was cured.

Golda worked as a fund-raiser in the United States to pay her daughter's medical bills. Ironically, it was this experience that helped make her a great speaker and diplomat for the Israeli cause. And by the time Golda returned to Palestine, the cause seemed to her more important than ever; a German politician named Hitler wanted to remove the Jewish presence from Europe.

MOTHER OF CHILDREN, MOTHER OF A COUNTRY

Young Menachem and Sarah grew to understand that their mother was dedicated to a goal that required tireless service. They probably came to terms with her life's work better than Golda did. Even though she recognized the international significance of her work, on some levels

Golda never stopped regretting the speeches and meetings that kept her away from her children.

When World War II ended, Golda became a leader in a successful rebellion against British rule. In 1948 she signed Israel's Declaration of Independence. Her children (Sarah, on a kibbutz, and Menachem, a muscian in New York) celebrated the triumph of their mother's dream. A homeland for her people was now a reality.

A WORKING MOM DOES GOOD

Golda served Israel as an ambassador, a Knesset (parliament) member, and a cabinet minister. In 1969, Golda Meir became Israel's fourth prime minister. In an era when many believed that women were too emotional to cope with the pressure of running a business, Golda showed that mothers and grandmothers could run a country. She was famous for making coffee for her guards and making chicken soup for "the boys and girls" in the Israeli army. When Israel was attacked by its neighbors, she became famous for leading her army and her nation through the Yom Kippur War to emerge victorious.

It could be argued that her experience as a working mother helped make her a great leader. In politics Golda stood up to pressure with the same decisiveness that she'd developed when she kept her career on track and raised two kids, just as when she defied the experts and successfully saved her daughter's life by taking her to New York. Golda's own experiences in raising a family gave her a rare perspective, humility, and compassion for all families around the world.

Jigalong Home

"They told us we had no mothers.
I knew they were wrong."—Molly Craig Kelly

Two Aboriginal Mardu women have attracted a lot of attention in Australia. Molly Craig Kelly, 84, and Daisy Kadibil, 78, who appeared in the acclaimed film *Rabbit-Proof Fence*, are fueling a small tourist boom. Dedicated fans from all over the world travel to the women's home, a remote desert outpost called Jigalong.

Going to Jigalong is not like taking a Hollywood bus ride past movie-star homes. Fans must brave heat, dust, and a lack of four-star hotels, but still they come to meet the heroines of Australia's stolen generation. The pair who—when they were girls—overcame the dangers of the outback and the power of the Australian government to get home to the mothers who loved them.

MARDU MOLLY

In 1931, Molly, 14, her cousin, Gracie, 10, and sister Daisy, 8, lived in close-knit families, enjoying a life that still followed many of the Mardu traditions. The Mardu live in the deserts of western Australia. Molly, Daisy, and Gracie were fast friends, bound together by their common mixed race. While their mothers were Mardu, their fathers were white and chose to live with the Mardu.

THE STOLEN GENERATION

From 1905 to 1971, the Australian government forcibly removed half-white, half-Aborigine children from their mothers. Some think it was an attempt to "save" partly white children from a culture the Australian government considered savage. Others believe that these children would have ultimately been rejected and become social outcasts had they remained with their families. Either way, these children were taken from their birth parents and sent to institutions where they would be assimilated into white Australian society. They became known as the "Stolen Generation."

In 1931 Molly Craig was taken from her tearful mother, Maude. Along with Gracie and Daisy, Molly was sent to the Moore River Native Settlement located near the southwestern city of Perth and roughly 1,000 miles away from home. At Moore River, Molly, Daisy, and Gracie were locked in an overcrowded dormitory with bars on the windows; they were forbidden to speak their own language. Meals weren't any better, usually consisting of weevily porridge or watery stew.

What was toughest for Molly was the government's attempt to make her forget her mother. Over fifty years later, Molly still remembers her feelings when she was told that her mother no longer wanted her. "Those other kids," Molly has explained, "they were much younger. They didn't know their mother. But I was older. I knew my mother. I wanted to go home to Mother."

Molly had been warned that no child ever successfully escaped from Moore River. Those who tried were brought back to face floggings and solitary confinement. Still, the teenager gathered up Gracie and Daisy, and instead of going to school, the three ran off, crossing a rain-swollen river and heading into the bush. Traveling as fast as she could, Molly searched for her guide home—the rabbit-proof fence.

THE RABBIT-PROOF FENCE

Molly's father was an inspector in charge of maintaining the rabbit-proof fence, a barrier built in 1907 to keep out rabbits that were eating farm crops. Her father had explained to Molly that the fence crossed western Australia in an unbroken line from south to north. Once Molly found the fence, she knew she could follow it to Jigalong. What she didn't know was that she was about to lead her cousins on one of the longest walks in Australian history.

Chased by government trackers, the girls hiked north along the path of the fence. Rumors spread that they'd drowned, but the three used the bush survival techniques they'd learned from their mothers and grandmothers to make it across the harsh desert outback. Gracie was eventually captured, but Molly and Daisy hiked about 1,000 miles back to home and her mother.

DORIS'S HOMECOMING

The girls were taken to the desert upon their return. But when Molly had children of her own, Doris, 3, and Annabelle, 18 months, all three were returned to Moore River. Ten years after her first journey, Molly escaped again with her baby, eluding the trackers to return to Jigalong. She had to leave Doris behind because she could not carry two children during the long journey home. She hoped that Gracie, who was still at Moore River, would look after young Doris.

Doris grew up at Moore River and Roelands Native Mission, where she seemed to be one of the government's successes. She became a nurse's aide, married, and had four children. But the institutions left a troubling mark, and Doris was ashamed of her Aboriginal family.

It was 21 years before Doris and Molly were reunited. (Three-year-old Annabelle was retaken from Molly. They were never reconciled.) Doris then began to appreciate her culture and family history, and she decided to write Molly and Daisy's story in the memoir *Follow the Rabbit-Proof Fence*. The book was a runaway success.

THE STOLEN GENERATION ON FILM

Based on the popularity of Doris's book, the film *Rabbit-Proof Fence* was made in 2002. The movie exploded on the Australian scene and caused the country to revisit that dark period in its history. Molly's longing to be with her mother gave many Aussies a realization of how much suffering had been caused by misguided policies and old-fashioned ideas about race.

Sadly, Molly has recently passed away, but the impact of her life will always be felt. What may be most important is that members of the Stolen Generation now know what Molly knew, that they were never despised and abandoned. Many have begun to search for their families and begin a journey home.

Advancing Adoption

Adoption is on the rise!

It used to be bad manners to ask people whether they were adopted—even if you were a census taker. For years adoption was considered such a private matter that census takers didn't keep track of the number of adoptions in the United States. In fact, adoption agencies used to just place children without consulting the birth parents.

It wasn't until the late 1970s that adoption agencies allowed open adoptions, where biological and adoptive parents could establish a relationship with each other. As adoption came further out into the open, curious researchers were standing at the door, eager to finally ask questions. They got surprising answers. Adoption was far more common than anyone had guessed, adopted families were on the rise, and the numbers would likely keep going up.

BY THE NUMBERS

The Evan B. Donaldson Adoption Institute ran a significant national poll about adoption in 1997 that amazed even adoption professionals. Fifty-eight percent of respondents declared a "personal experience" with adoption—meaning that they, a family member, or a close friend had been adopted, had adopted a child, or had placed a child up for adoption. Ninety percent had a positive view of adoption, and a third had "somewhat seriously considered adopting." Adoption was far more common and accepted than the experts had ever suspected.

In 2000, for the first time the U.S. Census calculated how many adopted children lived in U.S. households. They learned that there were 2.1 million adopted children at that time in the United States, which constituted about 2.5 percent of all children in the country. The census did not ask, however, if participants themselves had been adopted, so the number of adopted persons in the United States could be much higher. Will there be a much higher percentage by the end of the decade? Seems likely.

Given the numbers, that's hardly surprising since the estimated total number of adoptions has more than doubled in the last century. In 1944 there were a recorded 50,000 adoptions that year. Fifty years later that number had almost tripled. There were approximately 120,000 annual adoptions in the 1990s!

MOVIN' ON UP

So what's up with these upward trends in adoption? Statisticians point out that women in developed countries are delaying their plans for motherhood until they are older. And older would-be moms have a greater likelihood of infertility, problems conceiving, and difficulties in carrying a child to term. In the United States almost one third of childless married women who had problems becoming biological mothers were in the 35–44 age group. About 6.1 million American women had impaired fertility in 1995—that's over a million more than in 1988.

Infertility is the common motivation for adoption. In one survey, more than 80 percent of the respondents gave the inability to have a biological child as the reason they chose to adopt. With more women delaying marriage and motherhood and facing biological problems with pregnancy, there are also more potential moms searching for a child to adopt and raise.

Luckily, adoptions are a good thing for everyone involved. The Search Institute, a nonprofit research organization, concluded after a four-year study that most teenagers who were adopted as infants "show no signs that adoption had a negative effect on their identity development, mental health, or well-being." Adopted or biological—loving mothers have an equal chance to produce healthy children.

"A mother is not a person to lean on but person to make leaning unnecessary." —Dorothy Canfield Fisher

"Bitter are the tears of a child: Sweeten them.
Deep are the thoughts of a child: Quiet them.
Sharp is the grief of a child: Take it from him.
Soft is the heart of a child: Do not harden it."
—Pamela Glenconner

Lit 101:
A Novel Approach

In the second part of our literature quiz, we're taking a "novel" approach to the question, "What's a mom to do?" Multiple choice for you again—read closely and don't peek at the answers before you're through!

1. The Novel: *Anna Karenina* by Leo Tolstoy, 1875–1877

The Plot: Anna, the beautiful and spirited mother of Seryozha, is bored and restless in her marriage with the dull Karenin. She has fallen in love with the dashing Count Vronsky.

What's a mom to do?

__ A. Introduce Karenin to a charming, but conventional, woman and hope they fall in love and let you off the hook.

__ B. Run off with Vronsky and then tire of him.

__ C. Jump in front of a train.

__ D. None of the above.

__ E. Both B & C

2. The Novel: *Moll Flanders* by Daniel Defoe, 1722

The Plot: Moll's mother "pleads her belly" (pregnancy) to avoid being executed as a thief. Her baby remains in England while she is transported to the colonies (the United States), where she prospers. Moll is raised by others and has many adventures, lovers, and husbands. Eventually, she marries an American sea captain and travels to his home in Virginia. After bearing the captain two children, Moll meets his mother and then discovers they have more in common than she thought. She's shocked to learn that she is married to her half-brother.

What's a mom to do?

__ A. Leave your husband, return to England, and remarry.
__ B. Jump in front of a train.
__ C. Kill your husband and his/your mother so no one will ever know.
__ D. Become a prostitute.
__ E. Both A & D.

3. The Novel: *The Scarlet Letter* by Nathaniel Hawthorne, 1850

The Plot: In Puritan New England, Hester Prynne gives birth to a daughter whose father is not Hester's husband. She is forced to wear a scarlet "A" (for "adulteress") and is publicly shamed.

What's a mom to do?

__ A. Blame your youth and the man who led you astray.
__ B. Rail against the hypocrisy of the town's so-called solid citizens.
__ C. Wear the scarlet letter proudly and raise your daughter with tenderness and good values.
__ D. Become a prostitute and jump in front of a train.
__ E. All of the above.

4. The Novel: *Uncle Tom's Cabin* by Harriet Beecher Stowe, 1852

The Plot: Eliza, a slave, overhears her owners talking about selling her five-year-old son, Harry, to another plantation owner.

What's a mom to do?

__ A. Move to a cottage by the woods, become a prostitute, and then jump in front of a train.
__ B. Grab your son and run away to Canada.
__ C. Plead with your owner's wife and appeal to her Christian values.
__ D. Ask kindly Uncle Tom, who is to be sold along with Harry, to take good care of him.
__ E. Both B & D

Answers on page 300.

Ante Up, Mom!

We're not bluffing. Be sure to bet on this poker-playing mama.

In the never-ending quest of working moms to find the best way to raise a family and earn a living, moms have moved into such traditionally male-dominated careers as steel workers, firefighters, and investment bankers. But card sharks?

You can bet on it. Today's working mother can just as easily be a professional gambler who ambles up to a green-felt poker table as an office worker who spends the day with a computer in a cubicle. Just ask Annie Duke, a working mother of four and one of the top-rated poker players in the world.

The Bellagio, a luxury hotel in Las Vegas, Nevada, features an 8.5-acre lake and more than a thousand fountains; it houses luxury stores, art masterpieces, botanical gardens . . . and, oh yes, slot machines and poker tables. Thirty to forty hours a week, Annie Duke takes leave of her husband, Ben, and her kids, Maud, Leo, Lucy, and Nelly. Then, often clad comfortably in jeans and a T-shirt, she heads off to the cushy casino, where she is one of but a handful of women who are serious contenders in the world of high-stakes poker.

A MAN'S GAME?

The origin of the game of poker is somewhat in doubt. Some say it began in China, some say Persia, others Egypt or even India. The version played in the United States probably came from a "bluffing and betting" card game called "poque," which French settlers brought to New Orleans. Poque was likely the origin of the game that card sharks used to fleece travelers on the steamboats of the Mississippi River. By the time of the Civil War, poker and draw poker were popular pastimes—for men.

Today the World Poker Tour and the World Series of Poker fascinate both tournament crowds and TV fans at home. If the popularity of poker hasn't faltered since the Civil War, neither has its reputation as a man's game. So in 2000 it was quite an event when a thirtysomething soccer mom who was over eight months pregnant came in tenth place in the World Series of Poker. No small accomplishment. For Annie, it was just evidence that the high-stakes world of poker could be a great career choice for a mother.

THE DUKES OF VEGAS

Big money, job flexibility, time for her kids . . . it's all a dream come true for Duke, who came to her unusual profession in the usual way. She had to juggle marriage and kids and she badly needed money. But some say that gaming is in the lady's genes.

Born into the Lederer family, Annie grew up on the grounds of a preppy boarding school in New Hampshire where her father taught English. Card games and chess were family obsessions, and poker playing seems to run in the family. Annie's older brother, Howard, dropped out of college to play chess, but he eventually moved into the world of professional gambling. Now he is also one of the world's poker greats.

Annie stayed in school and attended Columbia University, where she was a member of its first coed class, and then went on to graduate school to study cognitive psychology at the University of Pennsylvania. She was finishing up her dissertation for her PhD when she realized that she didn't really want to spend the rest of her life in academia. With a boldness that would eventually serve her well at the poker tables, Annie proposed to her boyfriend, who said yes. The two married and went to live in Montana.

A scarcity of jobs and a need to help keep the roof over her family's head inspired Annie to call her brother Howard and ask him to teach her to play poker. She did so well that the Duke family eventually moved to Las Vegas. Her husband, Ben, who ran his own investment business from home, agreed to take on the child-care chores when she was away at the casino . . . and the rest, as they say, is poker history.

STRAIGHT FLUSHES, STRAIGHT PRIORITIES

For Annie, her "beautiful family" remains her first priority. This responsibility to her family may help keep her ego in check and make risk management a lot easier. It may be that self-control that has contributed to her great success. Very few players can win as consistently as Annie Duke does—or cope with losses as well. But win or lose, Annie considers poker the perfect job. That's because she's an involved, hands-on mom with a simple strategy. "If I have a sick child or a soccer game, I don't have to play." Sounds like the perfect work schedule for any parent!

She was even a no-show at a game where she could have taken home a six-figure pot. Why? She had decided it was more important to be at her daughter's sixth birthday party. "I didn't care what kind of money was at stake . . . I'm not missing that party," she said. "You know what?

When she's 25 and in therapy, she's going to be talking about how I missed her sixth birthday party."

PLAYING IS WORK

So play is actually work for Ms. Duke, but rest assured it's no easy gig. She relies on skill, not luck, to make her living. She has to memorize cards and calculate the odds in order to bust some bluffs and second-guess her opponents' moves. She considers her gender an asset, as it rattles some men who are a little touchy about losing to a woman. When they're rattled, they lose more.

She treats the game as strictly business, managing her money carefully. Annie has a separate cash stash specifically set aside for her playing stake. She never gambles her winnings on other games, unlike some poker players who will immediately gamble their winnings at the craps or roulette tables. Annie doesn't take her work home, either. Her kids have no playing cards. Guess gambling isn't a family affair.

"My mother used to say, 'He who angers you, conquers you!' But my mother was a saint."—Elizabeth Kenny

Mom Goes Buggy

Courageous insect moms risk their lives for their offspring.

You just never know where you're gonna run across a heroic mom. The kind who would risk her own life to save her child. We've all heard the stories about super-charged moms able to lift cars to save their children. But would you expect to meet such a supermom in, well, a pile of dung?

I DON'T KNOW HOW SHE DUNGS IT

The insect world isn't known much for decent parenting. Many insects lay their eggs, hide them, and then it's bye-bye baby. And if most insect moms see a hungry predator go after their eggs, they will, not very bravely, run, wriggle, crawl, or fly away. But among the multitude of species of insects on Earth, there are a few dedicated and even heroic moms.

Some insect moms—like those among dung beetles—can be quite devoted. Most species of dung beetle moms simply lay their eggs in underground tunnels, then take off after leaving the babies with a supply of dung for food. Others form brood balls, actually enclosing the eggs in a ball of dung, but then they, too, are off to enjoy carefree, childless days.

But for *Copris lunaris*, a special type of dung beetle, such behavior is unthinkable. The *Copris lunaris* mom carefully cares for her eggs after they're packed in the brood ball.

She will turn the brood ball so that the egg and porous areas are at the top and not in contact with damp soil, making the ball less susceptible to fungus or parasites. She will repair the surface of the ball and smooth out irregularities—keeping her eggs in the best environment possible until they can hatch and fend for themselves.

Copris laeviceps, a smaller dung beetle, is even busier. In addition to keeping the brood balls round and repaired, mom will defend her little dung heap (actually called the "nest chamber") by killing the larvae of any unrelated species— because these might become a predator to her eggs.

DON'T BUG MOM

Other insect moms can be downright fierce when protecting their brood until the babies are old enough to fend for themselves. A praying mantis mom camouflages her eggs or hatchlings and then stands guard over them. If another insect approaches, wanting to eat the praying mantis nymphs (babies) who can't defend themselves, the formidable predator mom will attack to kill.

The European shield bug takes on any bird or insect that wants to chomp on her clutch of eggs. She will not back down, even if the confrontation means certain death. She protects the eggs by keeping them behind her shield. If a predator insect or a bird tries to eat them, she stands fast, tilting her body bravely toward her enemy.

The Brazilian tortoise beetle mom also stands up to her attackers, but in her case the whole family works together until her hatchlings are mature. The Brazilian tortoise beetle arranges her newly hatched larvae so that she can perch atop them. Then, when a predator attacks, she makes a fighting stand while the little ones back her up. They have hooks on the end of their tails to which their feces are attached. If a predator bug tries to chomp on this family, it will get a mouthful of beetle feces instead of young and tender beetles. That can really discourage a hungry enemy (or at least ruin its appetite).

Just as with human moms, you can't tell a courageous bug mom by her outer appearance. Even seemingly delicate creatures like the lace bug mother can turn ferocious in times of danger. A damsel bug is a deadly predator to the flimsier lace bug. But a mother lace bug will attack a damsel bug if necessary. Creating a diversion, she will fan her wings at the damsel bug to distract it from her offspring and allow her nymphs to escape.

WHAT MAKES A BUGGY HERO?

Scientist Douglas W. Tallamy has found a reason why some insect moms could be careless and others are so full of motherly love. His theory is that fiercely protective moms are "semelparous," meaning that they breed only once in a lifetime. So instead of laying many clutches of eggs, the semelparous moms have only one shot at having kids. The protective moms spend their time and energy defending their one clutch of eggs and making sure their offspring survive. Other insect moms breed often, which gives them plenty of time to get busy and makes protecting their young less important.

Of course, what works in the primitive insect world isn't comparable to what works in the complex and socialized world of human beings. A human mother with an only child isn't necessarily more protective than one with more children. Still, it is nice to know that courageous moms can be found in so many dung-gone shapes and sizes.

Cool Stepmoms Keep Their Royal Heads

*In a crisis, a good stepmom keeps her cool
when others are losing theirs.*

R aising stepkids is never easy and any stepmom can
have a bad day. But if you were married to King
Henry VIII, a bad day might be your last on earth.
Altogether, head-lopping Henry was married to six women:
Catherine of Aragon, Anne Boleyn, Jane Seymour, Anne
of Cleves, Kathryn Howard, and Catherine Parr. Two
queens he divorced (Aragon and Cleves), and two he
beheaded (Boleyn and Howard). But two of the queens,
Henry decided were keepers, noggins and all.

Both Jane Seymour and Catherine Parr kept their heads
about them and managed not only to keep horrible Henry
happy but also to nurture his abused royal brood. Without
the efforts of these kindly stepmoms, the history of Merry
Olde England would have been decidedly different.

A LOVE 'EM AND CLEAVE 'EM KINDA GUY

Whatever else you can call Henry, "nice guy" probably
doesn't leap to mind. He wanted a son and heir and was
willing to get rid of anyone who stood in the way. That
included his first wife, Queen Catherine of Aragon, who
gave him a daughter, Princess Mary. Henry waited for
Catherine to have a boy . . . and waited some more. After

twenty-plus years of waiting, he decided to play "let's make an heir" with a new contestant.

When he dumped his faithful wife, Henry also dissolved the English association with the Roman Catholic Church because the pope refused to let him divorce Catherine in order to marry Anne. In 1533, the king declared himself Supreme Head of the Church of England. Then the king annulled his first marriage, exiled his old queen, and married a new one—feisty, flashy Anne Boleyn.

Unfortunately for Queen Anne, her first child was a daughter, Princess Elizabeth, instead of the son Henry desired. Henry sighed and gave her another chance, but Anne's second child was a stillborn son. The disappointed father didn't even bother to ask the once-loved Anne for an annulment of their marriage; he axed Anne's head off instead.

POOR LITTLE RICH GIRLS

Henry wasn't only tough on wives. His kids suffered too. When Henry annulled his marriage to Catherine of Aragon, his daughter Mary was 16 years old and the pampered princess of England. After the annulment, Mary was declared illegitimate—a waif in danger of losing her life. Her bad dad demoted her from princess to lady, sent her to live away from court, and forbade her from seeing her beloved mother.

After he executed Anne, Henry spread the pain around to his three-year-old daughter Elizabeth. He also denied her legitimacy, revoked her title, and ordered the once-pampered little princess to stay away from Windsor Castle.

PLAIN JANE

The day after Anne lost her head, the king and his new fancy, Jane Seymour, were betrothed. They married ten days later. The courtiers bowed low to Henry's new wife and privately wondered how long she would last. She wasn't even crowned queen, since Henry was waiting to see if he'd get a son from this woman before he decided to place the crown on her head—that is, if she still had a head.

But plain Jane became Henry's favorite wife. Whether from natural sweetness, shrewdness, or sheer terror, Jane was gentle, meek, and obedient. And Henry liked that. She made no attempt to seize power in affairs of state and he liked that too. The one point that Jane would take up with him was his cruel treatment of her stepchildren.

ROYAL REUNIONS

Jane begged Henry to reconcile with his daughters—a dangerous proposition, since the king had a nasty temper and an executioner . . . and wasn't afraid to use them. In the beginning, tyrant Henry told his wife to back off and stop meddling. Surprisingly, though meek in other areas, Jane didn't back down; she continued to work for a reconciliation.

Jane wasn't completely selfless. She wanted to restore Roman Catholicism to England, and Mary, who was a Catholic like her mother, would be a valuable ally. Finally in 1536, due in large part to Jane's efforts, Henry and Mary affectionately reunited, ending over 5 years of estrangement. After the reconciliation Mary was often invited to court, where Jane proclaimed her the "chiefest jewel of England" and made a show of sitting near the young woman and insisting that Mary walk beside her instead of behind her. Such courtesies were a signal to the court that Mary—who'd been marked for arrest and even death—was restored to high status and should be respected.

Jane had less to gain from giving attention to Elizabeth, but once again she braved Henry's wrath to have the little girl brought to court. When Jane, Mary, Elizabeth, and Henry celebrated Christmas together, they were, at last, a unified family. They might have stayed that way too if Jane hadn't been such a dutiful wife. The queen finally provided Henry with his long-sought-after male heir, Edward. But twelve days later she was dead from childbed fever. Mary was Jane's chief mourner, riding a black-draped horse to Windsor Castle to attend her step-mother's funeral.

SIXTH TIME'S THE CHARM

After Jane Seymour's death, Henry married three more times. He divorced his fourth wife, Anne of Cleeves, because she was ugly (one wonders why he married her to begin with). And his fifth, Kathryn Howard, was beheaded for having an affair. What would happen to wife number six, Catherine Parr?

Catherine Parr was not envied when she went down the aisle. By now, few women wanted anything to do with Henry, king or not. But Catherine kept her head by cater-ing to Henry's health and his king-sized ego. Courtiers breathed a sigh of relief as this new queen attentively nursed the aging, gouty king and made him feel respected and powerful. They saw that this wife would manage the volatile monarch and manage to survive.

SMART STEPMOM CATHERINE

After Jane Seymour's death and two wives later, Henry had begun neglecting his children again. But Catherine used her influence with Henry to humanize him, just as Jane had. Thanks to his new queen, Henry restored Mary's title as princess and she was once again in line for succession to the throne.

For six-year-old Prince Edward, Catherine was a lifesaver. She gave the motherless prince love and affection, and she made sure that Henry provided Edward with the best education available. The young prince had a reputation for being a cold, withdrawn child with a princely temper, but for Catherine Parr he showed only deep affection and called her "my very dearest mother."

Shrewd ten-year-old Elizabeth wasn't as quick to take to the new stepmother. But ultimately it was Elizabeth who benefited most from her new stepmom. Catherine brought the girl to court and made sure that Elizabeth was restored to princess status and able to inherit the crown. Catherine also made sure that Henry gave Elizabeth a "male" education with the same scholars from Oxford and Cambridge who taught the prince.

Like Jane, Catherine also had her own religious agenda. Her Protestant beliefs had no effect on the devoutly Catholic Mary, but their stepmother encouraged the younger children to follow in the Protestant faith.

STEPMOMS RULE!

Catherine survived her notorious husband Henry only to marry again and die as a result of childbirth just as Jane had. But this queen had a huge influence on history. Without Catherine's efforts, Mary and Elizabeth might never have become queens themselves. Perhaps Queen Elizabeth I would not have been so well-educated, and one of England's most glorious eras might never have occurred. Thanks in part to her stepmother, Elizabeth was better prepared to preside over a literary and scientific renaissance and to oversee an expansion of British power.

Jane and Catherine may have influenced history in another way. After watching both her stepmothers cater to horrible Henry and after mourning both of their deaths from childbirth, it's no wonder that the great Elizabeth decided to remain a virgin queen.

Yes, Minister's Mom

Born Jeanette Jerome in Brooklyn, New York, in 1854, she became better known to the world as Lady Randolph Churchill and even better known as the mother of Sir Winston Churchill, Prime Minister of Great Britain (1940–1945, 1951–1955). Jennie moved with her family from New York to Paris at age 11 and entered fashionable society. Then in 1873, she met Lord Randolph Churchill and charmed him into marriage. Little Winston was born in 1874; some say he arrived a little earlier than was proper. It seems Winston was always ahead of his time!

Reel Moms & Kids

Can you match these celebrity moms to their famous offspring?

1. Blythe Danner

An acclaimed character actress whose first love is theater, she won a Tony in 1970 for her performance in *Butterflies Are Free*. She has been nominated for Tonys for her performances in *A Streetcar Named Desire* and *Betrayal*. Well-known for playing motherly roles on the big screen, such as in *Meet the Parents*, she's no stranger to the small screen either.

Danner is also famous for her dedicated supporting role as mom to her superstar daughter, who won an Oscar playing Shakespeare's true love. Mom and daughter recently shared the big screen in *Sylvia*, a biopic about Sylvia Plath.

Who is the reel daughter?

    ___A. Cameron Diaz
    ___B. Gwyneth Paltrow
    ___C. Minnie Driver
    ___D. Jennifer Aniston

2. Ingrid Bergman

You can see this gorgeous Swedish actress in classic films from the 1940s, such as *Casablanca* and *Gaslight*. Bergman's beauty and portrayals of strong, sophisticated women made her famous, but her love affair with an Italian director nearly ruined her career. Bergman abandoned her family to run away with her lover. The scandal was so overwhelming that Bergman fled the United States in 1950, and it was 6 years before her comeback Oscar for the 1956 film *Anastasia*.

Ingrid's famous daughter inherited her mom's acting and beauty genes. Along with work in movies, she's been a spokeswoman and feature model for Lancôme cosmetics.

Who is the reel daughter?
___A. Chastity Bono
___B. Andie MacDowell
___C. Isabella Rossellini
___D. Elizabeth Hurley

3. Judy Garland

From her role as Dorothy in the 1939 classic *The Wizard of Oz* to her beloved recorded concert in Carnegie Hall, Garland remains a show-business legend and one of the world's greatest entertainers. Sadly, her personal life was fraught with personal problems, including struggles with drugs and alcohol.

Before her death at age 47, Garland performed in concert with her eldest daughter and both received rave reviews. Her daughter went on to follow in mom's footsteps, both as a film star and renowned singer, in addition to her turbulent personal life.

Who is the reel daughter?
___A. Liza Minnelli
___B. Barbra Streisand
___C. Britney Spears
___D. Tammy Wynette

4. Janet Leigh

She was a Hollywood celebrity in the 1950s and 1960s, starring in multitudes of films with everyone from Anthony Hopkins to Lassie. Leigh's most famous film, Hitchcock's classic thriller *Psycho*, terrified her so much that she reportedly never took showers again.

Her daughter became a scream queen herself in the 1970s as the star of a popular horror movie, *Halloween*. She's made memorable comedies too, including *A Fish Called Wanda* and *Freaky Friday*. Like mother, like daughter.

Who is the reel daughter?
___A. Debra Winger
___B. Demi Moore
___C. Jamie Lee Curtis
___D. Madonna

5. Debbie Reynolds

A famously sunny actress, singer, and dancer, Reynolds was an MGM star in the 1950s who brightened up the classic *Singin' in the Rain*. Her personal life became tabloid fodder when her seemingly perfect marriage was broken up by Elizabeth Taylor. But through triumphs and tragedies, Reynolds kept on dancing (and singing and acting) in films, television, theater, and Las Vegas nightclubs.

Reynolds also raised a famous daughter who made a splash as a galactic princess and a heralded writing debut with *Postcards from the Edge*, a novel about growing up in Hollywood.

Who is the reel daughter?
___A. Sissy Spacek
___B. Carrie Fisher
___C. Natalie Portman
___D. Angelina Jolie

6. Vanessa Redgrave

Famous for her radical politics and her brilliant acting, Redgrave's successes began with Shakespeare at London's Old Vic in 1961, continued on with starring roles in Chekov plays, and have not stopped in more than 40 years. Redgrave's films include *Julia*, *Howard's End*, and 1997's *Mrs. Dalloway*.

Vanessa's famous daughter followed mom's lead, appearing onstage in Chekov plays and in Shakespearean roles at the Old Vic. Her films include *Nell* and *The Parent Trap*. She's also known for her devotion to her sons and hunky husband, Liam Neeson.

Who is the reel daughter?

___A. Jane Seymour

___B. Kristen Scott Thomas

___C. Natasha Richardson

___D. Meryl Streep

7. Goldie Hawn

A bubbly goofball on screen, Ms. Hawn made her mark on TV's *Laugh-In* and in film comedies like *Cactus Flower* and *Private Benjamin*. But Hawn is actually a bright businesswoman who has managed to negotiate a Hollywood career spanning four decades.

She's also a hands-on mother to her kids, including a look-alike, kooky blonde daughter who made Academy Award history as one of only three daughters to follow their mothers in landing an Oscar nomination for *Almost Famous*.

Who is the reel daughter?

___A. Charlize Theron

___B. Kate Hudson

___C. Frances McDormand

___D. Gretchen Moll

or a washing machine, but string allowed her up and haul them from one place to another. at, string allowed women to make nets, which ing smaller animals for dinner possible. sites show the remains of small animal bones and marmots, exactly the kinds of animals ould have caught. That meant no one would let that woolly mammoth get away. In fact, it eant that dad didn't need to hunt big, danger- all.

-bye to the image of an ice-age woman er a fire in a cave, waiting for her mate to bring mammoth bacon. The prehistoric mom was sing children, gathering plants, making crea- , and maybe even hunting to have much time d at all. If only one day those researchers find ner. It could probably give her modern coun- great tips!

n do not have to sacrifice personhood if they hers. They do not have to sacrifice mother- order to be persons. Liberation was meant to women's opportunities, not to limit them. The em that has been found in new pursuits can found in mothering." —Elaine Heffner

8. Patty Duke

A noted television star, Ms. Duke is fondly remembered for starring as "cousins, identical cousins" in *The Patty Duke Show*. But it was her Oscar-winning portrayal of Helen Keller on the big screen in 1962's *The Miracle Worker* that eventually landed her her own show on the small screen and lasting fame.

Ms. Duke is also a mother of three sons. Her eldest became famous as a goonie in the early 1980s, but more recently he has drawn raves for his big-screen portrayal of a hobbit in *The Lord of the Rings* trilogy.

Who is the reel son?
___A. Corey Feldman
___B. Heath Ledger
___C. Elijah Wood
___D. Sean Astin

ANSWERS: 1. B; 2. C; 3. A; 4. C; 5. B; 6. C; 7. B; 8. D

"My mother was the most beautiful woman I ever saw. All I am I owe to my mother. I attribute all my success in life to the moral, intellectual and physical education I received from her." —George Washington

Cave Mom Couture?

Cave moms were more fashionable than you might think.

Pity the poor cave mom. We picture her walking along, draped in smelly animal hides, when her future mate sees her. He bops her on the head, yanks her off by her tangled hair, and deposits her in his cave. There she spends the rest of her life raising little cave people and cooking up whatever her mate drags in. Ugh.

But picture this instead: a woman uses a delicate bone needle to stitch up a linenlike fabric or make a lacy skirt. Now take this mental image of our seamstress and place it during the Upper Paleolithic period, about 27,000 years ago.

Surprised? Modern archaeologists have discovered evidence that cave couture was more sophisticated than we once thought. Move over, Wilma Flintstone! It may be that the concept of life as a prehistoric mom needs a total revision.

FINDING A GOOD IMPRESSION

One of the scientists changing our view of a prehistoric mom's life is a mother herself. Professor Olga Soffer, an archaeologist at the University of Illinois at Urbana-Champaign, worked for ten years as a fashion promoter before she began her academic career. Now she's promoting (and proving) the view that cave women were fashionably clever.

Textiles don't usually survive
Soffer and her colleagues Dr. A
realized that fabric impressions
ric fell to the mud floor of a hu
always live in caves), it would g
the ground where it made an im
studying thousands of pieces of
clay, they've found impression
27,000 years. The professors
knotting patterns in the fabric.

Prehistoric bone and antler
hunting tools have researche
objects could also be battens
Soffer believes that prehistori
nettles, then the fibers were w
even cloth. Working with p
work, so it was most likely the
the fiber into thread and twin

In addition to the clay in
small, stylized carvings of wom
also gave more clues that
women. The various figurines
lacy, string skirts; sashes; and l
resentations of intricate fiber
that likely existed nearly 30
but Professor Soffer, fashion
that the textiles are quite st

NET GAIN

But our prehistoric mom w
brave fashion statements.
twine, it changed her who

refri
to ti
Not
mad
Preh
from
that
starv
may l
ous g

So,
hunch
home
too bu
tive te
to sit
her da
terpart

"Wo
are
hood
expa
self-
also

Goddess Moms' Divine Woes

Being a goddess is no guarantee of an easy ride!

You would think that being a goddess would be a pretty sweet deal—immortality, beauty, people worshipping you. But no mom has it easy—even if she's a goddess!

ISIS IN CRISIS

The great mother goddess of ancient Egypt, Isis was also a queen and the consort of the god-king Osiris. Unfortunately, all that power didn't keep her from having a life like those afternoon soap operas. Just when she got it all together—wham! It fell apart again.

To start, Isis's husband, Osiris, was murdered by his jealous brother, Set, who dismembered and hid Osiris's body. The flooding of the Nile was said to come from Isis's teardrops as she wandered its banks, collecting every part of Osiris's corpse. She then used her powerful magic to bring Osiris back to life and the couple conceived their son, Horus. Alas, their reunion (and hanky-panky) was short-lived. Osiris was forced to return to the land of the dead and Isis was again a single mom.

Fearing Set would kill her son, Isis and Horus hid out in the reeds—without so much as a pup tent. Isis watched over Horus night and day, but Set was able to take advantage of Isis's single-mom isolation. One day while she looked for food, he disguised himself as a scorpion and gave nephew Horus a lethal sting. When Isis found Horus dying, she was so distraught, all her magic powers of healing deserted her.

Good thing she could scream hysterically. Her cries reached the other gods, who helped Isis heal her son. From then on Isis was more careful until Horus came of age, killed his wicked uncle, and became the new god-king of Egypt. Let's hope he thanked his mom.

RHEA-GURGITATION

Rhea was a Greek goddess lucky enough to be married to the king and lord of everything, Chronos. Unfortunately, her status was no guarantee against winding up in a dysfunctional family. Chronos had heard predictions that he would be knocked off his throne—or simply knocked off—by one of his kids, who was destined to be greater than dad. Choosing power over papahood, Chronos simply swallowed all his offspring. Guess he figured being lord of all he surveyed was worth a little indigestion.

Rhea, on the other hand, was miserable. After watching all five of her precious infants go down Chronos's greedy gullet, Rhea decided enough was enough. She hid her sixth son, Zeus, in a cave and tricked her husband into swallowing a rock wrapped in swaddling clothes. The ruse worked and Rhea got to raise her boy. The grown-up Zeus forced his father to disgorge his two brothers and three sisters, who were able to overpower their papa, just as he had feared. Zeus and his siblings then became the Olympian gods, all thanks to Rhea's motherly ingenuity.

CERIDWEN'S UGLY SON

When even your mom thinks you're ugly, you know you're ugly. The Welsh goddess Ceridwen had a son who was no great beauty and was, in fact, quite a great ugly. Despite being the goddess of fertility, death, regeneration, and wisdom, Ceridwen could not cure her son's serious case of the uglies. She worried about him getting along in the world.

Since beauty is only skin deep, Ceridwen knew her son could get by with his bad looks as long as he possessed great wisdom. Ceridwen possessed the Cauldron of Inspiration, which allowed her to cook up a magical brew to give her son the smarts he needed to overcome his aesthetic shortcomings. One drop of this potion and the boy would possess all the knowledge of the world.

The brew required a year and a day of stirring. She hired a boy named Gwion to help her with the task. On the 366th day, Gwion stirred in the last three ingredients and accidently burned his finger on the potion. He stuck his burned finger in his mouth and instantly gained supreme knowledge from the tiny taste he had. Ceridwen returned, realized what had happened, and had a goddess-sized fit. If Gwion had all the knowledge, then there was none left to help her son.

Gwion wisely fled, but Ceridwen chased after him. With his new powers, Gwion became a hare and tried to elude her. But she turned into a dog and continued the chase. Gwion became a fish; Ceridwen became an otter. He flew off as a bird, so she went after him as a hawk. Finally Gwion flew to the threshing floor and hid himself as a grain of wheat. Not so smart since Ceridwen became a hen and promptly ate him up.

After eating the wheat, Ceridwen found herself pregnant (these things happen in myths). A smart cookie herself, she figured that the baby would be Gwion and planned to finish him off after he was born. But the baby was so beautiful that she let him live, and he became the greatest bard of Wales. And the poor ugly son? He had to earn his own wisdom and do it with a face that only a mother could love.

THANK GOD, IT'S FRIGGA

Frigga is the Norse cosmic mother, the goddess for whom Friday is named. That alone is enough to make anyone love her! Frigga was the goddess of households and in charge of married and motherly love. Like most moms, Frigga knew everything, but in her case, Frigga knew everything because she was the goddess of fate and could foretell everyone's future. Frigga would never tell anyone their fate since she knew they were powerless to change it.

Only once did Frigga decide that she would go all out to change fate. She did it to save her son, Baldur, a favorite among the gods, beautiful and pure. When it was learned that Baldur was fated to die, Frigga made an effort to save him by making everything in the world—pointy sticks, hard rocks, singing birds, heavy anvils, you name it—promise not to harm him. And everything Frigga asked was granted. Only she forgot to ask the mistletoe to not kill her boy.

Enjoying his newfound invulnerability, Baldur invited the gods and goddesses to hurl things at him for fun. Baldur may have been loved, but he sure wasn't too bright. Loki, the Norse god of mischief, knew of Frigga's omission and made an arrow out of mistletoe. He then convinced Hodur, a blind god, to shoot this arrow at Baldur to join in the fun with the other gods. Hodur shot; the arrow struck

Baldur and killed him. The gods mourned long for Baldur and for the fact that even a cosmic mother couldn't control the fate of her child.

MY KID'S GREAT—BUT NOT HIS FRIENDS!

Selu was the great corn mother of Cherokee myth. She and her husband Kanati had it all. Kanati could miraculously provide game for the table, while Selu always had baskets of corn. It was a sweet family life, and you can guess what their son was like, as they named him "Good Boy."

Unfortunately, Good Boy had a best friend. This friend, Wild Boy, was born from deer blood spilled into a creek. Under Wild Boy's influence, Selu's son got into trouble. Despite warnings that he must never follow his parents, Wild Boy convinced Good Boy to follow Kanati. They saw him go into a cave and come out with a freshly killed deer to feed the family. When Kanati was gone, the boys rolled aside a big boulder from the cave entrance and suddenly all the game animals in the world fled the cave. From that day on, hunting was a very difficult labor, requiring great skill.

Wild Boy and Good Boy followed Selu too. They saw her go into a storeroom, shake her body, and miraculously fill a basket with corn. Startled, the boys screamed out that Selu was a witch. The corn mother feared (now that her secret was out) that she would be killed, so she left the world. Before going, Selu gave the two boys careful instructions of what to do to have corn for nourishment. But they didn't follow her directions completely. To get corn today, farmers must tend it carefully. Corn will not even grow in some parts of the world.

Kanati left to follow Selu. Without the Cherokee couple's wisdom, people had to work hard to put food on the table. Selu had raised a good boy, but like many other moms, she would probably admit that she should have been more careful about who she let her son hang out with.

Japan's Most Novel Mom

Shikibu Murasaki (978–c. 1031) was always a smart cookie. Her father knew that she had a quick wit and he gave her a good education and allowed her to read many classic Chinese tales that weren't considered proper for young girls. If she had been a man, she certainly would have been a scholar, but instead Murasaki was married off to a relative and had a daughter.

When Murasaki's husband died, she and her daughter went to live at court to become ladies-in-waiting to the empress. At court, Murasaki wrote much of *The Tale of Genji*, which is considered the greatest Japanese literary work and which is thought by many to be the world's first true novel. *The Tale of Genji* is the story of a talented, beautiful son of the emperor who could not rule because his mother was too low in status. Some scholars have speculated that Murasaki's daughter wrote the last section.

Get Down, Mama!

*A celebration of mothers—good, bad, sappy,
and even sexy—over six decades of song. Get down, mama!*

"Apron Strings" by Everything But the Girl
(album: *Acoustic*, 1992)

British pop duo Everything But the Girl is best known in
the United States for the cool techno longing of their
dance hit "Missing," but before that singer Tracey Thorn
expressed a warm longing for something else: babies!
"Apron Strings" tells of a woman besotted with the idea of
motherhood and domesticity, singing to her as-yet-unborn
child, "You'd be happy wrapped in my apron strings." Film-
maker John Hughes used the yearning song to sappy cinematic effect in his mostly ignored pregnancy comedy *She's
Having a Baby*, but don't let that dissuade you. It's a really
lovely song and a reminder that even club divas can hear
the beat of the biological clock.

"To Daddy" by Dolly Parton
(album: *The Essential Dolly Parton*, 1995)

Dolly Parton spins a tale of the perfect, long-suffering, poor
country mama, who silently accepts deprivation and mari-
tal neglect: "Mama never wanted any more than what she
had / and if she did, she never did say so to Daddy," Dolly
sang. But if you think this is just another one of those of
those "stand by your man" sort of ditties that makes modern women gnash their teeth, just you wait. At the end of

the song, with the kids all grown up, Mama up and disappears, off to find the love she didn't get at home. Passive-aggressive on her part? Possibly. On the other hand, Daddy's a real jerk who should have given up some cards and flowers. So there you have it. In addition to Dolly's original version, there's a fine cover by Emmylou Harris on the recent Parton tribute album, *Just Because I'm a Woman*.

"Dear Mama" by Tupac Shakur
(album: *Me Against the World*, 1995)

Your average gangsta rappers may not come off as the sentimental types, that's fo' shizzle, but get 'em talking about their sainted mamas and they may start blubbering like 10-year-old boys. The disturbingly posthumously prolific Tupac Shakur is no exception. "Dear Mama" finds him representing for his mother, who raised him right even though he was a bad kid. It's a sweet, yet tough, tribute to all his mama did for him: "Cause through the drama / I can always depend on my mama / And when it seems that I'm hopeless / You say the words that can get me back in focus." Warm and sincere, Tupac's thanks to his mama could make anyone shed a tear or two.

"Mama, Come Home" by Ella Fitzgerald
(album: *The War Years*, 1994)

Whipsaw yourself back to the 1940s for this Ella Fitzgerald gem in which a little girl begs her mom to come home from jitterbugging at the local juke joint: "Papa's been mending the holes in his socks / While you stick nickels in the jitterbug box!" Ella exclaims. They've even eaten all the crackers and cheese. But then Ella adds this note—seeing as dad likes to jitterbug too, mama should just drag the jukebox home with her. They'll all still be hungry and have holes in their socks, but at least they'd be dancing as a family. And isn't togetherness what family is all about?

"Mama Liked the Roses" by Elvis Presley (album: *From Nashville To Memphis: The Essential 60's Masters I*, 1993)

Elvis Presley was the biggest mama's boy in the entire known universe, and it's a good thing too. If he hadn't have stopped off at Sun Records to record a song for his mama as a gift, thence to be discovered, he might still be a trucker today and then all those Elvis imitators would have to have found something else to do with their lives. Hmmm. Anyway, you can see how Elvis would do this song, which talks about the roses Mama used to grow and how now they use those same roses to decorate Mama's grave. It's kind of schmaltzy—but, come on. You know Elvis's mama, Gladys, would have loved it.

"Stacy's Mom" by Fountains of Wayne (album: *Welcome Interstate Managers*, 2003)

The song's main character is asking teen pal Stacy if he can come to her house after school. Does he have a thing for Stacy? Well, no, as the exuberantly poppy chorus explains: "Stacy's mom has got it going on!" Yeah, way to make *Stacy* feel special there, pal. It's a deeply silly song, but it's also insanely catchy, down to the Cars-like guitar riffs. And it pretty accurately reflects what it was like to be a deliriously hormonal teenage boy fantasizing about a Mrs. Robinson experience from one of the local suburban divorcées. Advice to you potential Stacys out there: a good cold blast from the garden hose will get the boys back to reality.

The True Story Behind Mother's Day

A daughter's answer to her mother's prayer creates Mother's Day. Trouble is, the success of the holiday made her want to quash it.

The American Mother's Day had its origins after the Civil War, when Ann Maria Jarvis worked hard with other mothers to start Mother's Friendship Day in an effort to bring together a community divided by the Civil War. Inspired by her mother's work and words, Anna Jarvis lobbied for Mother's Day to become a national holiday.

MOTHER'S FRIENDSHIP DAY, THE ORIGINS

The daughter of a minister, Ann Maria (1832–1905) gave birth to twelve children, but, sadly, only four survived to adulthood. She lived in West Virginia and was very active in her church. There she formed the Mother's Day Work Clubs, where local moms could raise money for the poor.

In 1861, Ann Maria and the Mother's Day Work Clubs faced a terrible challenge. When the Civil War began, the inhabitants of West Virginia were deeply divided. Some West Virginians served the Confederacy while others stayed true to the Union. Determined that the political division wouldn't end the Mother's Day Work Clubs, Ann Maria and the other mothers declared themselves neutral, serving both Rebels and Yankees. Blue and Gray mothers worked together to nurse, clothe, and feed all the sick solders.

When the war was over, Ann Maria set out to heal the civil wounds by initiating a Mother's Friendship Day in the summer of 1865 for all the mothers and their families living in Taylor County, West Virginia. The occasion marked the reunion between Blue and Gray, and the event was an amazing success, as humble mothers and housewives were able to bring once-bitter enemies together. For several years after, Mother's Friendship Day was an annual celebration. Ann Maria's unexpected success inspired Julia Ward Howe and then her own daughter, Anna, to propose special mother's days of their own.

MOTHER'S DAY, THE BEGINNING

It started innocently enough. Ann Maria's daughter, Anna Jarvis (1864–1948) centered much of her life on the church where Ann Maria taught. The legend goes that Ann Maria gave a stirring talk on the mothers of the Bible and concluded with a prayer that someone would establish a day to commemorate mothers and their service to humanity. Twelve-year-old Anna committed that prayer to memory and silently vowed to fulfill it.

After her mother died on May 9, 1905, Anna began serious work to answer Ann Maria's prayer. Being the daughter of a dedicated activist, she knew how to get things done. By the second anniversary of her mother's death Anna had convinced the minister of Andrews Methodist Church in Grafton, West Virginia, to hold a Mother's Day memorial service. Anna passed out white carnations, her mother's favorite flower—an act that would later come back to haunt her. Eventually those whose mothers had died wore white carnations, while those whose mothers were living wore pink or red carnations.

MOTHER'S DAY, THE HOLIDAY

Anna kept on fighting to make Mother's Day an official holiday. With the help of some wealthy supporters, her efforts began to pay off by the third anniversary of her mother's death. By May 10, 1908, the Mother's Day Sunday service in Philadelphia brought out a crowd of more than 15,000! The idea really took off in the following year, and by 1909 forty-five states, plus the territories, Canada, and Mexico, observed the holiday.

Congress finally woke up and smelled the flowers. They voted in 1913 to have government officials from the president on down wear carnations on Mother's Day. By 1914, Woodrow Wilson proclaimed it an official holiday.

MOTHER'S DAY GOES COMMERCIAL

Anna wanted Mother's Day "to brighten the lives of good mothers. To have them know we (their children) appreciate them, though we do not show it as often as we ought." What Anna didn't appreciate were the commercial interests that looked at moms and began to see dollar signs. She opposed the sale of Mother's Day cards, "A printed card . . . means nothing except you're too lazy to write." She opposed candy sales too, since she thought that adult children brought a box of candy to mother, then ate most of it themselves! But it was the florists who made her blood boil. They had turned Mother's Day into a day to purchase flowers. "I wanted it to be a day of sentiment, not profit," Anna said.

She tried urging practical gifts like new eyeglasses or comfortable shoes. When that failed, she worked to get rid of the darned day altogether. But this time, letters and lobbying didn't work. In 1923, her lawsuits to stop Mother's Day celebrations in New York failed and her protests even landed her in jail. In the 1930s, perhaps a little unbalanced from the long battle, Anna was removed by police after she disrupted a sale of carnations . . . by the American War Mothers.

MOTHER'S DAY, THE LEGACY

Despite Anna's best efforts, she could not undo her work, nor the work of greeting card manufacturers. Mother's Day lived on and thrived. Nations across the globe now formally honor mothers with their own special day. But we wonder, in answering her mother's prayer, did Anna create a monster? We don't think so. Even though commercialism can run amok, the sentiment of the holiday does shine through. Grateful women fondly remembered Anna as the mother of Mother's Day and sent her cards for years. Oh, the irony.

"Mother's Day is in honor of the best Mother who ever lived—the Mother of your heart."
—Anna Jarvis

"Time is the only comforter for the loss of a mother."
—Jane Welsh Carlyle

Great Mama Ape!

Binti Jua shows some maternal moxie!

Mom saves a little boy from ferocious gorillas! Showing a calm intelligence when everyone around her had panicked, a brave mother (with her own baby still clinging to her) saved a three-year-old toddler who'd fallen approximately 20 feet to the floor of the gorilla enclosure at Illinois's Brookfield Zoo. The catch? The heroic mom was one of the gorillas.

SAVED BY THE MOM

On August 16, 1996, at the Brookfield Zoo's Primate World exhibit, a rambunctious toddler climbed the stone-and-bamboo barrier and then fell to the floor of the gorilla compound. The horrified crowd panicked and the boy's mother screamed, "The gorilla's got my baby!" A female gorilla, Binti-Jua (whose name means "Daughter of Sunshine" in Swahili) was the first to act. Carrying her own baby, Koola, on her back, she approached the unconscious boy and picked him up.

Gorillas are five and a half feet tall when they stand straight up on their hind legs and can weigh from 200 to 600 pounds. Their fierce reputation is undeserved, but even the zookeepers who were familiar with the gentleness of giant apes were worried. The helpless child was suddenly under the control of a wild animal.

Binti-Jua cradled the child in her arms and rocked him gently. She seemed to hesitate as to where best to take the little boy; then, keeping other gorillas away, she crossed the compound and placed him near the door where the zookeepers usually entered. She placed the child gently down in a place where waiting staff and paramedics could easily take over. Then, as a stunned crowd watched, the rescuer casually returned to her comfortable spot and began to groom her own baby. The little boy spent a few days in the hospital and was released as good as new.

MOTHER OF ALL CONTROVERSY

Binti-Jua's actions hit the headlines. Celebrated for her amazing rescue, she also became the focus of controversy. Dr. Morris Goodman, a molecular phylogeneticist and the man who discovered the small genetic differences in the coding between human and gorilla DNA, believed that Binti-Jua had some sort of thought process similar to a human's regarding the safety of the child. She had recognized the toddler as vulnerable and displayed intelligent behavior by moving him to safety. Others praised her ability to cope intelligently in a new and unexpected situation.

Skeptics argued that Binti-Jua was only trying to win the approval of her keepers and avoid punishment by retrieving something for them. They pointed out that Binti had been reared by humans, and when she became pregnant, the zoo staff gave her mothering lessons. This led some researchers to argue that Binti-Jua acted more like a human mom because she'd been raised and learned parenting skills from human keepers.

Witnesses, however, claimed that regardless of what did or did not go on in her brain, Binti treated the boy with as much gentleness and care as if she'd been his own mother. And as the rescued toddler recovered from his injuries, Binti was praised as a genuine heroine. Letters and gifts (including pounds of bananas) poured in from all over the world. The heroine received a medal from the American Legion, an honorary membership in a Downey, California, PTA, and a spot as one of the 25 most intriguing "people" in *People* magazine.

Did You Know?

Largest Dog Litter: 23 Puppies
The record is held by three different dogs: an American Foxhound in 1944, a Saint Bernard in 1975, and a Great Dane in 1987. All had 23-puppy pregnancies.

Largest Rabbit Litter: 24 Baby Bunnies
Two separate New Zealand rabbits mums each gave birth to a litter of 24 kits: one mama in 1978 and the other in 1999.

Largest Bird Egg: 5 pounds, 2 ounces
In June of 1997, a big mama ostrich laid a very big egg in Datong, Shanxi, China.

The Dalai Lama's Mama

From an overworked peasant wife to the mother of a
god-king and the heroine of a country in exile, Diki Tsering
rose to the challenges of an amazing life.

What if you were a religious, hard-toiling peasant
mother who suddenly learned that your two-year-
old toddler was the incarnation of a god? Not only that,
but he was preordained to become the leader of a nation?
It's an event that seems impossible, almost beyond imag-
ining, but it was exactly what happened to Diki Tsering,
the mother of Tibet's Dalai Lama.

Born in the year of the ox, her grandfather gave her
the name Sonam Tsomo, after the goddess of fertility
and longevity. Sonam was a peasant girl from the north-
eastern edge of Tibet. Though she had many chores and
was never formally educated, she was quite happy growing
up on her parents' large farm. She wanted to stay there,
close to her family, but Tibetan customs were rigid—a
daughter must marry and serve her husband's family in
his household. At the age of 16, Sonam left home a reluctant bride.

CINDERELLA STORY

Her new in-laws wanted a daughter-in-law to help them in
their old age. The 16-year-old was put to work at home
and in the fields. Like Cinderella, Sonam was expected to

be on the job 24-7. She fetched water, swept the floors, fed and milked the animals, collected fuel for the fires, made the meals, and tended crops. Despite the harshness, the bride accepted her life, believing as a devout Buddhist that suffering would ennoble her character and make her a better human being.

A few years after her marriage, Sonam's in-laws died. She helped her husband manage the farm and she was also responsible for running the household as well as caring for her children. But some things didn't change: she was still working 'round the clock, and when she had a child she simply tied the baby on her back and returned to her chores. In fact, Sonam was hard at work shoveling snow when she had an important visit from government officials. They told her that, like Cinderella, her drudgery was over and that she would live in a palace; she'd even have a new name, Diki Tsering, which means "ocean of luck." The enormous change in this mother's life was all because of her two-year-old toddler, Llhamo Dhondup.

A CHILD'S DESTINY

The strangers, who arrived at Diki Tsering's door in 1937, had been led there by dreams, divination, and oracles. They were an official search party scouring the country for the reincarnation of the late thirteenth Dalai Lama. The title "Dalai Lama" means "teacher of wisdom as vast as the ocean," and he's considered a god-king, Avalokitesvara, the Bodhisattva of Compassion, spiritual and political leader of Tibet. Each new Dalai Lama is believed to be a reincarnation of the previous one. When little Llhamo Dhondup passed the search party's official tests (like being able to identify possessions of the thirteenth

Dalai Lama), the toddler was recognized as the fourteenth Dalai Lama. And his mom became Amala, the great mother of the nation.

Overwhelmed and more than a little frightened by the fate of her family, the peasant mother set off for the palace in the forbidden city of Lhasa. Later in her autobiography she wrote, "Ever since I went to live in Lhasa, I tried to become Diki Tsering, with all the social forms and graces that go with that name." But it wasn't easy to take the unspoiled peasant girl out of the new Amala, which turned out to be a darned good thing.

CINDERELLA MISSES HOME

Diki Tsering lived in the palace where she was treated like a queen—but she soon longed for her hard life on the farm. She disliked being idle while servants did all the work. She valued simple honesty and hated the devious court intrigues for power. She missed her son, as his Holiness had to live with the monks in a monastery.

And oh, those impractical royal fashions! Government officials gave Diki Tsering garments laden with pearls and coral. Scorning the heavy gowns, she wore her comfortable, peasant *hari*, a simple embroidered overdress. Haute couture was definitely not her style.

While Diki Tsering adjusted to a queenly lifestyle, danger swirled around her. The young Dalai Lama was a regent and the men that ruled in his stead were constantly fighting. One of those ruling officials even assassinated the regent's father. Feeling alone and helpless without her husband, the Amala soon had to help her son face a new threat from Communist China, which was imprisoning and killing Tibet's religious leaders.

NO FAIRY-TALE ENDINGS

By 1950, the Chinese forced the Dalai Lama and his family to flee to India, where they set up a government in exile. In India, the Amala spent the rest of her life helping Tibetan refugees and fostering Tibetan traditions, keeping them alive despite the destructive efforts of the Chinese. The exiled Tibetans grew to love and revere her. The Dalai Lama praised his mother's calm kindness and credited her with helping the royal family to be compassionate while never forgetting their humble origins.

Infighting, death, warfare, and exile: it wasn't exactly a fairy-tale ending to her Cinderella story, but the Amala coped just as she had when she was a peasant bride. Diki Tsering thought of herself as an ordinary wife and mother, but those who experienced her compassion or were inspired by her humility and strength of character—they considered her extraordinary.

"The reason why mothers are more devoted to their children than fathers: it is that they suffer more in giving them birth and are more certain that they are their own." —Aristotle

"All mothers are working mothers." —Unknown

Ladies' Man,
Mama's Boy?

Good guys got a good thing goin' with mom.

He's strong, he's suave, and women go weak in the knees when he walks into the room. And of course he's close to his mom.

Huh? Do "ladies' man" and "mama's boy" go together?

You bet they do. Researchers have investigated how a guy's relationship with his mom might affect his relationship with his significant other—and they came up with some surprising results.

GOOD SON = GOOD BOYFRIEND

Researchers at Ferrum College in Virginia found that when a woman was highly satisfied with her man, he tended to get along well with his mother. They questioned couples, asking the women about their relationships with their husbands and boyfriends and surveying the men about their relationships with their mothers. The findings showed significant correlations between the way a man feels about his mother and the way the woman feels about him.

Overall, it's good news for men who are valued and respected by their moms. Turns out that the men who thought highly of their mothers were also close to their wives and girlfriends. Their mates rated these guys as affectionate and good communicators, calling them both good lovers and best friends.

Sarah Roberts, who ran the study, noted that in many homes the mother is a child's first experience with femininity, as well as his first influential teacher. A son who has a happy maternal experience may be more open to a woman's affection. Men who had a high-quality relationship with the first important female in their lives seemed to be able to go on to have high-quality relationships with females in their love lives too.

HOW MUCH IS TOO MUCH?

But can a man be too close to his mom? What about the guy who treats his mom so well that he makes his girlfriend second best? The study may have spotted that guy too.

Men who rated moms as their "best friend" didn't get such a strong nod of approval from their honeys. These men were rated as "less than considerate" by their mates. So for mom and son, it seems to be a question of degree. When mom and son are too close, wives and girlfriends aren't as happy.

How close is too close? That's a question only a woman can answer. (Seriously, we're not touching that one.)

"Few misfortunes can befall a boy which bring worse consequences than to have a really affectionate mother."
—W. Somerset Maugham

Mama Presley's
Pink Cadillac

*Millions of girls got all shook up over sexy Elvis,
but here's the story of the King's greatest love*

In 1956 Presley-mania swept the country. You couldn't turn on a radio without hearing "Heartbreak Hotel." Millions of TV viewers tuned in to *The Milton Berle Show* to watch a sultry teenager with slick-backed hair and sideburns rush onstage to belt out "Hound Dog" while accompanying his bluesy singing with a pelvic bump and grind that drove the girls and the TV censors wild. Some authorities declared it the end of civilization. Others said, nah, it's just the birth of rock and roll.

At Presley's performances, girls screamed, cried, fainted, and tore off his clothing—behaving in a highly unladylike manner. As for Elvis, he loved his female fans. But he always declared that his greatest fan and the woman with the deepest hold on his heart was Gladys, better known as his mama.

ELVIS ENTERS THE BUILDING

Gladys Love Smith was a descendant of sharecroppers and moonshiners who lived through hard times that never seemed to improve much. A striking woman, family said Gladys owed her dark-haired good looks to her Cherokee great-great-grandmother. Folks in her hometown of Tupelo praised Gladys's singing talent. And Gladys could move. In the dance halls, friends stood back to gawk open-mouthed when the girl hip-swiveled into buck dancing, a frowned-upon 1930s version of dirty dancing. Nobody shook up Tupelo like Gladys.

Alas, Gladys's partying days were short-lived. She came of age in the Great Depression and dropped out of school early to help care for seven brothers and sisters. She worked 12-hour days in a garment factory, and her marriage to Vernon Presley didn't improve her chances for enjoying leisure time. Vernon might have been handsome, charming, and funny, but he was poorer than Gladys and was said to be allergic to steady work.

Vernon borrowed money and built the young couple's first home, a two-room shotgun shack. In that little house in Tupelo, a pregnant Gladys went into labor. On January 8, 1935, Elvis entered the building.

A LEGEND IS BORN

The night of Elvis's birth was at once the happiest and the most tragic of the young mother's life. She delivered twin sons, but one, Jessie Garon, was stillborn. The loss of one baby made Elvis all the more precious to her. She took to heart the folk belief that if one twin died it meant that the "one that lived got all the strength of the other." But the trauma surrounding her son's birth left Gladys fearful for his safety. Along with her powerful faith that Elvis could do great things out in the world, his mama was always terrified that the world might destroy him.

THAT'S NOT ALL RIGHT, PAPA

Vernon managed to support their little family, with Gladys taking on jobs like picking cotton to help out. Family friends, church meetings, and tent revivals dominated their social life, making the Presleys an "average" Tupelo family. That is, until Daddy got arrested for forgery.

Vernon and two companions had placed an extra zero on a four-dollar check they'd received from the Presleys' landlord in payment for a hog. They were all sentenced to three years in prison. Gladys, left alone with a two-year-old to support, was dealt a second blow when the landlord evicted her from her home for lack of payment.

Somehow, Gladys managed. She stayed with relatives, got a job in the laundry, and cared for her son. While Vernon was locked up, Gladys and Elvis were two against the world. They loved and protected each other fiercely, spent all the time they could together, and even invented a language that only the two of them understood—and which they would communicate in for the rest of their lives. Elvis became the man of the house before he was three. He often called his mother "baby" and vowed to one day make her life easy. Most kids forget promises they make when they're young, but not Elvis.

YOU CAN LEAVE THE BUILDING NOW

Believe it or not, there was a time when people actually wanted Elvis Presley not to sing. Once Gladys noticed that her boy loved music, she gave him his first guitar and even arranged for him to take lessons. Elvis practiced that guitar everywhere and sang to everyone. He was an immediate success with his teachers and classmates, but his tendency to sing the same songs over and over caused some pals to beg him to stop!

Mama never tired of hearing Elvis sing his favorite songs like "Old Shep." As for Elvis, he noticed the way kids who had once looked down on him suddenly admired him when he sang. Maybe with music, Elvis could give his mama everything she'd ever wanted.

MOVING TO MEMPHIS

The Presleys moved to Memphis after Vernon was released from prison, but unfortunately, Vernon still had problems holding down a steady job. Gladys came to the rescue again and took on odd jobs to make sure her son didn't have to drop out of high school. In fact, there were few limits to Gladys's support of her boy. Coeds might one day swoon when Elvis shook his locks, but at Humes High the girls turned up their noses at the shy, polite boy from Tupelo. They didn't like his weird sideburns or hairstyles that looked shot from a grease gun. It was loyal Gladys who understood Elvis's search for his own look; she even home-permed his soon-to-be-famous pompadour when Elvis asked for a Tony Curtis style.

Elvis Presley was a model son. The summer after graduation he took a job driving a truck for an electrical company and faithfully brought home his paycheck. But inside, Elvis was restless. He longed to sing his way to stardom. Then he'd buy his mama a real house—along with a pink Cadillac.

A RISING SON BECOMES A STAR

Elvis went down to Sun Records and paid them to cut a record as a belated birthday present for his mama. He sang "My Happiness" and "That's When Your Heartaches Begin." This record led to a professional session at Sun, where Elvis cut his first single, "That's All Right." When Elvis's voice hit the airwaves, Vernon and Gladys were glued to the radio. When Gladys heard them say Elvis's name, she went into such shock that she "couldn't rightly hear the record." But it didn't matter—the song was played again and again. It was an immediate local sensation.

Elvis's first recording was a triumph for Gladys (and payback for all those times she'd had to listen to "Old Shep" over and over and over). But pride in her son's success turned to panic when Elvis quit truck driving in favor of the music business. Overanxious Gladys, who'd walked her precious boy safely across the highway for about eight years longer than necessary, now had to watch him head out on tour. And the rest, as they say, is rock and roll history.

THE PINK CADILLAC

Once Elvis was a star, he did keep his promise and bought his mama a big pink Cadillac. Gladys was proud and grateful, but she never drove that car—she didn't like to drive. As for world-famous Graceland, it was Gladys who saw the estate and fell in love with it. So Elvis bought it for her.

In August 1958 Gladys was stricken with hepatitis, which would eventually bring on a fatal heart attack. Before her death, her beloved pink Cadillac was placed outside the hospital, where she could see it from her window. Elvis, who'd been drafted into the army, got special leave to rush to her side. Friends claimed Elvis was never the same after Gladys died. Overcome with grief, he parked the pink Cadillac at Graceland, where it remains to this day.

Lullaby Power

There's power in rocking a baby to sleep with a lullaby.
If you don't believe the world's moms, just ask the scientists.

Did you know that lullabies sound the same the world over? Or that a mother's singing can decrease stress hormones in her child? How about the fact that rocking a baby helps it to develop faster? Scientists are beginning to take note of the centuries-old power of a mom's lullabies.

BABIES ARE NOTEWORTHY

All around the world, mothers sing lullabies to their children to soothe them to sleep. Lullabies are distinguishable as simpler and more repetitive than other types of songs. And not only are all lullabies similar, but all mothers sing them in a similar manner: at a high pitch, in a slow tempo, and with a distinctive tone.

What drives this worldwide warbling of lullabies? University of Toronto professor Sandra Trehub has done experiments that show babies are very responsive to music and quicker to notice a "sour" note than adults are. She believes this infant affinity for music is connected to a lullaby's power to soothe a fretting baby. Trehub's research has also shown that moms can mesmerize babies with lullabies and even lower their children's stress hormones!

Lullabies may be an important survival tool. The sweet sounds make a baby less fussy, which, in turn, makes a mom's demanding job easier. When a mother can more successfully care for her infant, the infant is more likely to survive and thrive.

GIVE ME A LULLABY, STAT !

More evidence of lullaby power was discovered by Rosalie Pratt, a music professor at Brigham Young University. Pratt conducted a study showing the effect of lullabies on the health of newborn babies in hospital intensive care units (ICUs). For four days, newborns in the ICU were exposed to lullabies for two 20-minute sessions each day. Video cameras recorded the infants' responses, and their heart and oxygen response measurements were calculated. These "lullaby babies" were compared to a carefully matched, "lullaby-free" control group.

The result? Lullaby babies showed lower heart rates, increased oxygen saturation, and reduced stress behaviors than the lullaby-free babies. Biological signs of relaxation were accompanied by other positive results. Lullaby babies were able to settle down faster and eat more. They consistently grew faster and had a healthier weight gain—two important goals for infants.

How were lullabies helping the babies? The theory is that the noisy ICU overstimulates a baby's nervous system. Noise keeps babies from resting and provokes stress movements that use up calories needed for growth. Soothing lullabies distract babies from stressful sounds. They help the babies rest, relax, eat, and grow stronger.

A LULLABY A DAY REDUCES THE HOSPITAL STAY?

Whatever the reason, other studies are confirming that premature babies benefit from lullabies. A two-year study on premature infants at Children's Hospital in Akron, Ohio, showed that lullaby preemies gained more weight and grew faster than lullaby-free preemies. Lullaby preemies were discharged from the hospital an average of 12 days earlier.

An ongoing study in the Akron hospital is testing the healing value of familiar lullabies. Classic tunes such as "Rock-a-Bye Baby" and "Hush, Little Baby" are now filling the neonatal ICU. In addition to the recorded tunes, the babies also hear a heartbeat in the background to simulate the sound they hear in the womb. You can get relaxed just thinking about it.

YOU AIN'T GOT A THING IF YOU AIN'T GOT THAT SWING

Turns out that "Rock-a-Bye Baby" is good advice—except for that whole treetop thing. The common rocking motion that mothers use while they sing to their babies can make a lullaby even more beneficial. Some scientists believe that rocking soothes babies by mimicking the sensations they felt in utero.

Dr. Mary Neal constructed a swinging bassinet for premature babies. The preemies placed in her hammock were faster to develop reflexes like crawling and grasping at objects than preemies who didn't experience the movement of the hammock.

TO CROON OR NOT TO CROON

The verdict of science? Keep the lullabies coming! Studies show that you don't have to sing like Ella Fitzgerald to soothe a baby. Even musically challenged parents enhance their child's development by warbling a soothing lullaby and rocking their baby to sleep. Just try to stay on key.

TV Moms III:
TV Gets Real(er)

Check out these TV moms who finally got real, man.

Moms started to become a bit more real in the 1970s and 1980s. As the number of single parents soared from 3.8 million in 1970 to 6.9 million in 1980, TV writers introduced moms in not-so-great marriages, as well as single and working moms.

EDITH BUNKER: A REAL DINGBAT?

The Show: *All in the Family* (1971–1979)
At first glance, *All in the Family* seemed like a step backward. Ditzy Edith Bunker (played by Jean Stapleton) seemed a deferential housewife to her boorish husband, Archie, who called her "Dingbat" and often told her to "Stifle!" But a closer look shows that *All in the Family*'s unflinching comedic take on social issues and family life was quite revolutionary.

Edith didn't have a glamorous life; the Bunkers were staunchly blue-collar. She dressed simply (no pearls for her!), and her house was clean, but a little on the shabby side. Her grown daughter, Gloria, and son-in-law, Mike, brought the generation gap to the table and Archie's prejudiced ways out in the open. As a balance, Edith became the heart, soul, and conscience of the show. The Bunker clan reshaped family TV, introducing "gritcoms."
Fun Fact: In 1972, the show won an Emmy for the episode called "Edith's Problem." What was Edith's problem? Menopause. And it was the first real mention of it on TV.

MS. ANN ROMANO: A REAL SINGLE MOM

The Show: *One Day at a Time* (1975–1984)

Ann Romano (played by Bonnie Franklin), on the series *One Day at a Time*, was in a tough spot. Divorced after 17 years of marriage, with little job experience, she found herself single with two teen daughters to support. So the family moved to an apartment where every week a new family drama played itself out. Luckily for the audience, the building's superintendent and resident Romeo wannabe, Schneider, served up the comic relief to keep things light.

Nothing was easy for Ms. Romano, certainly not finding a job or raising her two daughters alone. Ann tussled with the same troubles that faced divorced mothers of her day— tight budgets, deadbeat dads, rebellious teenagers, the need for a career, and the longing for romance. The series walked a fine line between drama and comedy. The issues were serious, but the humor was there and was genuine.

Fun Fact: Mackenzie Phillips, who played the eldest daughter, Julie, was the real-life daughter of John Phillips, one of the founding members of the singing group the Mamas and the Papas.

KATE AND ALLIE: A REAL ODD COUPLE

The Show: *Kate and Allie* (1984–1989)

Kate and Allie (Kate was played by Susan Saint James, Allie by Jane Curtin) followed the friendship of two single moms who were high-school buddies and now found themselves recently divorced moms. To save money and find mutual support, they shared a Greenwich Village apartment with their combined family of three kids.

Kate was trendy and a little more independent. Allie was old-fashioned and a bit uptight. They leaned on each other while coping with the ups and downs of romance, the trials of raising kids in New York, and the oddities of their family unit.

Fun Fact: As an original cast member on *Saturday Night Live*, Jane Curtin can be seen in reruns as an out-of-this-world mother and conehead, Prymaat, who insisted that she was from France.

CLAIR HUXTABLE: A REAL SUPERMOM

The Show: *The Cosby Show* (1984–1992)
In the 1980s, *The Cosby Show* dominated Thursday nights. It seemed everyone was tuning in to watch the Huxtables—the five lively children, funny father Heathcliff, and supermom Clair (played by Phylicia Rashad). A successful attorney, as well as a down-to-earth parent, Clair managed the pressures of her profession, cared for an upscale home, and coped with the antics of five lively children—all without taking any backtalk along the way.

Critics complained that the Huxtables weren't realistic, but some say that have-it-all, do-it-all Claire realistically reflected the spirit of the times. The notion of the modern woman succeeding was celebrated, and Claire's seemingly impossible achievements gave us something to strive for.

Fun Fact: Credited as Phylicia Ayres-Allen, Phylicia Rashad played a munchkin in the 1978 film *The Wiz*.

Barbie Doll's Mom

It takes a mother of invention to create a great gal.

In her long career as one of America's most popular toys, the glam Barbie doll has been a teacher, a singer, a stewardess, and even an astronaut—but never a mother. Too bad, since Ruth Handler was one of the world's most creative entrepreneur moms.

BARBIE'S IMMIGRANT ROOTS

Barbie's creator had few toys when she was growing up in Denver, Colorado. Ruth was born in 1916 to Jewish immigrants who'd fled persecution in Poland. As the youngest of ten children, Ruth's family situation wasn't exactly easy. Her mother was illiterate and in such poor health that Ruth had to leave home to live with her older sister.

When she was in high school, Ruth fell head over heels for a guy named Elliot Handler. She eventually moved to California and the two were married there in 1938. The Handlers' marriage wasn't only a love match that lasted 63 years, but also a strong business partnership. Elliot became an expert at creating giftware, while Ruth was a whiz at marketing and merchandising his products. By 1944 the successful couple could afford a house that Elliot designed for Ruth, himself, and their two children, Barbara (nicknamed "Barbie" or "Babs") and Kenneth (nicknamed "Ken"). Barbie and Ken sound familiar, right?

In 1945, Ruth and Elliot formed a company that would become one of the largest toy companies in the world—Mattel. The first Mattel products were wooden picture frames, but the company branched out into toys when Elliot started making dollhouse furniture from leftover frame scraps. For the next decade Mattel grew exponentially, with Elliot and a partner creating toys and Ruth successfully marketing them.

RUTH'S OWN LITTLE DOLL INSPIRES HER

As a mom in the late 1940s and early 1950s, Ruth noticed that her daughter Barbara didn't have many types of dolls to play with—mostly baby dolls; dolls that looked like little girls; and paper dolls. Ruth noticed that Barbara preferred paper dolls, which looked like fashionable young women and had multiple gorgeous outfits that could be changed frequently. This observation gave Ruth an idea. She wanted Mattel to create a teenaged doll or a career-woman doll for her girls to play with, but Mattel's male executives discouraged her until she gave up.

A BARBIE IS BORN

Then in 1956, the Handlers went on a European vacation. In a little store in Lucerne, Switzerland, Barbara finally saw a three-dimensional molded plastic doll that interested her. It was a Lilli doll made in Germany. A mature German lady, Lilli had an alluring female shape and face. She was actually created as a takeoff on a bawdy comic strip character and designed to appeal to the male bar crowd, but little Barbara didn't know that, and Ruth didn't much care. She bought Lilli dolls for her daughter and herself. Based on her daughter's reaction to the doll,

Ruth became convinced that this idea for a new type of doll would be a runaway success.

Ruth used Lilli as a prototype for her own doll, Barbie, named after Barbara Handler. With Barbie, a little girl could act out the fantasy of growing up and having beautiful clothes to do it in. "My whole philosophy of Barbie was that through the doll, the little girl could be anything she wanted to be," Ruth wrote in her autobiography. "Barbie always represented the fact that a woman has choices." Barbie would be a fashionable young woman with a fashionable wardrobe that could be changed and varied.

BARBIE TAKES OFF

Ruth presented her idea to the suits at Mattel. At first they resisted the doll's zaftig figure and the idea that any mother would buy a doll with—well—large breasts. Ruth insisted that the doll would sell, so Barbie made her first appearance at the 1959 Toy Fair in New York City, wearing a zebra-striped bathing suit and costing all of three dollars. The male buyers didn't like the doll themselves, but the little girls sure did. Mattel was deluged with orders and sold more than 350,000 dolls that year.

Five years later, Barbie was a million-dollar doll. Ruth used all her marketing skills to keep Barbie current and on top of the latest trends. As women took on more varied careers, Barbie took them on too, including becoming an astronaut in 1965. Barbie's social circle began to expand with the introduction of the Ken doll, which was named after Ruth's son. Then came Midge and Skipper. And eventually Stacie, Todd, and Cheryl, who were named for Ruth's grandchildren.

Despite big earnings, Barbie's figure remained controversial. The National Organization for Women argued that Barbie gave girls an unhealthy body image. If she were five foot six instead of 11 inches tall, her measurements would be "unrealistic" and rather top heavy. An academic expert once calculated that a woman's likelihood of being shaped like Barbie was less than one in 100,000. Feminists, concentrating on Barbie's chest, missed the fact that her creator—who by now was a grandmother—had become one of the top executives in the male-dominated toy industry. Ruth liked to point out that successful women—and feminists—would come up to her and admit they'd loved to play with Barbie. Today a new Barbie doll is sold approximately every three seconds. Barbie is a $1.5 billion business for Mattel, so tomorrow's feminists probably have Barbies as well. All in all, Ruth's creation has become an icon of American life.

Mother Knows Breast

Ruth Handler's life took a new entrepreneurial turn after a battle with breast cancer and subsequent mastectomy. Finding an acceptable breast prosthesis proved difficult, so Ruth developed her own and founded Nearly Me, a company that manufactures breast prostheses for cancer survivors. Summing up her career, Ruth liked to say, "I've gone from breast to breast."

Labor Pains

Could you afford a mom's services if you had to pay for them?

What would it cost to pay someone to do all the jobs that mom does during the day? What would it cost to hire a mom to cook for you, keep your house clean, help solve your personal problems, and nurse you when you're sick—not to mention walk your dog? Get ready for sticker shock.

WHAT IS WORK, ANYWAY?

In 1934, economist Margaret Reid developed a way to measure the value of unpaid labor—the third-person criterion. If a third person could be hired to do a job, then the job would qualify as work. So technically, the hours Mom spends cleaning the house, balancing the checkbook, and acting as a taxi driver for her kids can be considered work.

DETERMINING MOM'S NET WORTH

Ric Edelman, chair of Edelman Financial Services, put together a list of all the different job tasks and titles that seems to come close to all the stuff moms do every day. Then Edelman tried to quantify a mom's market value in the 2002 job market based on all these job descriptions.

Here are just a few positions and their annual salaries:

Animal caretaker	$22,256
Chef	$25,110
Child-care worker	$18,179
Computer systems analyst	$60,860
Financial manager	$70,366
Food service worker	$14,710
Housekeeper	$15,410
Management analyst	$52,457
Psychologist	$56,576
Registered nurse	$45,614

And that doesn't even begin to consider her transportation and property management services. Or making sure that the species continues. When Edelman Financial Services added up all of Mom's salaries (which included more than the ones listed above), her total deserved pay came to a hefty $635,000.

Not everyone agrees with this nice six-figure salary. Economic journalist Ann Crittenden, author of *The Price of Motherhood*, has a more conservative estimate of Mom's market value, putting it at about $60,000. Crittenden sees motherhood as a very skilled, mid-level management job. Whether worth $600,000 or $60,000, getting two economists to agree on anything is about as easy as attaching an accurate price tag on all that Mom does for us.

The Real Migrant Mother

*The portrait of a weary migrant mother and
her hungry children struck America's heart
and made Florence Thompson an American icon.*

The famous photograph shows a tired mother staring into the distance, her fingers nervously touching her cheek. Two of her young daughters huddle against her for comfort and a baby rests in her lap. Taken as part the National Farm Security Administration's (NFSA) photography project during the Great Depression, "Migrant Mother" put a human face on the hardships of that era. The powerful image became so symbolic that people tended to forget that the subjects of the photo were not just symbols. They were real people: Florence Owens Thompson and her three daughters, Katherine, Ruby, and baby Norma.

THE LEGEND

On a miserably cold, wet afternoon in March 1936, photographer Dorothea Lange drove into a migrant camp near Nipomo, California, after seeing a sign advertising pea-picking work for farm laborers. For over a month, Dorothea, a staff photographer for NFSA, had been documenting the plight of migrant farmer workers. Because of an early frost, most of the pea harvest had been destroyed, and she knew the workers were down on their luck.

Near the entrance to the camp, Lange saw a woman and her children in a ragged tent. As Lange later described:

I saw and approached the hungry and desperate mother, as if drawn by a magnet...I did not ask her name or her history. She told me that she was thirty-two. She said that they had been living on frozen vegetables from the surrounding fields and birds that the children killed. She had just sold the tires from her car to buy food. There she sat in that lean-to tent with her children huddled around her, and seemed to know that my pictures might help her, and so she helped me. There was a sort of equality about it.

She snapped six images and hurried home to develop them. She rushed her prints to the *San Francisco News*, along with the story of starvation in Nipomo. The *News* ran two of the photos with the story, which was picked up and syndicated nationally with the headline "Ragged, Hungry, Broke, Harvest Workers Live in Squalor." As a result of the coverage, 20,000 pounds of federal food supplies were sent to the hungry in Nipomo within a week. But the food never reached Florence or her children because, by that time, they had moved on to Watsonville, California.

NO OKIE FROM MUSKOGEE

Though Lange never asked the woman her name or her history, most people assumed her to be a typical Okie. In the mid 1930s, drought had turned the Midwest into what became known as the "Dust Bowl." The drought and lack of jobs resulted in small farmers (particularly those from Oklahoma) losing their farms and homes. Many packed up their cars and headed to California, where there was seasonal work picking the harvest.

Florence Owen Thompson's story was unique. Most Okies were of European descent, but Florence was a Native American, born in 1903 in Oklahoma's Indian Territory. Most Okies were new to California, but Florence had been living there for ten years before she was photographed. The death of her first husband in 1931, not the Dust Bowl, had forced her to work in the fields in order to support her six children.

As for the pea-picker camp, according to Florence's son Troy Owens, they had only stopped in Nipomo because the car broke down. Florence set up their tent near the entrance to the camp and waited while the boys went into town to fix the car. Florence's family wasn't starving, although many in the camps were. As for selling tires for food, they had no extra tires to sell. Their car, once it was running again, certainly wouldn't get very far without tires.

After they had moved on to Watsonville, one of Florence's sons happened to see a copy of his mother's photo in the *San Francisco News* and rushed home to see her for fear she was dead. He couldn't think of any other reason why his mother's picture would be in the newspaper and was relieved to find her very much alive. He showed her the photo, but she just looked at it in silence and remained silent about it for many years. Perhaps she even forgot about it. The photo's popularity never helped her family to survive the hard times. Florence and her family continued to move from town to town, harvesting crops and taking odd jobs whenever they could.

In the 1940s Florence took a job at a state hospital and eventually married her second husband, George

Thompson, a hospital administrator. She settled down in Modesto, California, having finally made it along with her family (make that ten kids now) into the middle class.

TIME TO SET THE RECORD STRAIGHT

Florence had moved past those bleak moments in a cold, wet camp in Nipomo, but her photo remained frozen in time. Time, in fact, only increased the popularity of "Migrant Mother". Finally in the 1970s, after seeing her own face reproduced continually and after hearing her story told incorrectly, Florence wrote to the *Modesto Bee*.

She complained that Dorothea Lange had promised that the photos would only be used to help the people in the camp. She had never been consulted about the use of her photo, nor had she made a dime from the many reproductions of the picture. Florence might have believed that Lange profited from the photo, but the photographer never received money for the reproductions either, since the photo belonged to the NFSA.

But Florence did admit that she had lived the hard times Lange tried to capture in photographs. "When Steinbeck wrote in *The Grapes of Wrath* about those people living under the bridge at Bakersfield—at one time we lived under that bridge. It was the same story. Didn't even have a tent then, just a ratty old quilt." Florence remembered how she walked miles to work at a diner for scant wages and leftovers to feed her family. And in Fireball, California, she harvested cotton and received only 50 cents for every 100 pounds she picked. Florence summed up those years up by saying, "We just existed . . . we survived."

Maybe because she was hardworking and proud, Florence disliked what she saw as the photo's portrait of her as a victim, a woman who sat still in the face of starvation, almost paralyzed with despair. Only that impression isn't what most viewers took away from that powerful image.

MIGRANT MOTHER'S POWER

In 1983, Florence suffered a stroke and needed around-the-clock medical care. Her children, unable to afford the cost, issued a public plea for help. From across the country, letters of good will poured in, along with $15,000. Many grateful people had been helped by the strength and dignity they had seen in "Migrant Mother." Rather than making her an object of pity, the image made Florence an inspiration and a comfort to people struggling with adversity. Roy Stryker, the head of the NFSA photography project, probably summed it up best: "She has all the suffering of mankind in her, but all the perseverance too. A restraint and a strange courage . . . She was immortal."

Did You Know?

A psychological survey from Mount Holyoke compared Mother's Day and Father's Day. Though fathers got less attention (3.5 hours for dads as opposed to 5.5 for moms to be exact) they found their day more enjoyable than moms did.

Can't We All
Judd Get Along?

The Judds didn't always have it easy.
The road to country music success was sure paved with
hardship for this mother-and-daughter team.

At age 17, Diana Judd was pregnant and worried. Diana and the baby's father were already having problems—their future didn't look too bright. And her own parents were coping with Diana's brother Brian, who was dying of Hodgkin's disease. How, Diana wondered, could she possibly care for a child with a not-so-great husband and limited support from her family?

On May 30, 1964, Diana, now Mrs. Michael Ciminella, forgot her worries when she held the baby girl she named Christina Claire. As Diana soothed the crying infant with a song and their voices blended, history was being made. One day those voices would create a diva duo that enchanted millions.

SINGLE MOM STRUGGLES

Michael and Diana left Kentucky for college and a brighter future. In time they made it across the country to Los Angeles, where they had another daughter, Ashley. Unfortunately, their rocky marriage foundered and the two divorced, leaving Diana a single mother with no college education and two children to support. For a time she took advantage of her good looks to do modeling work, but the money was too uncertain. So Diana enrolled in nursing school while she worked at other jobs to earn money.

Diana once described her life on the edge: "I was a paycheck away from the streets all the time with a minimum-wage job . . . I was traipsing around with two young children, alone. That film of desperation coats everything when you have no emotional support." Despite hunger, cold, and constant worry about paying for school clothes and braces, the divorced mom kept searching for a solid future—not realizing it was sitting in the backseat of her car.

SINGING AND HOLLERING

Mom and daughters were united as a team against the world. But within their little clan, tempers often exploded, especially between Diana and her oldest daughter, Chris. Both feisty and quick tempered, they've been described as "two cats with their tails tied together and thrown over a clothesline."

One thing did bring them together: music. Noticing Chris's fascination with her guitar, Diana bought the eleven-year-old a guitar of her own. Mother and daughter started playing and singing Kentucky hill-country music together. Finally there was at least some harmony in their squabbling household—two-part harmony, that is. The new duo gave their first performance on Mother's Day when they sang for Diana's mother Polly Judd, who declared that they sang like angels. Even allowing for motherly prejudice, the record does show that Polly was probably right.

BIBLES, ROUTE 66, AND NEW NAMES

Diana and Chris kept singing while Mom was finishing her nursing education in Northern California. Ready to shed her old life, Diana took back her family name and added the biblical first name, Naomi, symbolic of love, loyalty, and, of course, moving on. Chris took a new name too: Wynonna, after a town from the song "Route 66."

Some of Naomi's precious extra pennies paid for Wynonna's professional music lessons. The pair met people in the recording industry who encouraged them to keep singing. By the time Naomi had her nursing degree, she had a new goal for herself and Wynonna. Good-bye, California. Hello, Nashville, Tennessee, the center of the country music business!

As mother and daughter appeared together locally, Naomi vowed they'd make it in Nashville. Even though Naomi had her nursing degree, times remained tough for the Judd family. Still broke, Naomi and family were renting an abandoned farmhouse and burning furniture for warmth before they got an unexpected break.

In 1983, a hospital patient who appreciated Naomi's nursing and her singing just happened to be the daughter of an RCA record producer. Luckily for the Judds, her dad liked Naomi's singing too. From there it was live auditions at RCA, a first album, first concert tour, and huge success when "Mama, He's Crazy" hit number one on the country charts.

THE HITS JUST KEEP ON COMING

For the next eight years, the Judds reigned as the queens of country music, with shining platinum albums and six Grammys. Ashley took her own route to fame from the University of Kentucky to Hollywood, where she would go from an ensign on TV's *Star Trek: The Next Generation* to starring in major features like *A Time to Kill, Kiss the Girls,* and *Double Jeopardy.*

With all the Judds so wildly successful, Naomi felt herself to be the "Queen of Everything." Then hard times returned with a vengeance. Naomi was diagnosed with the hepatitis C virus and given three years to live. Forced to retire in 1991, Naomi once again fought to survive, this time using the power of her mind and spirit to aid her body.

And she triumphed again. Naomi won a rare remission of hepatitis. She now enjoys vastly improved health and the continued success of her girls—Wynonna's spectacular solo career and Ashley's Hollywood stardom. The doctors were baffled, but the younger Judds were less surprised. They've always known that "Mom is a force to be reckoned with."

"Death and taxes and childbirth! There's never any convenient time for any of them!"
—Margaret Mitchell's character, Scarlett O'Hara, in *Gone with the Wind*

"If you talk bad about country music, it's like saying bad things about my momma. Them's fightin' words."
—Dolly Parton

Mom's Sensational Senses

There's no limit to what a mom "nose" about her own child.
And no limit to the importance of staying in touch.

Many mothers say they can identify the cry of their own infant. And they soon learn to know them by sight. But humans aren't known for their good sense of smell. So it was something of a surprise to find that most human mothers could recognize their new baby by smell alone. Not only that, but most new mothers can identify their offspring with just a simple touch on the hand.

A new mother's senses of smell and touch are much more sensitive than expected, and these two senses affect moms and their families in ways that are only beginning to be understood.

MOM'S AROMAMEMORY

A key to the complexity of motherhood can be found in smelly shirts, of all things. In a famous "sweaty T-shirt" experiment, women were asked to sniff T-shirts worn by men for two nights. They were asked to describe the odor of the shirts—which by now were filled with the "perfume" of male sweat—in terms of intensity, pleasantness, and sexiness. The unexpected results made headlines. Women unfailingly preferred the T-shirts of men who had MHC genes (the genes that can detect disease) that were the least like her own. Amazingly, women could sniff out a guy's genetic code. On a biological level they seemed to know that it would aid their offspring's health to have varied MHC genes and their noses told them which guys would help them create healthy offspring.

Which brings us right back to babies and those smelly shirts again. This time, in a Jerusalem hospital, the sniffers were new mothers who had spent at least one hour with their newborns. These moms took a whiff from three bags. Each bag contained identical undershirts that had just been removed from three newborn infants—one from their new child. Every single mom could identify her own child by smell—sometimes after only an hour of being together.

It seems a mom's nose knows how to pick a mate that will give her healthy children. And a mom also has the scent-ual ability to recognize and bond with her own infant—instead of a stranger's kid from down the hall.

MOM'S MAGIC TOUCH

Like her sense of smell, a new mom has a heightened sense of touch. At the Shaarei Zedek Medical Center in Jerusalem, volunteer mothers tried to identify their own infants from a group of three babies asleep in their bassinets. The catch was that they had their eyes and noses covered with a heavy scarf and they were only allowed to stroke the skin of the infants' hands. Even so, 69 percent of the moms knew their own infants, more than double the number that would be expected by random guessing. When asked how they recognized their own babies, most moms said texture and temperature, though some couldn't explain it.

So why do new mothers have such a heightened sense of touch? The pleasure from skin-to-skin contact with their babies may help them ensure their infants' development. Animal and human studies show that touch is important to brain development in newborns. Human babies also benefit from touch. Premature infants who receive massages gain weight faster and come home from the hospital earlier than nonmassaged infants.

Lots of touching, skin-to-skin contact, and just plain old cuddling aren't only pleasurable to sensitive new moms, they're a way for her to give her babies a good start in life.

DAD'S GOT THE MAGIC TOUCH, TOO

Fathers of newborns also tried to identify their own offspring solely by touch. And they did almost as well as moms, with a 61 percent success rate. Dr. Marsha Kaitz, who ran the Jerusalem study, found dad's style different from mom's. Touching between fathers and babies was less caressing and soothing, more patting and playful.

Preemie babies benefit when dads give them massages and "kangaroo care." For kangaroo care, the dad opens his shirt and the baby lies on his chest with nothing on but a diaper. Then they put blankets on the baby, and dad and baby have some bonding time together. Babies relax and show the benefits of a decrease in their heart rates and oxygen consumption; they're less stressed when they do kangaroo care with dad.

Dad, mom, and baby: they all benefit from the scent-sations of smell and touch.

Secret Agent Mom

Espionage was all in a day's work for this
Civil War mother and daughter.

During the Civil War, two of General Grant's most valuable soldiers never fired a shot. Instead, a well-born mother and her brilliant daughter risked their fortune and their very lives while pouring tea and serving soup. Widow Eliza Van Lew and her unmarried daughter ran one of the Union's most ruthless and successful spy operations.

THE MANSION ON CHURCH HILL

Eliza Baker always moved in privileged circles. The daughter of the mayor of Philadelphia, Eliza married John Van Lew, a wealthy hardware merchant, and moved to Richmond, Virginia. She might have been born a Yankee, but she became a true Southern aristocrat and presided over one of the city's finest homes, the mansion on Church Hill.

Here, amid the splendid marble fireplaces, crystal chandeliers, damask hangings, and mahogany furniture, Mrs. Van Lew raised her children and entertained the distinguished of her day with lavish balls and receptions. John Marshall, chief justice of the Supreme Court, frequently came to dinner. The famous "Swedish Nightingale," Jenny Lind, sang in the music room and Edgar Allan Poe recited verses in the conservatory.

THE WIDOW AND DIZZY MISS LIZZIE

Even though she lived in the South, Mrs. Van Lew did speak out about the need to end slavery despite the family's owning fifteen slaves. Her daughter, Miss Lizzie, was even more outspoken about the evils of slavery than her mother. Actually, she ranted so much that the locals suspected Miss Lizzie was a few stays short of a corset. After John Van Lew's death, his widow and daughter freed their slaves, a move that must have had the town gossiping! But talk in Richmond quickly turned to larger matters. Tensions between North and South were heating up—war could come at any time.

On April 17, 1861, the Confederate flag flew over Richmond, which had become the capital of the rebel nation. Even though the Van Lew women considered themselves patriotic Virginians, they disagreed with secession. In despair, mother and daughter vowed to battle until the Stars and Stripes returned to Richmond. They never wavered.

THE WAY TO A MEN'S PRISON
IS THROUGH THE STOMACH?

When Northern prisoners of war were brought to Libby Prison in Richmond, Lizzie saw her chance to actively help the Union. Miss Lizzie first asked for permission to bring food and medicine to wounded Union soldiers, but was denied. Undeterred, Miss Lizzie won the day with buttermilk and homemade gingerbread for the head of Confederate prisons, Lieutenant Todd, who was the half-brother of Mary Todd Lincoln, interestingly enough.

Soon Miss Lizzie began regular visits to the prison. She and her mother provided clothes, bedding, books, stationery, and medicine to the Union soldiers. But helping the wounded wasn't their only goal—picking up military secrets became an important objective.

Imprisoned soldiers picked up military information overheard from Confederate guards and officers, vital news for Union generals! Miss Lizzie took information from the prisoners and passed it to the Union secret agents that had also infiltrated Richmond. When visting the prison, she often hid written messages in the bottom half of "double bottom" dishes, a set in which the bottom dish was supposed to hold hot water to keep the food warm. The soldiers' food may have been cold, but the information was sure hot! Once, knowing a suspicious guard was onto her, Miss Lizzie brought in a double bottom dish wrapped in her shawl. When the guard tried to examine the dish, he howled in pain, since Miss Lizzie had filled the bottom dish with boiling water!

HIDDEN IN PLAIN SIGHT

Most spies are careful to hide or disguise their political sympathies. Not the Van Lews. They used their politics as a cover. Miss Lizzie openly championed the Union and Mrs. Van Lew vowed to help its wounded men. Friends, neighbors, and even the newspapers railed indignantly against the two for "spending their opulent means in aiding and giving comfort to the miscreants who have invaded our sacred soil."

Both Lizzie and her mother could have been executed for treason to the Confederacy had their spying operation been uncovered. By being open about their politics, both women were able to hide their operations in plain sight by being underestimated. Richmond Confederates tolerated the pair as just a couple of oddballs—a charitable, but misguided, widow and her overwrought daughter. The pair played their role to the hilt. Miss Lizzie, who knew everyone thought she was a little off, even began muttering to herself and acting so strangely that she soon had a new nickname, "Crazy Bette."

THE SPY SQUADRON

In addition to their prison exploits, the team had developed a squadron of spies to help supply information to Union agents. Some of the Van Lews' freed slaves stayed on as paid servants, tending a small family farm outside of Richmond, carrying messages in their shoes or inside buckets of vegetables. Crazy Bette's open criticism of the Confederacy actually brought many of Virginia's humbler folk to her door. Farmers and shopkeepers admitted they were loyal to the Union and were soon secretly enlisted in the spy ring. As she became more adept at espionage, she sent and received coded messages directly from Union General Benjamin Butler and even General Ulysses S. Grant. She kept the key to the codes until her death.

Though too frail to do much active work herself, Mrs. Van Lew used her own formidable weapon—her mansion. When Union agents crossed into Confederate territory for information, they hid in the back bedrooms on the third floor. A space behind a panel under the roof hid escaping Union soldiers if the house was searched. The two women even hid a horse in an upstairs bedroom to keep it from being seized by the Confederate government.

Perhaps the Van Lews' greatest achievement arose from an action they'd taken before the war. When they'd freed an exceptionally intelligent slave, Mary Bowser, they also sent her to school in Philadelphia. Mary returned to Richmond and Elizabeth, through a friend, secured a job for Mary in the Confederate White House. Of course Jefferson Davis never suspected that Mary could read or write. But while she dusted his desk, Mary also read his secret papers and quietly relayed that important information back to the Van Lews.

STARS AND STRIPES AGAIN

On April 2, 1865, the day came that mother and daughter had longed for. The Confederacy evacuated Richmond as the Union soldiers marched in. Their neighbors could hardly believe it when Crazy Bette and her servants clambered up to the roof and unfurled a huge American flag. The Stars and Stripes were once again waving in Virginia.

After General Grant arrived in Richmond, he sent his calling card to the Van Lews. He wanted to thank the two women for all they'd done for their country. As Eliza and her daughter served tea to General Grant and his wife at the Van Lew mansion, we can just imagine the polite conversation. "General Grant," they might have said, "When we said we'd help the Union, we weren't just whistling 'Dixie.'"

There's No Mummy Like an Egyptian Mummy

Dr. Spock would have felt right at home with the nurturing moms of ancient Egypt.

Egyptian moms loved kids—and lots of 'em. In ancient Egypt, mothers nurtured and cared for their children with a devotion unmatched in the ancient world. All babies were welcome, boys and girls, and a woman with many children was the envy of her barren sisters and the apple of her husband's eye.

GET YOUR FREE PREGNANCY TEST!

Since Egyptian moms were often anxious to know if they would soon hear the patter of lots of little feet, Egyptians developed fertility aids and even an ancient home-pregnancy test.

To increase her fertility, a wannabe mom would "squat over a hot mixture of frankincense, oil, dates, and beer, and allow the vapors to enter her." To discover whether or not she was pregnant, she used her urine to moisten seeds of emmer and barley. If a plant grew in a few days, she would bear a child. If the plant didn't grow, it was time to go back to bed (so to speak).

Though the fertility aids are suspect, modern scientists have tested the Egyptian pregnancy test and found that watering either seed with the urine of nonpregnant women resulted in no growth for many of the seeds, just as the ancients said it would. Although the "no growth" test did fail in about 30 percent of the cases, this was cutting-edge thousands of years ago!

HELP, HORUS, HELP!

Once a happy mother-to-be was in labor, she often went to a cool spot like the breezy roof of a house or to a special pavilion made of papyrus stalks and decorated with vines. Midwives or friends came to help the mother give birth.

Though children were a blessing, every mom knew that childbearing could be a fatal pain, and they wanted all the divine help they could get. Since illness was often believed to be the result of evil spirits, women lined up divine allies like the powerful sun god, Horus, and the goddess Hathor, guardian of women and domestic bliss. Sometimes the god Amun blew in as a northern breeze to cool mothers during the hard work of labor.

You would be hard-pressed to find an epidural in ancient Egypt, so women sought relief in spells and amulets. An amulet was placed on the mom-to-be's forehead when this spell was repeated four times:

> "Come down, placenta, come down! I am Horus who conjures in order that she who is giving birth becomes better than she was, as if she was already delivered . . . Hathor will lay her hand on her with an amulet of health! I am Horus who saves her!"

Unfortunately, Horus's help wasn't foolproof. Many women died in childbirth, even in royal families. In King

Horemheb's tomb, the body of his queen, Mutnodjmet, was found along with the tiny bones of a fully developed fetus who is believed to have died inside the dying mother.

WHAT'S IN A NAME?

If Mom and her precious baby survived the birth, she named that baby immediately. In case of sickness or death, a name ensured the infant's survival in the afterlife. Some names expressed a mother's joy, so a baby might be called "Welcome to You" or "This Boy I Wanted." A baby might also be named for his or her physical characteristics, with a handle like Pakamen, meaning "The Blind One." Names of gods and goddesses abounded, along with names from the pharaoh's family.

Babies were given constant care. To keep them close, mothers carried babies in a sling around their neck and breast-fed their children for up to three years. They were even encouraged to eat sour barley bread to increase their breast milk—talk about devotion! As babies grew up, doting moms provided plenty of toys. The children of ancient Egypt played with carved animal figures, painted wood or simple rag dolls, boats and balls, and even pets like dogs or kittens or birds.

THANKS, MOM!

Since children were so valued in Egypt, it comes as no surprise that grown children were expected to cherish their moms right back. That didn't always work out, of course. A will still exists that preserves the indignation of Lady Naunakhte, who declared: "I am a free woman of Egypt. I have raised eight children and have provided them with everything suitable to their station in life. But now I have grown old and behold, my children don't look after me anymore. I will therefore give my goods to the ones who have taken care of me. I will not give anything to the ones who have neglected me."

However, most Egyptians agreed with the ancient text that read: "Repay your mother for all her care. Give her as much bread as she needs, and carry her as she carried you, for you were a heavy burden to her. When you were finally born, she still carried you on her neck and for three years she suckled you and kept you clean." Sounds fair to us.

"If your mother tells you to do a thing, it is wrong to reply that you won't. It is better and more becoming to intimate that you will do as she bids you, and then afterwards act quietly in the matter according to the dictates of your better judgment."
—Mark Twain, "Advice for Good Little Girls"

"My mother had a great deal of trouble with me, but I think she enjoyed it." —Mark Twain

Just the Facts, Ma'am

*Test your knowledge of fascinating factoids
about moms and their nearest and dearest.*

IT ALL STARTED WHEN YOU WERE A BABY

T__ F__ 1. More boys are conceived in the summer, which is
why they're called sons.

T__ F__ 2. Girls are daintier eaters than guys—even before
they're born!

T__ F__ 3. If your mom was assaulted by morning sickness,
you're probably putting extra salt on your food.

T__ F__ 4. The average baby weighs more than a lightweight,
six-pound bowling ball.

T__ F__ 5. New moms who are too tired to go to jazzercise to
lose weight should try "milkercise."

AS TIME GOES BY

T__ F__ 6. A "family moon" is when the entire family bares
their bums at passersby.

T__ F__ 7. If a guy hates his chrome dome, then tell him to
call home—and blame mom.

T__ F__ 8. Jet lag is mom's baggage.

T__ F__ 9. If daughters catch matrophobia when they're
teenagers, they can still recover.

T__ F__ 10. The pressures of modern life have been killing the
bond between mothers and kids.

Turn the page for the Answers.

ANSWERS

1. False
Statistics show that fall is the time to try for a baby if you want to have a boy.

2. True
In a Harvard medical study, pregnant women carrying boys ate up to 190 more calories than those who were carrying girls. Does this mean that girls come into the world on a diet?

3. True
University of Washington researchers found that if their mom suffered from moderate to severe morning sickness their babies showed a preference for salted water over regular water. Older children whose moms had similar levels of morning sickness also craved salty foods.

4. True
The average baby weighs about seven pounds at birth. Only about 10 percent of all babies weigh more than eight pounds 13 ounces. Rarely do babies weigh more than 10 pounds.

5. True—sort of
Breast-feeding burns about 500 calories a day, so a breast-feeding mom can lose weight faster—unless, of course she starts eating more.

6. False
The familymoon is a new trend among remarrying couples that have kids from a previous marriage. They invite the kids along on their honeymoon! How's that for togetherness?

7. False
If a man is bald, it's a myth that he inherited the hair loss problem from his mother's side of the family. Baldness is a very complicated genetic trait that may be inherited from either the mother's or the father's side of the family (or both). And it can even skip generations. So, don't blame mom!

8. Seems to be true
French scientists have found in zebra fish the genes that run a body clock are similar to the ones found in humans. They believe they'll find similar

genes controlling the human body clock (which controls whether or not you're badly bothered by night work or a transatlantic flight) in mom's eggs, which means a baby inherits jet lag from mom's genetic material.

9. True

Despite conflicts, complicated emotions, and even matrophobia (a fear of becoming like mom), a Pennsylvania State University study found that by the time they were middle-aged, from 80 to 90 percent of women reported good relationships with their mothers.

10. False

The numbers on the relationship between mom and her kids are strong:

- 88 percent of adults say their mother has had a positive influence on them.
- 92 percent say their current relationship with their mother is positive.
- 88 percent of all mothers say their family appreciates them enough.

Poem by Holmes

"Youth fades; love droops,
The leaves of friendship fall;
A mother's secret hope outlives them all."
—Oliver Wendell Holmes

TV Moms IV: Work It

*Put on your overalls and test yourself
on these sitcom working moms.*

As time marched on, more TV moms were marching into the workplace and facing even more complicated issues. Single motherhood, financial burdens, turning 40—playing a mom on TV was no picnic!

ROSEANNE CONNER: DOMESTIC GODDESS AT WORK

The Show: *Roseanne* (1988–1997)

This show didn't shy away from the harsher realities of family life. Blue-collar Roseanne Conner (played by Roseanne) took low-paying jobs to make ends meet. Working in a beauty parlor, a factory, and a diner, Roseanne braved annoying managers and snarky coworkers. She and her husband, Dan, struggled to raise their three kids and keep food on the table. Roseanne's kids were constantly in trouble. Sarcastic, loud, opinionated, and overweight, Roseanne was far from being a "perfect" mother. But she was a loving mom who told it like it was. (Despite the fact that this family spouted TV's most brilliant wisecracks, they couldn't seem to use their smarts to get ahead.)

Fun Fact: Roseanne's oldest daughter, Becky, had a lot in common with Darrin from *Bewitched*. Wonder why? No, they didn't both have witches in the family. Becky was played by two different actresses and Darrin by two different actors during each series' original run.

MURPHY BROWN: TV'S UNWED MOM

The Show: *Murphy Brown* (1988–1998)
In 1992, Murphy Brown (played by Candice Bergen) became famous as the tough, impatient TV newswoman who'd managed to tick off Vice President Dan Quayle. And he wasn't a character on television! What had Murphy done that caused a real, powerful politician to wag his finger at her?

She was single and pregnant and had decided to keep her baby. In the summer of 1992, during a speech in San Francisco, California, Quayle announced that Murphy was glamorizing unwed motherhood and mocking the importance of fathers. With that speech, *Murphy Brown* became the eye of a media storm on family values. By the time the storm blew over, both sides seemed the worse for wear. Murphy *did* have trouble adjusting to unwed motherhood and so did her ratings, which began to sink. As for Dan Quayle, he lost his job in the 1992 election.
Fun Fact: Avery Brown, Murphy's young son, was played by Haley Joel Osment. Luckily he didn't start seeing dead people until his breakout performance in *The Sixth Sense*.

CYBILL SHERIDAN ROBBINS WOODBINE: GETTIN' UP THERE

The Show: *Cybill* (1995–1998)
Finally, a sitcom for women over 40! An unconventional comedy, *Cybill* took an unflinching and funny look at the problems confronting an older mom who happens to be an aging, twice-divorced actress looking for work in Los

Angeles. Cybill Sheridan Robbins Woodbine (played by Cybill Shepherd) had two headstrong, nearly grown daughters (one from each marriage) and two clingy ex-husbands who never got out of her life.

Fortunately for Cybill, she had her sophisticated, boozy friend Maryann (played by Christine Baranski) to confide in. The friendship between the two women and their adventures proved hilarious and also poked fun at popular ideas about youth and aging. Even over 40 with a nearly empty nest, Cybill showed that a mom's life could still be very complicated and very funny.

Fun Fact: Cybill Shepherd got her big break when director Peter Bogdanovich spotted her on a magazine cover. Bogdanovich went on to cast her in her first big role as Jacy in *The Last Picture Show*.

You Don't Say . . .

"Of course I don't always enjoy being a mother. At those times my husband and I hole up somewhere in the wine country, eat, drink, make mad love and pretend we were born sterile and raise poodles."
—Dorothy DeBolt,*Winner of the 1980 National Mother's Day Committee Award. Natural mother of 6 and adoptive mother of 14!*

Kids and Soul Mates Don't Mix

George Sand and Frederic Chopin made
beautiful music together, until her kids got in the way

She didn't care for feminists, but she's been called the world's first liberated woman. She was a French baroness related to Louis XVII, but she considered herself a woman of the people. She was famous for her scandalous love affairs. Men adored her, yet few friends thought her beautiful or feminine. She was best known for dressing like a man and constantly indulging a taste for smelly cigars. She was France's famous romantic, but she was actually a hardheaded working mother whose practical business sense supported a wild, bohemian life.

This contradictory mom was Amandine Aurore Lucile Dupin Baronesse Dudevant, Aurore to her friends. You may know her better as George Sand, the wildly popular and prolific French novelist. Sand was a romantic who believed that life was best fulfilled by the perfect passion. Her famous love affair with Frederic Chopin seemed perfect. But it was battered by a force that even strong-minded Sand couldn't control—her own children.

A NATURAL ROMANTIC

Aurore began her life the same way she lived it—as a scandalous romantic. The romantic part was that Papa

Maurice was an aristocrat who fell for Mama Sophie, a pretty but penniless dancer. The scandalous part was that in July 1804, less than a month after her parents' marriage, Aurore was born.

When Aurore was four, her father fell from a spirited horse and broke his neck, the nineteenth-century equivalent of a car wreck. At that point, Maurice's wealthy mother, Madame Dupin, kept Aurore at the family château, Nohant, in the French countryside and sent Sophie packing. Then strict, straight-laced Madame Dupin, aided by convent schools, somehow managed to raise the rebellious, head-strong young woman who would one day shock Paris.

MARRIAGE CAN BE MISERABLE

Had her grandmother lived, she probably would have forced Aurore into an unhappy, arranged marriage. As it was, Madame Dupin died before she got the chance. So, at age 18, Aurore made her own choice, Baron Casimir Dudevant. The marriage may have been voluntary, but that didn't mean it was happy.

Shortly after their first child, Maurice, was born, Aurore began to long for some good adult conversation (a familiar wish of new mothers). She also discovered her husband wasn't up for more than discussing cows or the health of his hunting dogs. He didn't care for music, art, or litera-ture—all as vital as food and drink to the brilliant Aurore.

SEEKING: ONE SOUL MATE

Quick-witted as she was, it didn't take Aurore long to notice that marriage vows didn't stop some men from seek-ing more perfect unions. Baron Dudevant, for example, had trouble keeping his mitts off the maids. If husbands could take a liberal interpretation of their marriage vows, then why not the wife? It should come as no surprise that when her second child, daughter Solange, was born, rumors persisted that the baron wasn't her biological pop.

Aurore protested that she was seeking a soul mate and had higher aims than mere physical pleasure. As it became more and more evident that the baron was hardly the "one," the unhappy couple separated in 1831. Aurore took her little ones to Paris, and since independence (especially with two kids) cost money, she took up writing. A year later her novel *Indiana* was published. The story of a wife struggling to escape the clutches of a tyrannical husband (who had more than a passing resemblance to Baron Dudevant) was a huge best-seller, and Aurore became a notorious celebrity under the name George Sand.

DON'T SEND ME FLOWERS

Sand supported her family and the estate at Nohant with the writing of more than 70 novels and a dozen plays. Readers were thrilled with her books, which asserted that marriage made slaves of women and (*mon dieu!*) explored female sexual desire. They were even more fascinated by the boldness of the author who enjoyed a good cigar and (*quelle horreur!*) wore men's clothing so she could prowl around Paris without being harassed.

"I ask the support of no one," Sand declared. "Neither to kill someone for me, gather a bouquet, correct a proof, nor to go with me to the theater. I go there on my own, as a man, by choice; and when I want flowers, I go on foot, by myself, to the Alps." So much for *The Rules*. Sand wasn't coy, but men flocked to her anyway—and often had their hearts broken.

THE PERFECT MATCH

Sand's love life became more discussed than her books and plays—if there'd been a *National Enquirer* in those days, she'd have certainly graced the cover. She had open affairs with well-known artitsts like poet and playwright Alfred de Musset. Always the equal opportunist, Sand even had a notorious liaison with actress Marie Dorval. Yet Sand claimed she believed in marriage as long as it was an ideal partnership between two free equals. Why settle down with less than perfection?

Sand's perfect soulmate seemed to have finally arrived in the form of Frederic Chopin. The handsome Polish composer played piano like an angel and had a genius that Sand openly admired. Chopin was frail and often ill, but strong, robust Sand instantly felt her love would nurture and save him. Chopin, wary of Sand at first, gradually came under her spell and the couple began a celebrated affair.

The couple settled into a grand passion for nine years. Sand tended lovingly to her frail Chopin, who composed some of his greatest works while living at Nohant. Chopin seemed to have adored Sand, who wrote some of her best novels while living with him. But their love finally soured. What could have caused these two lovebirds to split? You don't have to look any farther than home—sources say it was the kids.

WHAT'S THE MATTER WITH KIDS TODAY?

Sand saw herself as a loving, devoted mother, but what with all her writing and soul-mating, a child could feel neglected. Forget sibling rivalry, both Maurice and Solange had to compete with their mother's lovers and friends for her attention. Out of the two, Maurice had better luck. Aurore did seem to have a blind spot for her son and forgave his faults.

As Maurice grew older, he took over as head of the household. His doting mother encouraged him to throw his weight around. He even went so far as to fire one of Chopin's personal servants, making life harder for the ailing composer. It's not too hard to see that this mama's boy's star was on the rise, while soul mate Chopin's was on the decline.

But it was Solange who became the biggest problem between the famous lovers. She was becoming a beautiful woman and made the mistake of getting too close to Chopin. Sand may have been jealous not only of her daughter's youth and beauty but also of her daughter's relationship with Chopin. When Sand harped on her daughter's faults, Chopin defended Solange against unfair criticism—which made Sand even angrier. This couldn't continue forever.

SO LONG, SOLANGE

Over Chopin's horrified protests, Sand pushed her daughter into a bad marriage. Solange married sculptor Auguste Clesinger, a brutal and bullying man. Chopin's predictions of catastrophe came true. When Solange and her new husband came for a visit, the creepy Clesinger decided he needed more money, so he roughed up both Sand and her darling son, Maurice, to get it.

Outraged, Sand threw out Clesinger and her daughter too. Chopin could not overlook Sand's hardheartedness since Solange was now pregnant and Sand had introduced the smarmy sculptor into the family in the first place. Chopin appealed to the generous, loving spirit that he'd adored in Aurore, but his lover would hear none of it. In high indignation, Sand threw Chopin out too. It was a squalid end to the great affair. Chopin died two years later, destitute and in great pain. Solange came to comfort him before he died—Sand didn't bother.

The famous writer remained estranged from her daughter, who would eventually fall into poverty. Sand lived with and continued to dote on Maurice, who took over her estate, married, and gave her granchildren. Meanwhile, Sand continued to write about the joys of freedom, passion, and romance. So much for soul mates.

Uncle John's "Spiff" Notes

Another great read about the extraordinary bonds between mothers and daughters, Amy Tan's *The Joy Luck Club* traces the relationships of four Chinese American mothers and their American-born daughters. Showing how cultural differences can affect family life, the book draws contrasts between the mothers' lives in China with that of the daughters in the U.S. Will the girls better understand their moms and appreciate the hardships they had to endure? Pick up a copy and find out!

Mom's Haunted House

Mom's ghost becomes a celebrity.

Raynham Hall is the magnificent ancestral castle of the Townshends. Its most notorious occupant, the Brown Lady, came there by her marriage to Charles Townshend, 2nd Viscount, in the 16th century. She is the ghost of Dorothy Walpole, sister of Sir Robert Walpole, the first Prime Minister of England.

THE PAST CAN HAUNT YOU

The marriage was the viscount's second and Dorothy's first. However, before her marriage, Dorothy had been involved with Lord Wharton, a well-known womanizer who fled England to escape his debts. Several years into the marriage, Dorothy's old affair resurfaced as a source of tragedy. Some say the new Lady Townshend missed her old life with the no-goodnik Wharton, resumed their love affair, and her husband found out. Others say that Lord Townshend simply discovered Dorothy's past affair with Wharton. In either case, he was horrified by her loose morals and demanded that Dorothy be locked in her apartments and kept away from the children.

Despite Dorothy's pleas, Charles never relented. In 1726 she died, officially of smallpox. Rumors of murder persisted, from tales of her being poisoned to her being pushed down the stairs. Dorothy's presence persisted, too. According to residents, she became the Brown Lady (wearing a dress of brown brocade) and haunted Raynham Hall in search of her five children.

A GHOSTLY IMAGE

The Brown Lady became a ghostly celebrity. King George IV was staying in the Townshend castle when he awoke to find her at the foot of his bed. Recognizing her from a portrait, he immediately fled the house, saying, "Tonight I have seen that which I hope to God I never see again." Over the centuries the Brown Lady has terrified grown men, led servants to quit, and even caused police investigations. But the motherly ghost never seemed to scare children. In 1926, Lady Townshend's young son and his friend saw the Brown Lady, but she smiled so warmly they assumed she was a guest—until they gave the adults her description.

In 1936, Captain Provand and Indre Shira came to Raynham Hall on a photo shoot for *Country Life* magazine. Provand was focusing the camera for a shot of the staircase when Shira saw "an ethereal veiled form coming slowly down the stairs." He yelled to Provand, who snapped a photo of a ghostly woman floating down the stairs. Though some skeptics say that this now world-famous photograph is only a double exposure, many paranormal experts believe that the Brown Lady is captured on film— caught in the act of seeking her children.

Like Mother, Like Son

Joy Murray, a champion cowgirl, raises the "King of the Cowboys."

What kind of mother would let her baby grow up to be a cowboy? What kind of mother would put her kid on a 1,000-pound bull and watch to see if he stays on for a very long eight seconds through bucking and kicks—either of which could kill him?

A MOTHER WHO'S DONE IT HERSELF, FOR ONE

Joy Myers Murray—mother of Ty Murray, "King of the Cowboys" and the only seven-time world champion Professional Rodeo Cowboys Association All-Around Cowboy in history—is no stranger to bull riding. In fact, she's a two-time world champion bull rider herself, having won the event, as well as the all-around champion title for senior girls, in the National Little Britches Rodeo.

Born in 1942 into a rodeo family in rural Colorado, Joy Myers grew up with horses. Not only did her dad rodeo, all the kids in the family participated in Little Britches Rodeo, the Little League of the rodeo world. So it was natural for Joy to participate. A tomboy, she loved the thrill and excitement of racing horses and jumping them over barrels.

Joy liked the fun of a challenge. And what greater challenge than being judged on how well you rode eight long seconds on the back of a half-ton bucking bull? She never worried about staying on—she was having too much fun.

A RODEO FAMILY

Not long after winning her world champion titles, Joy gave up bullriding to marry Butch Murray four days after her eighteenth birthday. The couple moved to Arizona, where Butch worked on the racehorse circuit.

Soon, the Murray family grew. First came daughter Kim. Eleven months later, daughter Kerry was born. Joy enjoyed her daughters for six years, but from the moment she was pregnant with her third, she knew this one was a boy. "Baby Ty" came home from the hospital wrapped in a blanket and wearing diapers and cowboy boots. Two years later he was riding Joy's Singer sewing machine and declaring he was going to be a bullrider.

TEACHING THE COWBOY WAY

Joy and Butch raised their children in a traditional fashion. Butch worked at the racetrack, rode horses, and broke in colts; Joy worked at the family's tack shop, where she sold saddles and other riding equipment and broke in the kids.

One night when the girls were in the first and second grades, Joy and Butch attended a school meeting where a policeman spoke to parents about keeping kids off drugs. Thirty-five years later, Joy still remembers one woman asking the cop, "Do you find drugs more in rich kids, poor kids, or middle-income kids?" The policeman responded: "The only pattern we found for kids using drugs is that it is more common among kids who have nothing to do."

That did it. From that point on, the Murray kids always had something to do. Joy believed sports would keep her kids from experimenting with alcohol and drugs; rodeo was just the thing. In spite of their hard-working lifestyles,

Joy and Butch managed to get three children to different rodeos every weekend.

Joy not only took her kids to rodeo events, she also took them to school practices. Ty was also on the gymnastics and football teams, and at the end of the school day, Joy would race from the tack shop to the football field to pull up her chair and watch him practice! "I couldn't imagine my kid doing something without us being there to watch," Joy exclaims. She adds that the best thing she and Butch did for their children was to be there for them, to love them, and to support them.

Of course, raising a champion cowboy isn't something you set out to do; it's a mind-set and a set of values. Joy says that raising children is the hardest job anyone can ever do. Her philosophy was to raise each child as an individual. She tried not to focus on Ty more than the girls, but as the kids grew up, it became obvious that while the girls enjoyed rodeo, Ty was obsessed with it.

RAISING THE WORLD'S GREATEST COWBOY

Although the Murray kids learned early about doing without, they also learned about working hard to get what you want. Joy taught them the power of persistence. When Ty was a young teen, he worked all of one summer to save enough to buy a mechanical bull. By the time school started again, he'd earned $840. But mechanical bulls were selling for thousands. Joy never gave up. She searched the want ads and spent hours on the phone, and one day her persistence paid off. She found a mechanical bull for sale for $1,000, talked the man down to $840, and Ty had a career in bull riding ahead of him.

Inspired by his mother's determination and his father's work ethic, Ty Murray set out to become the world's greatest cowboy. He wanted to break the record held by Larry Mahan, who had earned six All-Around Cowboy titles.

Joy watched in the stands as Ty won rodeo title after rodeo title, including Professional Rodeo Cowboys Association's (PRCA) overall and bareback-riding Rookie of the Year and six PRCA World All-Around Championships.

In 1998, Joy Murray was in the stands yet again watching as her son finally achieved his goal and broke the world record, capturing his seventh PRCA world championship!

STILL RIDING AFTER ALL THESE YEARS

Unfortunately, kids grow up and leave home. "We spent our whole life on our kids," Joy Murray says. "Then our kids, dang it, grew up on us."

Fortunately, Riley entered Joy's life. Riley, a beautiful brown and cream paint horse with a white face and blue eyes, gave Joy something to do: learning how to ride all over again. Yes, even cowgirls who have been riding all their lives can learn a thing or two. Proving that you can teach a cowgirl new tricks, Joy recently began studying "Universal Horsemanship" with Dennis Reis to learn how to work with a horse's nature versus trying to control it.

Although her kids keep reminding her that she's 60 years old, Joy says she'll worry about getting old when she's 90. Until then, Joy Murray hasn't turned in her spurs, and even though her bulls riding days are over, she plans to keep riding until the trail's end.

Motherhood
by the Numbers

What the statisticians say about moms.

According to the year 2000 U.S. Census, there's a lot of interesting info about American moms.

STATE(US) OF MOTHERHOOD

- There are 75 million moms in the United States.
- 57% of women aged 15 to 44 are mothers.
- There are more single moms (with children under the age of 18)—the figures grew from 3 million in 1970 to 10 million in 2000.

HOW OLD IS MOM?

- 24.8 is the median age at which U.S. women give birth for the first time. Median age rose almost 3 years from 1970 to 2000.
- Over the past decade more births are occurring to women over 30 years of age.

TEEN MOMS

- The United States has the highest teenage pregnancy rate of all developed countries. Almost half a million teenage women (10% of all women aged 15–19) become pregnant annually.

- But teenage pregnancies are declining: by 17% from 1990–96 (from 117 pregnancies to 97 per 1,000 women). By 2000 the rate had declined by 21.9%.
- 78% of teen pregnancies are unplanned, accounting for about one quarter of all accidental pregnancies annually.
- Daughters of teen mothers are 22% more likely to become teen mothers themselves.

WHAT ARE THE ODDS?

- Of having twins? About 1 in 33. In 2001, twin births exceeded 3% of all U.S. births for the first time. The twinning rate has climbed 33% since 1990 and 59% since 1980.
- Of having triplets or multiple births? About 1 in 539. The triplet-plus birth rate has risen over 400% since 1980, largely due to older mothers taking fertility drugs.
- Of delivering by caesarean? About 1 in 4. The caesarean rate has increased steadily since 1996, climbing to 24.4% of all births by 2001.

IF THIS IS TUESDAY IT MUST BE YOUR BIRTHDAY

- In 2001, Tuesday was the most popular day for giving birth with 12,000+ births daily.
- In 2001, August was the leading month—360,000 births occurred.
- Most babies arrive in August and September meaning they were conceived around the holidays. (Can we blame it on the December eggnog?)

- The fewest babies are born in April meaning fewer are conceived during the hot summer months, particularly in the Southern United States.
- The hotter the U.S. summer, the fewer the number of babies conceived. (Although colder winters do not necessarily produce more babies.)

HOW MANY?

- U.S. families are shrinking. In 1976, 36% of moms had 4 or more children. These days it's closer to 11%.
- Most U.S. moms will have 2 kids.
- 3 is the average number of children that Utah women can expect—the highest in the nation.

NAME THE SCARIEST STATISTIC!

- The average child used 10,000 diapers before being toilet trained. With an average of 2 kids that's 20,000 diapers that need changing!
- An average-income family will spend $165,630 on a child by the time he or she reaches age 18.
- Stay-at-home moms put in 65% of the child-raising time compared to 60% put in by working moms.
- The College Board estimated that tuition, room, board, and other college expenses in 2000 came to about $11,000 a year for students at in-state public colleges and almost $24,000 for private institutions. Four years of schooling can cost $44,000 to $96,000.

Spot the Mom!

Is she or isn't she? Only Uncle John knows for sure!

Meet these political "first ladies." They were each the first to achieve a goal for their gender. They became legends in politics. Were they legendary moms too?

1. Indira Gandhi:
First woman to be prime minister of India

She was the only child of India's first prime minister, Jawaharlal Nehru. Oxford-educated, Indira was elected to India's parliament two years after Nehru's death following the death of his successor. Her party made her a compromise candidate for prime minister of India thinking she would be easy to control if she won. Oops, big mistake! Indira had political smarts to elbow out her would-be bosses and became a powerhouse of a prime minister who led India for 15 years (1966–1977 and 1980–1984), won a war with Pakistan, and established the state of Bangladesh.

Was Indira more than mother to her country?

2. Margaret Thatcher:
First woman to be prime minister of England

She went from a grocer's daughter to a baroness and in between (1979–1990) she ran the United Kingdom as the Conservative prime minister. Maggie Thatcher worked her way up in her party by holding cabinet positions like secretary of state for education and science. She was a hard-line Conservative, notorious for tough actions like abolishing free milk, which earned her the soubriquet "Maggie Thatcher, milk snatcher." As prime minister, Thatcher was the "Iron Lady," slashing government services, promoting business, and stomping Argentina in the Falkland Islands War.

Was Maggie Thatcher too tough to be a mom?

3. Wilma Pearl Mankiller:
First female principal chief of the Cherokee Nation

Wilma started life in 1945 on an Oklahoma farm until a drought forced her family to relocate to San Francisco, where Wilma later attended college. As a young woman, Wilma returned to her ancestral lands in Oklahoma outside of Tahlequah. She immediately began working for her people, and in 1983 won her first office as the Cherokee Nation's deputy chief. In 1985 when the former chief stepped down, as deputy chief she became the principal chief of the second-largest tribe in the United States. Mankiller faced death threats from those who refused to be led by a woman, but she persevered to be elected outright in the 1987 and 1991 tribal elections. She won respect for her focus on education and health care, and for tirelessly helping her tribe achieve economic independence.

Has Wilma continued the family line with children of her own?

4. Condoleezza Rice:
First female U.S. National Security Advisor

Condoleezza Rice, one of the most powerful women in the United States, grew up in a segregated Birmingham, Alabama. To combat prejudice, she concentrated on her education and being "twice as good" as everyone else to succeed. Rice was a political science professor at Stanford University when she was picked by President George W. Bush in 2000 to serve in his cabinet. A powerful member of the administration, she has helped manage the Afghanistan and Iraqi wars, but she says her dream job is to be commissioner of the National Football League.

Is Condoleezza Rice working to make the world safer for her own children?

Answers on page 301.

Did You Know?

According to the *Guinness Book of World Records*,
Shortest Interval Between Separate Births:
208 Days
Jayne Bleackley of New Zealand
Kid 1 is born on September 3, 1999.
Kid 2 arrives on March 30, 2000.

Longest Period Between Separate Births:
41 years, 185 days
Elizabeth Ann Buttle of the United Kingdom
Kid 1 is born on May 19, 1956.
Kid 2 arrives on November 20, 1997.

Africa's Joyful Moms

*Mothers raising kids in the heart of Africa may have
a unique lesson for the rest of the world.*

Don't all parents wonder how to raise kind, thoughtful children with healthy self-esteem? The answer to all their questions may lie deep within the equatorial rain forests of Africa with the Aka.

ALSO KNOWN AS AKA

The term "Aka" means "human," and these very humane humans are a tribe of pygmies. Adult Aka males usually reach a height between four to five feet. They once roamed most of central Africa, but now they make their home in the forests of the Central African Republic (C.A.R.) where they keep a thousands-year-old nomadic hunting-and-gathering tradition alive.

Under a canopy of foliage, the Aka hunt for game and gather berries, edible roots, protein-rich termites and caterpillars, and wild honey harvested from high trees. Their clothing is made of bark, and their housing from leaves and thatch, all taken from the forest. Among their neighbors are the chimpanzees, lowland gorillas, and forest elephants.

From time to time the Aka also entertain Western anthropologists like expert Dr. Barry S. Hewlett of Washington State University, who has studied this pygmy tribe's unique way of life and raising kids. Hewlett and others have found that Aka mothers bring up their children in a way that encourages a peaceful, cooperative society.

THEY LONG TO BE CLOSE TO MOM

Aka moms and babies are literally very close. As she does her housekeeping and cooking chores or goes into the forest to forage, mom will carry her baby in a sling strapped across her chest. Aka babies rarely are given a chance to have a good, long cry. As soon as they show signs of distress, either their mother or one of her close female friends is right there to rock them. Even at night, when she catches her forty winks, the baby remains physically close, resting beside her.

Dad is happy to be just as affectionate as mom. An Aka dad spends much of his time within close reach of his children and is always ready to take over the hugging, kissing, or cleaning of baby. With the amazing support system that dad and female friends or relatives provide, an Aka baby is sure to have his or her needs met on demand!

As they grow older these children are continually protected and affectionately indulged. They become part of a close-knit community that then takes on the task of teaching them to hunt and forage in the forest. There are few punishments and almost no beatings of children. In Aka society, beating a child is grounds for divorce.

RAISING PEACEABLE FOLK

According to Dr. Hewlett, the Aka may be a living embodiment of "attachment theory," which proposes that an infant's experience of mothering can influence the way a child relates to the world. For example, an attentive mom who promptly cares for her infant's needs creates a child secure in his environment, who trusts caregivers and the people in the world around him. In contrast, a cold or unresponsive mother can produce an anxious or aggressive child who lacks the ability to trust. According to attachment theory, the supernurturing Aka moms make their kids prime candidates for growing into secure, trusting individuals who are calm and peaceful as opposed to overly anxious or aggressive. And that's just the type of people that the Aka appear to be.

The cooperative Aka have no tribal headman or chief. Instead, they spread power among men and women in the small hunting bands. They share food and cooperate rather than compete. They use humor, tradition, and ritual to make group decisions. And they settle grievances in the same way—with cooperation and without aggression or violence. The worst punishment the community gives is usually to ignore someone. The Aka avoid battles that could tear their close hunting alliances apart. Because of the secure start Aka children have in life, they are able to carry over this peaceful, trusting way of life to adulthood. The United Nation Development Program describes Aka pygmies as a "joyful people." And that joy could be the result of the way Aka moms nurture their kids all day, every day.

THE LESSON THAT COULD BE LOST

Though the world wants to keep learning from the forest people, sadly, the Aka are under siege. C.A.R.'s forests are exploited by loggers, and murdering bands of militias have turned the country into one of the most dangerous places on the globe.

As the great African forests disappear, their people and traditions may disappear forever, but if the world can somehow help the Aka protect their forests, they may save themselves. Then Aka moms could teach the world more about fostering sharing, compassion, and nonviolence—not a bad deal.

Moms' May Days

Mark your calendar so you don't miss these maternal celebrations all over the world!

First Sunday in May
South Africa

Second Sunday in May
U.S.A., Denmark, Finland, Italy, Turkey, Australia, Belgium, Japan, and many other countries

May 10
Mexico, Guatemala, Bahrain, India, Pakistan, Saudi Arabia, Hong Kong, and many other countries

Last Saturday in May
Central Africa Republic

Last Sunday in May
France (it is called *"La Fête des Meres"* here!) and Sweden

Mom Takes a Dive

"If swimming would make his daughter grow up to look like
Esther Williams, then father was willing to pay for the lessons."
—*International Swimming Hall of Fame*

By the time she retired from film in 1961, Esther Williams had swum her way through 26 movies and into the hearts of American moviegoers. Young girls across the nation begged their parents for swimming lessons after seeing an Esther Williams's film.

POOL SHARK

Esther Williams was born on August 8, 1923, in Inglewood, California, a suburb of Los Angeles. It was Esther's mother, along with the Parent Teacher Association, who convinced the city to provide a swimming pool for the neighborhood. Esther learned to swim from her sister. Soon she was spending all of her time at the pool. In order to pay for swimming time, she counted towels in the locker room. During lunchtime, when the pool was virtually empty, lifeguards taught her more advanced swimming techniques. She even learned the butterfly stroke, which was not usually taught to girls at that time. At the National Senior Outdoor Championship in 1939, she led her 300-meter and 400-meter medley relay teams to victory by being the first woman to use the butterfly stroke in competition. By the age of 18, she had won four U.S. championships in breaststroke and freestyle. For the 1940 Olympics, she was

America's gold-medal hope. Unfortunately, Williams never competed because the games were canceled when World War II broke out.

GETTING ON SWIMMINGLY

After seeing Williams's picture in the newspaper, Billy Rose invited the young athlete to audition for his San Francisco Aquacade review, a musical performed by hundreds of swimmers and divers with singing and special effects. Rose handpicked Williams to star opposite Olympian and screen star Johnny Weissmuller. Swimming in the Aquacade at the 1940 World's Fair, Williams caught the eye of MGM moguls.

CHLORINE QUEEN

MGM quickly put the 18-year-old under contract and she made her film debut opposite Mickey Rooney in *Andy Hardy's Double Life* (1942). Two years later, she was starring in *Bathing Beauty* (1944), Hollywood's first swimming movie. Williams soon became one of the top-10 box office attractions. Her trademark aquatic musicals were wildly popular. By the end of World War II, she had become a pinup favorite with returning GIs.

MATERNAL MERMAID

Even with her busy film career, Williams found time to have children. She continued to work through all of her pregnancies until about the fourth month when she would get too sick. Sadly, during her fourth pregnancy, Williams's grueling schedule did take its toll and she miscarried.

"I don't know to this day how I managed to fit into those bathing suits when I was pregnant," she says, "but I did . . .

somehow I stayed a size 10 through it all." Even today, she refers to each child by the movie she was filming before they were born. She was pregnant with Benjamin during *Neptune's Daughter* (1949), Kimball during *Pagan Love Song* (1950), and Susan during *Easy to Love* (1953).

Williams taught her children to swim soon after birth. "One of the reasons I gave them this gift of swimming so early in their lives was because I loved having them with me in the water. And when I saw them take to it, it was a shared joy that we had in common."

MERMAID TYCOON

From early on, Williams knew that her movie career wouldn't last forever: "I mean, how many swimming movies could they make?" In 1958, she began a swimming pool company specializing in aboveground pools. Thirty years later, she and husband Edward Bell launched the Esther Williams Collection of fashion swimsuits.

FIGHTING GRAVITY

Williams started designing her own swimsuits when she realized that the designers for her movies didn't swim. She never asked for screen credit, but all of her swimsuits and many of the dresses she wore on the silver screen were her own designs. Aiming at a broader market, her designs are for more mature women. Some were even based on her classic costumes. "Somebody has to give a little thought to the woman who has nursed a baby and I want to apply my knowledge of what feels good in the water for that woman," she said.

The Power of
Motherly Love

*After decades under the microscope,
mom's love can get some respect!*

I f your mom gets on your nerves when she ruffles your
hair or smooches your cheek, relax. Scientific investi-
gators have discovered that a mother's loving stimulation
aids in the development of the brain's circuitry and
reduces stress.

DON'T MONKEY WITH MOM

In the late 1950s, a psychologist named Harry Harlow performed experiments that made him a villain in many
animal-rights circles. Harlow took infant rhesus monkeys
from their mothers and substituted a wire-mesh "mother"
with a bottle for the infant to nurse from and a cloth
"mother" that the baby monkeys clutched for comfort.
Harlow wanted to study the effects of severe affection deprivation on the little animals—and he got effects all right!

Harlow's monkeys all became severely disturbed. When
they weren't acting out aggressively, they often showed an
autisticlike syndrome, clutching themselves and constantly
rocking back and forth. Harlow's troubled animals revealed
how much they needed socialization, touching, nurturing
and . . . well . . . plain old motherly love.

WINNING THE RAT RACE

If mom's TLC—or lack thereof—could throw such a monkey wrench into behavior, could it also affect brain chemistry? Studies at McGill University in Montreal, Canada, proved that if baby rats got more licking and grooming from their mothers, their genes activated more brain receptors for benzodiazepines (tranquilizers). The added receptors increased the brain's response to the calming chemical.

When baby rats had more fondling from their mothers, they were also higher achievers. While they swam through a floating labyrinth to look for submerged objects (a ratty I.Q. test), the well-nurtured young'uns learned faster and had the best memories. Turned out that the ratty Einsteins each had a hippocampus (a part of the brain dealing with stress control, attention, and memory) containing more synapses than those pups that had less mothering. Attentive mothers could actually improve the neurological systems and even the genetics of the pups. So could foster mothers if they fondled their foster babies.

A MOTHERING CRISIS

Okay, the effects of motherly affection are powerful if you're a monkey or a rat, but what about in us humans? Most researchers never expected—or wanted—the chance to work with human children who lacked any maternal or parental care. But they got it anyway.

In 1989, a repressive dictatorship in Romania fell, and an international crisis arose. The state had forbidden birth control, but people were too poor to feed their big families. Thousands of kids had been left in Romanian state orphanages. They were warehoused in cribs or on dirty cots. Aside from being fed and changed, they were left alone without toys and with little touching or affection.

Sadly, many of these orphans showed autistic behavior problems (social withdrawal and repetitive rocking or movements) similar to Harlow's monkeys. Harvard researchers also found that the orphans' cortisol (a stress hormone) measures were very high compared with children brought up in family homes. The orphans also showed signs of being more anxious and fearful than other children.

THANKS, MOM!

The findings from these studies, along with other research, convinced many neuroscientists that our brains are molded not only by our inherited set of genes, but also by our earliest interactions. According to Alan Schore, assistant clinical professor at the UCLA School of Medicine, the most crucial component of these earliest interactions is the primary caregiver—usually the mother.

We don't know about your stress level, but if you can read this page—give mom extra hugs of thanks for helping make you so smart. And never underestimate the power of a mother's love!

"If you bungle raising your children, I don't think whatever else you do well matters very much."
—Jacqueline Kennedy Onassis

Bad Moms
Movie Festival

Moms gone wrong—They're no fun to live with, but they're sure fun to watch. Here are our flick picks for the best in bad moms.

Mommie Dearest—Come on, you know the words: "No more wire hangers ever!" This is a classic of the celebrity child-abuse genre (there is, thankfully, not that much competition). Faye Dunaway plays 1940s star Joan Crawford as completely unhinged and cruel, particularly to her adopted daughter, Christina, whose real-life memoir is the basis for the movie. Dunaway's portrayal and the breathless, trashy, camp vibe of the entire film are so over the top that even Christina Crawford was taken aback. "They've turned it into a Joan Crawford movie!" she memorably complained. It's no joke—this film was so successful in defining the public's image of Joan Crawford that these days when people think of Crawford, they don't actually think of the woman herself but of Dunaway's portrayal of her. That's some delicious Hollywood irony for you.

Cinderella—A classic evil-stepmother tale, lovingly animated and bibbity-boppity-boo-ilized by the folks at Disney. Some people prefer Snow White's wicked stepmother—and to be fair, the wicked queen *did* order one of her minions to cut out Snow White's heart. After all, most of us don't know anyone who would literally cut out our hearts, but we *do* know someone who would figuratively stab us in the back. What Cinderella's evil stepmom has going for her is a streak of pettiness as wide as the ocean. She doesn't want Cinderella dead (because then who would do the laundry?), she just wants to make sure Cinderella is very alive and dreadfully unhappy. Eleanor Audley, who also provided Maleficent's pipes in *Sleeping Beauty*, struck just the right tone of cruelty as the stemother when smugly telling Cinderella she could to go the ball only after her impossible list of chores was done. The scene where she breaks the glass slipper rather than let Cinderella try it on is a classic of cinematic venality. Sadly, the film never shows the stepmom getting her comeuppance, although a 1998 live-action version of the story, *Ever After*, has the evil stepmom ending up in a nunnery, doing the laundry. Turnabout is always fair play.

The Grifters—Anjelica Huston (who, it must be noted, plays the evil stepmother in the just-noted *Ever After*) does something terribly, terribly monstrous to her son, played by John Cusack in *The Grifters*. Scratch that—she does *two* terribly monstrous things to her son, one right after the other, and the reason she does is because she is a con artist for whom relationships take a back seat to the score and the cash. You might think that Cusack's character, a con artist himself, would know this about his own mother. But, see, he's not a very *good* con artist. And he's perhaps a little too trusting of people he shouldn't trust, including, alas, dear old mom. No, we won't tell you what horrible things Huston's character does. Watch for yourself. You'll be in awe of her.

The Manchurian Candidate—Angela Lansbury is best known these days for playing an animated teapot in *Beauty* *and the Beast* and a mystery writer who always seems to be around when people drop dead in *Murder, She Wrote*. But in this controversial 1962 film, she tried on another role for size—that of an ambitious and domineering political wife wrapped up in a plot to assassinate a presidential candidate, a plot that just happens to involve her war-hero son (played by Laurence Harvey), who'd been brainwashed to be the triggerman. It's a very complicated plot, and Lansbury's part is equally complex. She plays a mother happy to use her son for her own political gain. Call it "Assassination, She Wrote."

White Oleander—Prefer your bad moms to be from the 21st century? Look no further than 2002's *White Oleander*. Michelle Pfeiffer plays a mother whose somewhat impulsive murder of a boyfriend causes her teenage daughter to get shipped from foster home to foster home, each with foster moms of varying niceness. All the while Pfeiffer's character hovers over her daughter's psyche, offering her poisonous advice and commentary during visiting hours. Pfeiffer comes across as a marvelously interesting sociopath, which is why at least one film critic compared her character to Hannibal Lecter. Which is not usually a quality one wants in a mother, especially one's own. The movie's ultimate tagline: "No matter how much she damaged me, no matter how flawed she is, I know my mother loves me." Which is, indeed, one way of looking at it.

Haunting Dysfunction

Still angry after all these years.

At the ruins of Castle Rising, in Norfolk, England, tourists hope to glimpse the ghost of "She-Wolf" Queen Isabella, who has haunted the castle since the 14th century.

THE QUEEN TAKES A LOVER

Queen Isabella was born in France, and she had been given in a political marriage to King Edward II. Though they had four children, they also had one of the worst royal marriages in English history—which is really saying something. King Edward II was a weak king, who lavished his attention on lovers other than his queen. In 1325 the queen took a lover of her own, Roger Mortimer. Not only did she gain a boyfriend, she also found an ally against her husband. Roger and Isabella gathered an army, attacked, and defeated Edward. He was forced to abdicate and transferred the throne to his young son and heir, the future Edward III. Roger Mortimer, Earl of March, became the virtual king until the young heir came of age.

EXILING THE SHE-WOLF

Isabella didn't stop there. She had her husband imprisoned and schemed with Mortimer to secretly have him murdered. After that she and jolly Roger did quite well—until Edward III reached his majority, became king, and decided to avenge his father's death. King Edward III executed Roger but spared his mother's life. She "retired" to Castle Rising, where she was furious at her son for sending her away. Today, according to legend, she haunts the ruins of the castle, still furious after 700 years—and still screaming at Edward III and her fate.

The Joke's on Mom

So a doctor says to new mother: "You look exhausted! It appears that you're not getting enough sleep. If the baby starts to cry in the middle of the night, who gets up?" She says, "The whole neighborhood."

Tired of her son's misbehavior, a mom takes the guilt trip route and says, "Every time you act up, I get another gray hair." Without missing a beat, the son replies, "Then you must have been worse than me when you were young. Just look at Grandma!"

More Spot the Moms!

Catch the high-flying moms—if you can.

They were pioneers speeding through the air or orbiting into space. Did they ever come down to earth to raise kids?

1. Beryl Markham: First person to fly solo across the Atlantic from Britain to Canada

Beryl Markham grew up in Kenya, where she was a successful horse trainer until a friend took her for a ride in his plane. She knew she had found her calling. Taking lessons, she became a commercial "bush" pilot, flying to remote areas in Kenya. In 1936, Markham wanted prize money, so she made the first solo flight across the Atlantic "the hard way"—from Britain to Canada and against the headwinds. The flight, and her book describing it, *West with the Night*, made the pilot world famous.

Did the daring Markham ever dare to face the challenges of motherhood?

2. Jacqueline Cochran: First female pilot to break the sound barrier

Cochran, a beautician, had worked her way up from the rural South to the urban New York City. Once Jackie took flying lessons in 1932, she said so long to shampoo and hello to planes. Cochran began flying in competitions and won the Bendix transcontinental air race in 1938. During

World War II she trained female pilots for the British and the U.S. governments, receiving a distinguished service medal for her efforts. Cochran then became the first female pilot to break the sound barrier. She set more aviation records for speed and altitude. At the time of her death in 1980 she held more records than any other pilot—male or female—in history.

Did Jackie's kids ever break the sound barrier watching TV?

3. Valentina Tereshkova: First woman to fly in space and orbit the earth

Valentina came up (way up!) the hard way. Born in the small Russian village of Maslennikovo, she worked in a factory and studied engineering. Valentina was chosen as one of five women to join the Soviet cosmonaut corps based on her amateur parachuting experience. In 1963, she took off on *Vostok 6*, becoming the first woman in space. Orbiting the earth 48 times, her flight lasted just under three days. That same year she also married fellow cosmonaut Andrian Nikolayev.

Did Valentina and Andrian become the first set of "spacey" cosmonaut parents?

4. Dr. Sally Ride: First American woman in space

At 27, Sally Kristen Ride's four degrees, including a PhD in physics, seemed to propel her toward an academic career. Then she saw a newspaper ad placed by NASA calling for astronauts and, impulsively, she applied. Her impulse paid off and in 1983, Sally became the first U.S. woman in space when she orbited the earth in the space shuttle, *Challenger*. Sally found space work exhilarating. But back on the ground, she had to contend with reporters who asked her if she wept at work or needed a bra in space. ("There is no sag in zero-g" was Sally's reply.) Post-NASA, Dr. Ride worked to encourage girls to enter scientific fields. She is a physics professor at the University of California at San Diego.

Does Sally Ride have kids of her own that plan to be astronauts?

Answers on page 301.

Thanks, Son

A man could never give his elderly mom the right birthday present.

When he gave her a mansion, she said, "It's too big. I don't need so many rooms to clean. Thanks anyway."

When he gave her a new car she said, "I'm too old to be cavorting around, and I have my groceries delivered. Thanks anyway."

The man was in despair until he found the perfect gift. He knew his mother loved the Bible and her eyesight was failing, so he gave her a parrot that could recite any Bible verse she wanted.

His mother said, "At last you had the good sense to give a little thought to your gift. Thank you, thank you! The chicken was delicious."

The Age-Old Guessing Game

Can moms predict whether they'll have a boy or girl?

S hould the nursery be painted pink or blue? It's an age-old question for moms-to-be. These days there are ultrasound sonograms to determine a baby's sex with 95 percent accuracy. But ancient methods of foretelling whether baby will be a boy or a girl are still going strong.

When researchers investigated old-fashioned methods to predict a baby's gender, they made a surprising discovery. One method worked—mother's intuition!

PENDULUMS AND DRANO?

Before technology stepped in, mothers relied on folk wisdom to determine whether the occupant in their womb was male or female. If the mother seemed to carry the baby high, the child would most likely be a boy; if the baby was carried low, a girl was predicted. When visible clues weren't easy to spot, the pendulum prediction method was a popular standby. Mom-to-be, or a friend, would thread a string through a ring. The ring was dangled over the pregnant woman's stomach. If it swung back and forth, the baby was a boy; if the pendulum moved in a circle—break out the pink paint!

A popular urban legend claims that a mixture of Drano and the pregnant woman's urine can reveal the sex of her baby-to-be. If it turns green, is it a boy? Does red mean a girl? What about brown? The truth is that mixing Drano and urine won't tell you anything about an unborn baby at all. The only thing it will tell you, to paraphrase the great Ann Landers, is if your kidneys are working. Valuable knowledge? Yes. A predictor of boys and girls to come? No.

TESTING THE TESTS

When researchers from Johns Hopkins tested the accuracy of folk methods for determining a baby's sex for 104 women, the methods were accurate about 55 percent of the time— the same as random guessing. But there was one puzzling finding. Women who relied on their own dreams and intuition predicted the baby's sex with 71 percent accuracy.

Did mothers possess special insight to help predict the sex of their baby? The question was studied by Dr. Shamas of the University of Arizona. One hundred women were asked to use just their intuition to predict whether they would give birth to a boy or a girl. Mothers predicted gender correctly over 70 percent of the time, well above random chance.

But Mom can't let her personal preferences get in the way. Dr. Shamas's study also found that women who preferred one gender to the other had less successful intuitive abilities. "The point is that there's a big difference between what you want to happen and what your intuition tells you is going to happen," explained the doctor.

Does this mean mothers can forget about sonograms? Well, maybe not, but researchers have agreed that mom's surprising ability to predict the sex of her baby through intuition is a phenomenon worth serious study.

Of course, kids knew that all along. When Dr. Shamas did a survey of college students, nearly 75 percent of them claimed that their mothers could read their thoughts and feelings in ways no one else could.

Eskimo Mom Extraordinaire

Ada Blackjack was alone on an Arctic island with few supplies and no wilderness skills. All she had was a determination to survive for the sake of her child.

A da Blackjack was Inuit, a full-blooded Eskimo who had never seen an igloo. Ada was a city mom who lived in Nome, Alaska, where she cleaned houses and took in sewing to make money. Like many aboriginal people from an urban environment, Ada never learned the survival skills of her people. She certainly had no idea how to live in the Arctic without modern conveniences.

At 23, Ada had known hard times. She'd had three children with her first husband and had lost two of them. Only six-year-old Bennett had survived, but the boy had fallen ill with tuberculosis. Ada was desperate to get her boy good medical care, only she couldn't afford it—until it seemed she got a lucky break.

ESKIMO WANTED

In 1921, an expedition of four young men came to Nome to hire Eskimos to help them live off the land. They intended to camp on the Arctic island of Wrangel and interest the United States or Canada in its development. No Eskimo wanted to go to Wrangel, which was then controlled by Russia. Located north of Siberia, it was desolate, barren, and locked in ice floes much of the year.

But Ada needed money, and the expedition needed a seamstress to repair and sew warm clothing from animal skins. Leaving Bennett in a children's home, Ada went to Wrangel Island to make some money.

EXPEDITION TO TRAGEDY

Arctic explorer Vilhjalmur Stefánsson organized the expedition. He lectured that the Arctic was a friendly place and as bountiful a piece of real estate as Hawaii. Stefánsson's four recruits carried enough supplies for six months. After that they'd have to live off Arctic "bounty."

But when the expedition landed on Wrangel, they found no paradise. Isolated, bleak, and frozen—so much colder than Nome—Ada could barely tolerate it. Unlike the young men who believed in the importance of polar exploration, Ada was simply terrified, especially of the polar bears that roamed the island. Her biggest fear was that she'd never survive to see Bennett again.

GETTING BACK TO BENNETT

By the following summer the crew was desperately watching for a promised supply ship that never came. By winter their food was nearly gone and one of the men, Lorne Knight, had scurvy. Ada was left to care for Knight and the camp's cat, Vic, while the rest of the crew left with a dog team to find help. None of them was ever seen again.

Ada was malnourished, so she forced herself to learn new skills to survive. She learned to trap foxes and hunt birds and seals. Petite Ada invented a contraption to protect herself from the ricochet of a rifle so she wouldn't be knocked off her feet. She even managed to fend off the polar bears. She was determined to survive and return to Bennett.

Though Ada kept Knight warm and fed, he died in the spring. Now absolutely alone, Ada nearly despaired, and only thoughts of Bennett kept her going. When a rescue ship finally arrived, Ada had spent nearly two years in the Arctic and the last six months alone—except for the company of Vic the cat.

THE DISAPPEARING HEROINE

When Ada returned to civilization, she immediately took Bennett to Seattle for treatment. His health remained fragile and Ada's life remained difficult. She wanted to forget the horrors of Wrangel, but the press chased after her, demanding explanations for the disaster. When Ada wouldn't talk, wild stories circulated about her. Some portrayed her as a heroine; other accounts blamed her for Knight's death.

Ada married for the second time and had another son, Billy. This marriage didn't last, and the two divorced. Money from the expedition ran out, and there were battles with illness and poverty. She took her sons to Nome where she finally turned her luck around. She herded reindeer and used the hunting and trapping skills learned on Wrangel to feed her family.

ADA'S TRIUMPH

Bennett lived to be 56 and remained close to his mother all his life. So did her younger son, who became a leader of Alaska's native population. Billy understood the historic importance of Ada's ordeal, and he helped best-selling author Jennifer Nivens write Ada's story, in the book *Ada Blackjack*. When his mother died, Billy proudly put a plaque on her grave that reads simply, "The Heroine of Wrangel Island."

Mom Gets MADD

Candy Lightner didn't get even. She got MADD.

On an evening in May 1980, Candy Lightner was an average mother of three, driving her 13-year-old daughter, Cari, to a friend's house for a sleepover. When Cari opened the car door to leave, her mother suddenly was overwhelmed by the need to say, "Cari, you know I love you?"

"Oh, Mother, don't be so mushy," Cari replied. The ordinary evening probably would have been forgotten if it hadn't been the last time Candy ever saw her daughter alive. The following day, Lightner came home from shopping with a friend and learned that Cari was dead. Walking along a quiet street on her way to a church carnival in Fair Oaks, California, Cari was hit from behind. A drunken driver rammed her with his car, sending her flying 125 feet, with a force that knocked her out of her shoes and killed her. He never bothered to stop.

FROM SORROW TO RAGE

A few days later, Candy learned from the California Highway Patrol officers investigating the incident that the driver who ran down her daughter had several prior drunk-driving convictions, but that considering the way the system worked, she'd be lucky if the driver did any jail time. He wound up spending 16 months behind bars, but Lightner's sorrow fueled a new and consuming rage. If drunk driving maimed and killed people, then why didn't law enforcement take drunk driving more seriously?

Somehow Lightner made it through the funeral. Even while coping with unbearable loss while comforting her other children (Cari's twin sister, Serena, and her younger brother, Todd) the shell-shocked mother knew that she wanted to make something positive come out of Cari's death.

GETTING MADD

Lightner's friends were as enraged about Cari's death as she was and encouraged Lightner to take action. They supported her idea to found an organization to raise awareness of the deadly problems caused by drunk drivers and the relaxed penalties for those who were caught under the influence. One of her friends suggested a name: Mothers Against Drunk Drivers, which came to be better known by the acronym MADD.

At the time of Cari's death, Lightner was a divorced Sacramento real estate agent and focused on raising her kids. She had no idea how to launch political reform and no political connections to make her voice heard. But, supported by her friends and motivated by her anger over Cari's death, Lightner became an activist. She read books, did research, and consulted every possible ally she could think of. She eventually quit her job to begin a life of phone calls, meetings, and letter writing. Still wracked by crying jags, she forced herself to speak publicly, and calmly, about the daughter she missed so desperately. Otherwise she might be dismissed as an overwrought mother, too emotional to understand legal issues.

Candy stuck to her tactic with the first speech she wrote and delivered on her own at a traffic safety conference in Oregon. She began with a description of Cari and the details of her death. She was so clear-eyed and calm that when she told the audience that Cari was "my little girl," the crowd gasped in shock and the media went into a feeding frenzy. Soon MADD was national news. And so was MADD's founder, who appeared around the country as a keynote speaker, gave interviews for radio and television, and testified before Congress. Soon the victims of drunk drivers had a representative with a human face—the pretty, freckled face of Cari Lightner.

MADD SUCCESS

From 1980 to 1985, MADD went from a local crusade to a national organization with three million members and chapters in all 50 states. MADD eventually spread to the international community, with 600 chapters worldwide. During Lightner's tenure as head of MADD, alcohol-related accidents declined 14 percent and the legal drinking age was pushed from 18 to 21 in many states, saving an estimated 800 lives a year. In 1980, Cari was one of 25,000 people killed by drunk drivers. By 1992 the number was down to 17,000. Thanks to Lightner's work, Americans must have lost their tolerance for drunk drivers; from 1980 to 1994 the numbers of intoxicated drivers dropped by over 30 percent.

All this success came at a price. As MADD grew and grew, Lightner took on the executive tasks of running an organization with dozens of paid employees and hundreds of volunteers. With these responsibilities and commitments, Lightner feared she was neglecting her children. In 1985 Lightner resigned from MADD. She took the time to deal with personal issues and to coauthor a book, *Giving Sorrow*

Words, to help those who mourned the loss of a loved one. But her legacy continues; MADD, which changed its name in 1984 to Mothers Against Drunk Driving, still helps victims of drunk drivers, monitors the courts, and works to pass stronger anti-drunk-driving laws.

Arrangement in Gray and Black No. 1

Otherwise known as Whistler's mother, Anna McNeil Whistler has become one of the most famous women in the world because of a tardy artist's model. The story goes that in 1871, American painter James Whistler had arranged for a model to come to his London studio to pose for him. When she failed to show, Whistler asked his mother Anna, who was living with him, to pose instead. The painting became one of the most famous images in the world. Whistler called his mother's portrait *Arrangement in Gray and Black No. 1: The Artist's Mother*, but it is better known today as *Whistler's Mother*.

The painting helped establish Whistler's credentials as a serious artist when the French government bought it in 1891, an event that unfortunately Anna didn't live to see. The painting was eventually hung in Paris at the Musée d'Orsay, a great honor accorded to few American artists.

Name that Mama Diva!

*All moms can be divas, but can you ID
these chanteuses from their stories?*

1. Everybody knows I'm a diva Supreme. But most folks
don't know that I'm also a mama Supreme. I led my two
gal pals in our singing trio when we joined Motown and
our first hit record was "Where Did Our Love Go?" Want
to know where lots of my love goes? To my five kids.
They'll tell you I'm a devoted mom. I may be a star, but my
kids and I have dinner together with no phone calls or TV
allowed.

Who am I?

__A. Donna Summer   __C. Diana Ross
__B. Mary Wilson   __D. Gladys Knight

2. I'm the comeback queen who got her start as half of a
husband-and-wife singing duo. We had each other long
enough to have a darling daughter and star in a hit comedy variety show. Our love didn't last and we soon parted
ways, but my solo career kept my children and me going
strong. Whether listening to "Gypsies, Tramps, and
Thieves," "If I Could Turn Back Time," or "Believe," you'll
always recognize my distinctive sound.

Who am I?

__A. Natalie Cole   __C. Dolly Parton
__B. Joni Mitchell   __D. Cher

3. I used to be the Material Girl, but that was before I had two kids, a boy and a girl. I don't expose them to bawdy antics like the ones I've performed onstage. Instead of producing more adult books called *Sex*, I'm now writing children's books. People may call me immoral but my second children's book is based on rabbinical teachings that I learned while studying the spiritual lessons of the Kabbalah—so there!

Who am I?

__A. Debbie Gibson   __C. Cyndi Lauper
__B. Madonna   __D. Courtney Love

4. I made quite a name for myself as the raven-haired lead singer of the psychedelic rock band Jefferson Airplane. With hits like "White Rabbit" and "Somebody to Love," I was a freak-out queen in the late 1960s. Rumor has it that I named my daughter God, but that was just an unfortunate joke I made in the maternity ward right after her birth. Her name is and always has been China.

Who am I?

__A. Grace Slick   __C. Marianne Faithfull
__B. Michelle Phillips   __D. Carly Simon

ANSWERS: 1. C; 2. D; 3. B; 4. A

The Battle for Baby M

It was a trial that mesmerized the nation.
Who would keep Baby M?

I n 1985, a New Jersey homemaker and mother of two, Mary Beth Whitehead, and her husband, Richard, entered into a contractual agreement with biochemist William Stern to conceive a baby. Stern agreed to pay $10,000 to the Whiteheads for Mary Beth to be artificially inseminated with William's sperm. The contract stipulated that Mary Beth would not form a "parent-child relationship" with the baby and would surrender both the baby and her parental rights to William Stern. By signing the contract, Mary Beth agreed to become a surrogate mother for William and his wife, Dr. Elizabeth Stern.

THE NEW FRONTIER

There are two types of surrogacy. Gestational surrogacy involves a surrogate mother being implanted with another woman's fertilized egg; in this instance, the surrogate isn't genetically related to the baby she gives birth to. Advanced infertility treatments developed in the 1980s allowed doctors to fertilize an egg in a petri dish, then implant the zygote in a woman's uterus. This meant that many infertile couples would now be able to bear children. It also meant that if a woman could not carry to term, she could hire another woman to carry the baby for her. Mary Beth was different in that her egg was fertilized via artificial insemination. She was the baby's biological mother and Stern was the biological father.

Surrogate mothers help couples that can't have children by bearing a baby for them. According to the Old Testament, Sarah and Abraham had a surrogate mother, Sarah's maid Hagar, for their son Ishmael (Genesis 16). But if surrogacy is as old as the Bible, formal contracts like the one between Mary Beth and William were very new in 1985.

Though the contract was set down neatly in black and white, when the baby arrived things became very complicated. On March 27, 1986, 28-year-old Mary Beth gave birth to a baby daughter, with whom she immediately bonded. She decided that she had made a mistake in signing the contract and wanted to keep her daughter. Naming the baby Sara Elizabeth Whitehead, Mary Beth took the baby home and turned down the $10,000. The Sterns demanded custody of the infant they named Melissa Stern, and when Mary Beth refused to give her daughter up, the Sterns got a court order from Judge Harvey Sorkow ordering Whitehead to hand over her five-week-old daughter.

A MOTHER'S TRIAL

Whitehead escaped with her baby to Florida and threatened to kill herself and the baby if authorities tried to take her away. Private detectives hired by the Sterns tracked the pair down and took the baby away from the mother. They turned Sara over to the Sterns, who renamed her Melissa. On January 5, 1987, a custody trial began with both sides suing for custody. To protect the baby's privacy, the court referred to her as Baby M.

The highly publicized case was called the "trial of the century" at the time. The new use of surrogate contracts stirred curiosity. Could you really hire a woman to "rent out her uterus," as some newspapers described it? Mary Beth's dramatic flight to Florida gave the case an uncertain edge. What might this desperate woman do next? Finally, there was the prize of custody—everyone had an opinion about who should care for Baby M.

As the trial progressed, two issues were debated by the lawyers, pundits, and the public. The first was the contract between Mary Beth and William. The Sterns argued that Ms. Whitehead knew what she was getting into when she agreed to give the baby away. A famous child psychologist of the day, Dr. Lee Salk, testified that by signing the contract Mary Beth became a surrogate uterus—not a mother at all. Mary Beth supporters argued that she returned the money and that she loved her daughter. The two had formed a bond through pregnancy and delivery.

Next came the question of the most fit parent for Baby M. Mary Beth's attorneys attempted to show that the forty-something Elizabeth Stern had not had a baby because of possible interference with her medical career. The prosecution claimed that Dr. Stern hadn't become pregnant because she had self-diagnosed multiple sclerosis. Aiding the Stern's case were influential experts like psychiatrist Dr. Marshall Schechter. He called Ms. Whitehead an unfit mother, giving as examples her playing of patty-cake inappropriately—shouting "hooray" when the baby clapped her hands instead of reinforcing the behavior by clapping her own hands—and her giving the baby stuffed pandas for toys instead of simple pots and spoons.

WAS THIS DEAL IDEAL?

Outside the court, much public sympathy went to William Stern. "A deal is a deal," ran the popular verdict. Against the evidence of the contract she had signed, Mary Beth's love of her daughter was dismissed by many observers as overemotional and even a tad unbalanced. Though she was raising two healthy children, her former desperate outbursts and the verdicts of psychological experts convinced many that this mother shouldn't be trusted to even visit her daughter.

Still, there was growing public support for Mary Beth. Over 100 famous females—including Nora Ephron, Gloria Steinem, Betty Friedan, and Meryl Streep—signed a statement debunking Schechter's patty-cake test for judging motherhood. Other court watchers pointed out that the contract itself was unreasonable. It forced the Whiteheads "to assume all risks, including the risk of death" and insisted that Mary Beth not fall in love with her baby. Could a contract force a person to risk death and not feel love?

THE JUDGES GIVETH AND TAKETH AWAY

After listening to the evidence, Judge Sorkow granted William Stern full custody and denied visitation to the surrogate mother. Immediately following the decision, Elizabeth Stern adopted Baby M in Judge Sorkow's chambers. Mary Beth immediately appealed his decision, saying that the judge who had signed the original order taking the baby from her considered her "just a uterus with legs."

On February 3, 1988, the New Jersey Supreme Court heard Whitehead's appeal and reversed Sorkow's ruling. The original surrogacy contract was nullified, Elizabeth's subsequent adoption annulled, and Mary Beth's parental rights reestablished. The court recognized her as the baby's biological mother, giving her "generous" and unsupervised visitation rights. It also declared surrogate mother contracts invalid and illegal in the state of New Jersey. The

Baby M case led to strict legislation of surrogacy and bans on fee-based surrogacy arrangements in ten states. Mary Beth and the baby were now reunited. Some were glad. Some were horrified. And some called it "mothering by committee."

WHATEVER HAPPENED TO BABY M?

The little girl who'd been named both Melissa and Sara has since nicknamed herself "Sassy." According to Mary Beth, Sassy calls her "Mom," William Stern "Dad," and Elizabeth Stern "Betsy." Living mainly at the Sterns as an only child, Sassy also fits in comfortably with her half siblings when she visits her mother in Long Island, New York. Mary Beth feels she and her daughter still share a deep bond.

Though Mary Beth would never regret having Sassy and has described her relations with the Sterns as "civil," she speaks out against surrogacy and would like to prevent it from happening to anyone else. It's not known what the Sterns, who have fought hard for Sassy's privacy, think of the arrangement. On this and on the subject of surrogacy—they've kept mum.

"Children require guidance and sympathy far more than instruction." —Annie Sullivan

Swoopes, There It Is

Record Breaker, Olympic Gold Winner,
Basketball Maven, and Mom

Sheryl Denise Swoopes has been called the female Michael Jordan. The six-foot-tall forward for the Women's National Basketball Association (WNBA) Houston Comets certainly racks up points and awards like her male counterpart. But Swoopes has achieved something that Jordan will never accomplish—she's given birth.

RHYMES WITH HOOPS

Swoopes was born March 25, 1971, in Brownfield, Texas. When she was seven, she started playing basketball with her two older brothers with a homemade basket built from an old bike tire rim with the spokes popped out. Luckily, all the home practice paid off. A year later she went to the national championships with her Little Dribblers team.

As Sheryl got older, she became an even brighter star. As a high-school athlete, she led her team in scoring and earned the Texas female high-school player of the year award in 1989. Attending Texas Tech University, Swoopes and the Red Raiders won the national championship in the NCAA tournament in 1993. During the championship game, she even shattered the record for the most points ever scored in a Division I NCAA basketball championship game—a record formerly held by Bill Walton! Swoopes's 47 points are the most ever scored in the Final Four by any player—male or female.

JUST DO IT, MOM

In spring 1995, Nike announced the launch of a new basketball shoe—the Air Swoopes. Sheryl signed a multiyear deal with Nike to put her name on the first signature shoe named after a women. The black-and-white Air Swoopes is a high-top shoe, the first one named after any athlete since 1985, when the Air Jordan was introduced.

AWARD HIGHLIGHTS

After college, Sheryl's star continued to rise when, in 1996, Swoopes, as part of the U.S. women's team won Olympic gold. Then in 1997, she was the first woman signed to play basketball for the fledgling WNBA, a professional sports league for women. Since then, she has helped lead the Houston Comets to four consecutive championships.

BREASTFEEDING AND A GOOD SUPPORT BRA

On June 25, 1997, Sheryl Swoopes gave birth to her son, Jordan Eric Jackson. Swoopes claims that the first question she asked her doctor after giving birth was, "When can I start working out?" Two weeks later she was back in the gym working hard to lose the baby weight and get herself back on the court. In just six weeks, she returned to the hardwood floors having lost all but 5 of the 47 pounds she had gained during pregnancy. On August 7, she made her WNBA debut as a glowing new mom.

The life of a pro athlete is hectic. Often traveling and maintaining a crazy schedule, Sheryl took Jordan on the road with her and managed to breastfeed him for the first seven months. Swoopes credits the breast pump with her success, calling it the "second best thing ever invented." We're not sure what she thinks the first is.

DRIBBLES ON THE COURT, DRIBBLES ON THE BIB

Since little Jordan's birth, Sheryl has continued to be honored for all of her athletic achievements. She won the 2001 ESPY for Women's Pro Basketball Player of the Year and was voted the WNBA's Most Valuable Player in 2000 and 2002. She won another gold medal with the American women in the 2000 Olympic games as well.

Now, in addition to being an award-winning athlete, Swoopes is a single divorced mom facing the challenges of juggling motherhood and a professional basketball career. The WNBA does not provide childcare, so Swoopes must balance her parenting duties with the pressures of travel and night games. She credits her own mother, Louise, as her inspiration and role model. Louise worked three jobs and raised Sheryl and her brothers alone.

BUT WHOSE SHOES DOES HE WEAR?

Swoopes, like any mom, is proud of her son's accomplishments, but feels no need to pressure him into sports. "If he wants to play sports, then that's fine. If he doesn't want to play sports, that's fine too. I just want him to be happy," she says. He is involved with karate, ice-skating, gymnastics, and his favorite sport, basketball, of course.

Spot Those Moms, Again!

Are they or aren't they?

They are female movers and shakers. Are they power-houses too?

1. Annie Oakley:
International sharpshooting star

In Ohio, Phoebe Anne Oakley Moses took up hunting to help out her financially strapped mother. She was such a good shot that she sold game and used the money to pay off the mortgage on the family's farm. An admiring friend entered her in a contest against noted sharpshooter Frank Butler. Butler lost the match but won Annie; he became her manager and her husband. In 1885 Annie was the big star attraction in the Buffalo Bill Wild West Show. A famous part of the act included her shooting a cigarette out of Frank's mouth. What a trusting husband! It's no wonder they stayed married for more than 50 years.

Did Frank and Annie have any little sharpshooters?

2. Jane Addams: Founder of Hull House and Nobel Peace Prize recipient

At one time, Jane Addams considered a medical career, but eventually decided to work on social rather than medical ills. In 1899 in Chicago, Illinois, she helped to found Hull House, one of the first social settlements in

North America. Jane and her friends turned Hull House from an old mansion into a community center that delivered educational and social services to Chicago's immigrant poor. Jane wrote books on social reform and helped pass legislation banning child labor. But it was Jane's attempts to establish international efforts for peace that brought her the Nobel Peace Prize in 1931.

Did Jane hear the patter of little feet in her famous Hull House?

3. Sandra Day O'Connor:
First female justice of the U.S. Supreme Court

Sandra Day O'Connor studied law at Stanford University, where she ranked third in her class. But when she applied for her first job with a California law firm, they turned her down because she was a woman. Sandra persevered with her own practice in Arizona, and by 1979 she was a judge on the Arizona Court of Appeals. President Reagan was impressed by her conservative credentials and nominated her to the Supreme Court. A Supreme Court Justice since 1981, O'Connor shaped many of the court's decisions as a crucial "swing" vote.

What was Sandra Day O'Connor's verdict on motherhood?

4. Meg Whitman: CEO of a
billion dollar e-commerce company

Whitman was head of Hasbro's Playskool division (with 600 employees and $600 million annual sales of toys) when she made a very risky move. She accepted an offer in 1998 to head an unknown start-up called Auction Web, whose top-selling category was Beanie Babies. Her gamble paid off. Today Whitman is still President and CEO of the company—now better known as eBay—that hosts more than $20 billion in gross annual sales. More than seven million people visit eBay every day. In 2002 *Fortune* ranked Whitman as the third most powerful woman in business, *Worth* magazine ranked her numero uno on its list of best CEOs in 2003, and CBS *Market Watch* named her CEO of the Year.

Does Whitman have any children who trade Beanie Babies on eBay?

Answers on page 301.

Mom's the Word

"But you can't always tell—with somebody's mother, I mean. Mothers are all slightly insane . . ."
—J. D. Salinger, *The Catcher in the Rye*

"Whenever I'm with my mother, I feel as though I have to spend the whole time avoiding land mines."
—Amy Tan, *The Kitchen God's Wife*

"Having children makes you no more a parent than having a piano makes you a pianist."
—Michael Levine

Did She Eat Schnitzel with Noodles?

The true story of Maria von Trapp,
the world's beloved singing stepmom.

If you've never seen *The Sound of Music*, one of the world's most famous musicals—maybe you were locked in a cellar for the past few decades—here goes: It takes place in Austria as Hitler is coming to power. A sweet, impulsive nun-in-training named Maria leaves the convent to temporarily become a governess to seven motherless children and brightens their lives by teaching them to sing. She also falls for their stern widower father and retired naval captain, Baron Georg von Trapp, and gives up convent life to marry him. If all this isn't dramatic enough, the movie ends as the von Trapps leave everything behind to hike over the Alps to escape the Nazis, singing bravely all the way.

Thanks to a rousing score and stirring lyrics from Rodgers and Hammerstein, the stage version became a classic. After the creation of a film version starring Julie Andrews, Maria became one of the most familiar stepmothers around. But this tale was based on a true story. Maria actually existed and did become stepmother to the von Trapp children. But how closely does the musical resemble the facts?

WHEN FRUSTRATED, MARIA WAS KNOWN TO SING

False. (Did you really think this could be true?) Maria von Trapp, as she freely admitted, did not burst into song when hardship arose. She may have been as lively and impulsive as her movie character, but she also struggled with a scarred past. Her mother died when she was two, her father left her with an elderly cousin in Vienna for most of her childhood, and after her father's death she went to live with an abusive male relative. Despite her hardships, Maria was a strong woman who overcame much to support her beloved new family.

WHILE GROWING UP, MARIA ALWAYS WANTED TO BE A NUN

False. In the musical, we're led to believe that as a child, Maria was drawn to the church by the nuns' singing as they worked in the garden. In reality, Maria was actually raised to be a socialist and atheist. She became interested in Catholicism while she attended college. The story goes that she had ducked into a church hoping to hear a Bach concert but instead she heard and was moved by a sermon from a priest who sparked a new devotion in Maria. She would later join the convent.

MARIA WAS GOVERNESS TO ALL THE VON TRAPP CHILDREN

False. Maria only had to look after one of the baron's daughters who had rheumatic fever, and only for ten months, since the child was too ill to attend school. Still determined to be a nun, Maria was conflicted when she found herself falling in love—with the von Trapp children. Maria had grown up a lonely child, shuttled between different family members and had invented an imaginary family for herself, the Paultraxls, to keep herself company. Perhaps this von Trapp children reminded her of her imaginary playmates from childhood?

THE VON TRAPP FAMILY SINGERS WAS A REAL SINGING ACT

True. When Baron von Trapp's fortune was wiped out in the 1930s, Maria convinced him that there was no shame in singing for money. Maria organized her family into a choir and hustled the von Trapp Family Singers off on a well-paying tour. Maria's management solved more than financial problems. Baron von Trapp detested the Nazis, and a booking in America provided a chance for them to leave when Hitler took over Austria. After the von Trapps reached America, they continued to sing for their supper. They eventually settled down in Stowe, Vermont, and opened up the Trapp Family Lodge, which is still run by the von Trapp family today.

"Of all the rights of women, the greatest is to be a mother." —Lin Yutang

Where in the World Is Mom?

Vital stats about moms around the world.

Around the world, the five countries with the lowest birth-rates (births per thousand of population) were:

Bulgaria	8.02
Latvia	8.55
Germany	8.60
Czech Republic	9.01
Italy	9.18

Around the world, the five countries with the highest birthrates were all developing nations:

Niger	49.54
Mali	47.79
Chad	47.06
Uganda	46.57
Somalia	46.42

Source: 2003 CIA World Factbook

WHERE IN THE WORLD IS THE BEST PLACE TO BE A MOM?

You might be surprised! One essential of a good place for mothering is the likelihood of having a healthy baby.

In 2003, the ten countries with the lowest infant mortality rates per thousand live births were:

Japan	3.30
Sweden	3.42
Iceland	3.50
Singapore	3.57
Finland	3.73
Netherlands	4.26
Germany	4.23
Andorra	4.06
Norway	3.87
Netherlands	4.26

The six countries with highest life expectancy for moms (and dads) in 2002 were:

Andorra	83.5
Macau	81.87
San Marino	81.4
Japan	80.9
Singapore	80.4
Australia	80.1

Source: 2003 CIA World Factbook

In 2002 Save the Children Foundation published the Mother's Index comparing the well-being of mothers and children in 105 countries. Top-ranking countries have the best health care, nutrition, and education and lowest rates of infant mortality and deaths from childbirth. The three top-ranked countries were:

1. Switzerland
2. Canada
3. Norway

Puzzled Moms and Kids

Let's see how closely you were reading . . . Can you find seven other celebrated moms and their equally famous offspring from fact and fiction. Happy puzzling!

Across

1 Follows relentlessly
5 Moroccans and Libyans, e.g.
10 Wedding helper
15 Corrida cries
19 Heaps
20 Mt. Everest locale
21 "Lovergirl" singer ___ Marie
22 Ward of "Once and Again"
23 Run without moving
24 Melanie Griffith's mother
26 Vichyssoise veggie
27 This matter is settled
29 Become one
30 NASA concern
32 Just dumb
33 "Maybe" musical
34 Note after fa
35 Enters
37 "Deutschland ___ Alles"
38 Really lets have it
43 High degree
44 Bart, Lisa, and Maggie's mother
48 Hard to find
49 ___ end (finished)
51 Building wings
52 Marine eagle
53 52-Across's grabber
54 Misty who played Marilyn in "Goodbye, Norma Jean"
55 Seed cover
56 "Battle Cry" author Leon
57 Some cigars
58 Victoria's Secret specialty
60 Approximation words
61 Put a new handle on
62 Isabella Rossellini's mother
66 Taiwan capital
70 "Saving Private Ryan" event
71 Find work
76 Charlotte ___, V.I.
77 Become a member of
78 Disk on the ice
79 Poor, as excuses go
80 Copier, briefly
81 French denials
82 Of the hipbone: Prefix
83 Hose hole
84 Exile isle
85 Gwyneth Paltrow's mother
89 Bambi's aunt
90 Arranges again, as food or hair
92 Little dent
93 Comedian-actor-writer Steve
95 Continent north of Afr.
96 Common Bible word for "strike"

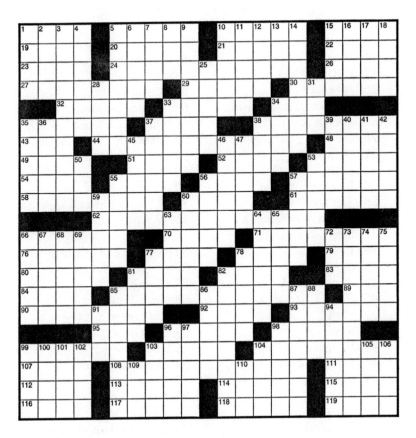

98 Philosopher of dialectics
99 Put under
103 Classic toothpaste
104 They go back on their word
107 "___ bien!"
108 Liza and Lorna's mother
111 Mideast money
112 Is under the weather
113 In flames
114 Davis of "Evening Shade"
115 Toaster waffle
116 Corn or Bible follower
117 Bear and Berra
118 Put one over on
119 Gorilla

Down

1 Oration station
2 Word often seen with "shoppe"
3 Kate Hudson's mother
4 Beer-garden sights
5 Disappearing rooftop fixture
6 Roi's spouse
7 Date with a Dr.
8 Religious sect: Abbr.
9 Goal of many dieters
10 Baby berths?
11 Grassy plant
12 "___ goes nothing!"
13 Chemical suffix

(continued)

14 Former name of Myanmar's capital
15 Capital on a fjord
16 Snidely Whiplash look
17 Part of G.E.
18 Japanese rice wine
25 ___ Bendel (trendy Fifth Avenue store)
28 "Look, ___ dancing!"
31 Winter woe
33 Hersey's "___ for Adano"
34 It's about a foot
35 Tree knot
36 10th-century German king
37 More like Lena the Hyena
38 ID's for the IRS
39 Orient Express, e.g.
40 Actress Hayek
41 Woolf's "___ of One's Own"
42 Keyed up
45 Fit again
46 Liverpool's river
47 Previous arrest, in police lingo
50 Photog's orig.
53 Poll revelation
55 Golfer Palmer, to fans
56 "___ Cowboy": Travolta film
57 Short-sheeting, e.g.
59 Letters for Old MacDonald
60 On the strange side
63 "___ care who knows it!"
64 Craft activity

65 Home of the Georgia State Fair
66 Circus star with a whip
67 What a miss is as good as, proverbially
68 Metrical feet
69 Cheerleader's skirt feature
72 Capp and Capone
73 Jamie Lee Curtis's mother
74 Muscat resident
75 Started
77 Delights
78 Woodworker's tool
81 N.Y. Met, e.g.
82 Longest dog sled race
85 Raucous bird on the feeder
86 City near Minneapolis
87 Corrected
88 Go ballistic
91 Up to now
94 Be sorry about
96 "Heidi" author
97 Wizards of yore
98 Skater Sonja
99 Rough guess
100 Buffalo's lake
101 Farmer's place, in a nursery rhyme
102 Mgr.'s helper
103 Beatnik's "Gotcha!"
104 Wood file
105 Prego competitor
106 Plug away
109 Vehicle for ET?
110 Shaq's alma mater

Answers on page 303.

Calling Dr. Mom

Down through the centuries mothers have been healers too.

Throughout time, mothers have always been called upon to "make it all better," especially when their families are under the weather. If you want to stock up your medicine cabinet with a few old-school remedies, here are a few that Dr. Mom would recommend.

Berries—Since pioneer days, mothers have touted cranberry juice as a way to prevent urinary problems. Turns out cranberries and blueberries contain condensed tannins. These little gems, called proanthocyanidins, prevent the infection-causing *E. coli* bacteria from attaching to cells in the urinary tract. You might say that they keep the bacteria swept off your insides—a bit of cleaning would appeal to a tidy mom.

Cabbage Juice—Imperial Roman mothers knew of an indigestion remedy that is still appreciated today—cabbage juice! The value of cabbage juice was upheld when a group of researchers from Stanford University School of Medicine found that 13 people with ulcers who drank 1 liter (about 1 quart) of raw cabbage juice every day healed six times faster than those who were cabbage teetotalers.

Chicken Soup—So many Jewish mothers used chicken soup as a restorative for a cold that it became known as

Jewish penicillin. According to researchers at the University of Nebraska, the garlic used in the soup has anti-inflammatory powers. In addition, the broth's heat stimulates the flow of mucus and the soup's liquid replaces lost fluids.

Garlic—Garlic was another remedy in a Chinese mother's pharmacy. To cure a bout of bronchitis, mom might make a tea of steeped garlic and honey. Thousands of years later (in 2001 to be exact), a U.S. trial showed that 72 volunteers who took a daily capsule containing allicin, the main active ingredient in garlic, were one third as likely to develop a cold as the 72 who took a placebo. If they did succumb, they recovered more quickly. Put another feather in the cap of Chinese mothers, grandmothers, and their remedies

Ginger—Ancient Ayurvedic remedies that have existed for thousands of years in India are making a popular comeback. But for many families where mothers and grandmother use traditional remedies—the ancient wisdom was never gone in the first place. Ma and grandma would often urge the chewing of ginger after a meal to ease indigestion. Ginger tea and honey were also given for a cough. Modern research has found ginger to have antinausea properties that aid digestion. And it is a powerful antioxidant with strong anti-inflammatory effects.

Green Tea—"Better to be deprived of food for three days, then tea for one," says an ancient Chinese proverb. For over four thousand years, with the simple act of brewing green tea for their families, Chinese mothers could combat everything from headaches to fatigue to tooth decay. But did they know they were pouring a miracle drug into the family tea cups? Scientific research hails green tea for reducing the risk of cancer, arthritis, heart disease, and immune function problems.

Potatoes—Thousands of years ago the ancient Incan civilization in Peru cultivated the potato. Incan mothers used potatoes as a tool for healing. Raw slices might be placed on an aching joint to help it heal. What was likely more useful was the Incan realization that cooked potatoes were a soothing bland food that helped prevent indigestion.

Tree Bark—If a child fell ill in ancient Egypt, chances were that her mom would give her a bit of willow bark to chew on. What for? Turns out that willow bark has many of the same chemicals as our modern day aspirin. Native American moms also knew the value of tree bark. Chewing on a willow twig eased pain and lowered fever, while the gummy bark of the slippery elm tree could treat coughs and sore throats by coating and soothing irritated mucus membranes. Today, there are cough drops that are still made with slippery elm as an ingredient.

Aztec mothers also used cinnamon bark to fight illness. This bark contains oil called cinnamaldehyde that fights nausea and reduces fever. If a virus had the family under the weather, an Aztec mother could make them an atole of masa harina (corn flour) flavored with a cinnamon stick to add both spice and healing power.

They Loved Lucille

The on-screen and off-screen lives of TV's funniest mom.

In January 1953, a record 44 million people turned on their TV sets to watch *I Love Lucy*, America's most popular TV sitcom. On that evening, the main character, ditzy housewife Lucy Ricardo, became a mom; her husband, bandleader Ricky Ricardo, rushed to the hospital to see his newborn son, Ricky, known thereafter as "Little Ricky."

DOUBLE WHAMMY

While that memorable episode was airing for the first time, actress Lucille Ball, who played Lucy Ricardo, and her husband Desi Arnaz, who played Ricky Ricardo, were actually in the hospital admiring their newborn second child, their own son, Desi, Jr. Life and art often blurred on episodes of *I Love Lucy*, but never more so than the day where their real son, Desi, Jr., and their fictional son, Little Ricky, were born.

Lucy's fans were enthralled by the double whammy. Congratulations and good wishes poured in from all over the world. But Lucy's TV life and real life didn't completely mesh. Lucy Ricardo was always an ideal (if wacky) mom, adored by her TV kids, but the real-life Lucille went home to serious challenges that mothers face, the kind that even the best screenwriters can't easily solve.

LUCY, I'M HOME!

Just like her irrepressible TV character, Lucille Ball had the show-biz bug. Coming to Hollywood in 1933 to audition for a bit part, she stayed on and eventually moved up to feature roles in small films. She starred in so many small films that she was known as the "Queen of the Bs."

In 1940, at age 28, the Queen of the Bs met a handsome Cuban bandleader named Desi Arnaz at RKO studios on the set of the movie *Too Many Girls* (foreshadowing, anyone?). There was instant chemistry between the two; he didn't even seem to mind that she was wearing a fake black eye for a scene in her current film. All he could see was Lucille. Within six weeks, the two were married.

Despite their strong attraction, Desi and Lucille weren't a heavenly match. Lucille was driven and hardworking, but remained insecure, a trait only exacerbated by Desi's problems with drinking and womanizing. The couple immediately began a long cycle of wrangling and reconciling. Friends gave the marriage six months.

LUCILLE IS PREGNANT, LUCY IS "EXPECTING"

By 1951 Lucille and Desi had been together for over a decade. Together they created Desilu Studios to produce the TV show *I Love Lucy*. The steady TV work would enable them to settle down on their chicken farm in Chatsworth, California, and get busy raising a family.

Neither Desi nor Lucille bargained on having both projects collide, but when it rains it pours. Less than two months after the birth of their first child, a baby girl named Lucie, filming began on the first season of *I Love*

Lucy. Lucille's antics as the starstruck Lucy Ricardo earned her legions of fans; by the end of the first season, *I Love Lucy* was a hit. But when Lucy found out that she was pregnant for a second time, the CBS execs got prepartum depression. This was the era when TV married couples slept in separate twin beds. Pregnancy meant that the couple had crossed the big divide between those beds. Viewers might be shocked and offended.

In a brilliant move that would make television history, Lucy insisted that her pregnancy become part of the storyline. The nervous TV executives gave in, but they substituted the word "expectant" for "pregnant" in the scripts and even hired a clergyman to ensure the morality of the episodes! Meanwhile, rather than being turned off by Lucy's expanding "expectancy," viewers were tuning in to set a ratings record.

Since Lucy was really pregnant, the show was able to tap into the emotions of parents-to-be. One of the show's most touching episodes is when Lucy is trying to tell Ricky that she is expecting, but she can't get a moment alone with him. Finally, she goes to his nightclub and makes an anonymous request for Ricky to sing *We're Having a Baby* to an expectant father. After searching the room for the dad-to-be, Ricky sees Lucy and realizes that he may be that guy himself. He rushes over to Lucy and the two are overcome with tears. Honest, emotional moments like these made *I Love Lucy* stand above most sitcoms of the 1950s and are part of the reason why the reruns are still enjoyed today.

STRESS OF SUCCESS

Back at the Chatsworth chicken farm, in real life, things weren't going as smoothly. Lucille adored her kids, but her work schedule meant she had to hire maids and nannies to help take care of Desi, Jr., and Lucie. There were plenty of good and loving times for the Arnazes, but the series that was supposed to help Lucille raise her family actually cost her time with her children and may have even hurt her marriage. It didn't help that Desi wasn't the most faithful of husbands and his problems with alcohol weren't improving. As Desilu Studios grew larger, the pressure increased and more money was at stake with every business decision. Lucille and Desi decided to end production of *I Love Lucy* in 1957. They worked together for 2 more years on *The Lucy-Desi Comedy Hour*, which ended in 1960. Sadly, they ended their marriage that same year.

HERE'S LUCY!

As always, the real Lucy was a trouper. In 1968 she starred in another hit TV series, *Here's Lucy*. This show was also a family affair and starred her two real kids as her character's two teenagers. Working with Lucille wasn't always easy, but the two children learned that getting laughs on TV was serious business. Problems with substance abuse forced Desi, Jr.'s early exit from the show. After much hardship, Lucille and her son worked through his problems together. Desi, Jr., not only gave up drugs, he also became a motivational speaker and worked to help other addicts recover.

LOVING LUCILLE

Lucille continued to perform in *Here's Lucy* until 1974. It was her last series except for a few episodes twelve years later in *Life With Lucy*, when the 75-year-old Lucille appeared as a grandmother. As her career wound down, Lucy moved to New York to be closer to her daughter and grandchildren.

Lucille Ball faced tough trials and heartaches that she couldn't always conquer, but like most real-life moms, she struggled to give her kids what she thought they needed. Her life wasn't a rose garden—or a sunny TV sitcom. But as Desi, Jr., later said, "We went through some painful stages but Mom's love was intense and tenacious." Reason enough to love Lucille.

Would You Like Novocaine with That?

While American moms value sparkling white smiles on their kids' faces, other cultures have different ideas about teeth. In Alor, Indonesia, a mom sends adolescents to a have their teeth stained black with a paste made of bark. Their six front upper and lower teeth are also filed down to reduce their height. An Alor Mom considers her teens much more attractive after this procedure is done. But is it cheaper than braces?

TV Moms V: Tough Mamas

In the 21st century, moms are tough!

There have never been TV moms like these. They can run their own lives and sometimes everyone else's too. These series' heroines are the matriarchs of the new millennium.

LOIS WILKERSON: RUNNING THE SHOW

The Show: *Malcolm in the Middle* (2000–present)
A master of psychological warfare, Lois Wilkerson (played by Jane Kaczmarek) stops at little to get her boys to behave. A mother to five boys (six, if you count her husband, Hal), Lois has to be on top of her game at all times in order to keep control of the household. Though Lois seems to be a frustrated major general, in reality she's a working mom trying to "hold on until the last one turns eighteen." Her family eats together in *almost* traditional fashion, although Lois has been known to shave her husband's back at the kitchen table. Nonetheless, she is law, or as her genius son Malcom would say, "the lord high magistrate and executioner, ultimate arbiter and dispenser of justice, inflicter of guilt." No wonder he thinks that the best thing about childhood is that eventually it ends.
Fun Fact: Jane Kaczmarek attended Yale Drama School and was a roommate of Kate Burton, the daughter of Richard Burton.

LIVIA SOPRANO: MURDERING MOTHER?

The Show: *The Sopranos* (1999–present)

Easily the most evil mother ever to appear on TV, Livia Soprano (played by Nancy Marchand) wins hands down. Widowed 70-year-old Livia claimed to be a weak, helpless lady, but underneath lurked a menacing force to be reckoned with. She often boasted that she gave her entire life to her children "on a silver platter," but mostly Livia gave her son, Tony, a series of panic attacks by tying him into emotional knots. Tony, a powerful mobster and a cold-blooded killer, couldn't easily gain the upper hand with his mother.

After Mrs. Soprano accidentally ran down her neighbor with her car and nearly burned her house down while frying some mushrooms, Tony moved her into a palatial retirement home; Livia angrily demanded that he kill her instead. When her guilt trip didn't work, she put a hit out on her son through another mob boss. Though that hit failed, until the moment that Livia died peacefully in her sleep (actress Marchand died of lung cancer), she gave Tony far more trouble than the FBI ever could.

Fun Fact: The series creator, David Chase, loosely based the character of Livia on his own mother.

SHARON OSBOURNE: DAD'S MANAGER

The Show: *The Osbournes* (2002–present)

Harriet and Ozzie started the reality tradition with their series based on their daily life. Today, Sharon Osbourne stars as "the mom" in today's version of the reality series. Married to rocker Ozzy Osbourne, Sharon allowed MTV cameras into her home in Beverly Hills to track the antics of her husband, her two teenagers, and a passel of California's most neurotic pets.

From Harriet to Sharon and Ozzie to Ozzy, TV moms have changed. For one thing, there's much more colorful language from Sharon. For another, Sharon is more than just a partner to her husband, she's also his manager. She's also the pillar of her family, making many of the decisions; the one the kids rely on if they get into trouble; and the one Ozzy turns to for just about everything. As always, Sharon shows that a good mom means good TV.

Fun Fact: Some say Sharon stole Ozzy away from her father, in a professional sense. Sharon's father, Don Arden, had been Ozzy's manager until Sharon, in a savvy business decision, "took over" for him.

"Women know
The way to rear up children (to be just)
They know a simple, merry, tender knack
Of tying sashes, fitting baby-shoes
And stringing pretty words that make no sense,
And kissing full sense into empty words."
—Elizabeth Barrett Browning, from *Aurora Leigh*

Uncle John's Stage Mother Awards

It's time for stage moms to stop hiding behind their talented kids and come out for awards of their own.

You've seen the Tonys, the Oscars, and the Golden Globes. But does the talent behind the talent ever get recognition? Of course we mean those pushy ladies who shoved their kids onto the stage and screen. It's time they got the recognition they deserve.

GERTRUDE TEMPLE: FOR PRENATAL EXCELLENCE

Gertrude Temple was managing Shirley Temple before the little tyke was even born. Believing in the abilities of thought to shape destiny, the pregnant Gertie set her mind to delivering a baby girl named Shirley Jane. Gertie then got busy with prenatal education. She went to museums, listened to classical music, viewed great architecture, and went dancing—all for the edification of her unborn Shirley. In 1928, when Shirley Temple finally did see the light of day, Gertrude continued to nurture her infant's musical abilities. Mom played the radio for her baby and danced her around the house.

It's hard to argue with success. Shirley Temple was a movie star by the time she was four. Shirley's singing and dancing and bouncing curls were so popular that she saved her movie studio from bankruptcy. She even won one of those golden statuettes—a special Oscar in 1934 "in grateful recognition to her outstanding contribution to screen entertainment."

ROSE HOVICK: OUTSTANDING ACHIEVEMENT IN VICARIOUS LIVING

What kind of mother would push her daughter into a career as a burlesque stripper? Rose Hovick, that's who. In her own words, Rose was "a woman alone in the world with two babies to support." In 1918, when daughter Louise was four years old, Mama Rose put her up on the vaudeville stage with her younger sister, June, who was the star of their act, "Dainty June and Her Newsboy Songsters." To ensure success, Rose would even sabotage competing acts, filching their sheet music or costumes.

When June was 13, she eloped with one of her Newsboys, leaving Louise the center of attention. Rose began to realize that vaudeville's days were numbered. Refusing to give up on vicarious stardom, she put 15-year-old Louise on the burlesque stage. Louise didn't reveal what she was supposed to, but her shyness and her teasing had appeal. With Rose's nudging, Louise became Gypsy Rose Lee, the most famous stripper of her day. Rose was delighted—after all, it was top billing.

In 1957, the stripper wrote *Gypsy*, a memoir about life with her overbearing stage mother. Adapted from the book, the hit Broadway musical immortalized Rose forever. The show may be called *Gypsy*, but it's all about Mama Rose.

ETHEL GUMM: BEST PHARMACEUTICAL EFFECTS

Ethel Gumm, a former vaudeville performer, realized that she'd never be a great success. Transferring her ambition to her daughters, she put them on the vaudeville stage as the

Gumm Sisters. The youngest girl, Frances "Baby" Gumm, was only two years old when mom started her in show busines. Frances was the most talented of the trio, and even as a toddler, she had a surprisingly full, expressive voice that could stop the show.

There were times when Frances wished she could stop the show, but Ethel knew that her daughter was special, and she was relentless about keeping her onstage. Mama moved the family to California, where she dragged her talented tyke—who by then had changed her name from Frances Gumm to Judy Garland—to every studio audition she could find.

Finally in 1935, at 13 years old, Judy was signed by MGM and launched on a path to stardom. Along the way she was also launched on a darker path to addiction. Studio head Louis B. Mayer wanted Judy thinner, and Ethel gave diet pills and sedatives to Judy to help keep her thin.

Judy won an Oscar for Best Juvenile Performance in *The Wizard of Oz*. For her efforts, Mama Gumm receives this award and a permanent place in the Hall of Shame.

SARAH BERLINGER:
BEST MAMA IN A SUPPORTING ROLE

Sarah Berlinger was determined that her son was going to be a star. Whenever he performed, she sat in the audience, watching and ready to criticize if one of his rapid-fire jokes fell flat. At a very early age, Sarah made little Mendel Berlinger a child model. (He later changed his name to Milton Berle.) By age 15, Milton had already appeared in silent films with stars like Charlie Chaplin and Douglas Fairbanks and sung in Broadway musical reviews. Sarah put him on the vaudeville circuit and began her career of monitoring every single one of her boy's performances, even if he did ten a day.

In 1948, funnyman Milton Berle became the first big star of television. Uncle Miltie's shows featuring cross-dressing antics and stand-up comedy routines earned him the title Mr. Television. He performed until the doctors made him stop at the age of 90.

Sometimes other comedians accused Milton of stealing material, but Sarah proudly defended her boy. "He wouldn't stoop so low!" she declared. "He stoops high!" It wasn't always easy being the mother of a comedian who was once called the "Thief of Badgags," but she supported him all the way.

The Last Words

"Mother's love is peace. It need not be acquired, it need not be deserved." —Erich Fromm

"Life began with waking up and loving my mother's face." —George Eliot

"The mother's heart is the child's schoolroom." —Henry Ward Beecher

"My mother was the making of me." —Thomas Alva Edison

Answer Pages

LIT 101: THE PLAY'S THE THING

Answers for pages 34–35.

1. E (Both A & D)

Medea kills everyone and escapes on her chariot drawn by dragons. Jason is left alone and robbed of all ambition since his former wife has taken everything from him.

2. C

The shepherd takes the child, Oedipus, away, but instead of killing him, arranges for him to be raised in far-away Corinth. When Oedipus grows up, he travels to Thebes, mistakenly kills the king, and marries Jocasta. When they realize what they have done, Jocasta hangs herself and Oedipus takes the pins from her robe and uses them to poke out his eyes.

3. B

Gertrude seeks out advice from elderly windbag Polonius, a court advisor and father to Hamlet's girlfriend, Ophelia. Polonius first suggests that Hamlet's madness is caused by his love for Ophelia. After Hamlet tells Ophelia to get lost, that theory is quickly ruled out. Next, Polonius from behind a tapestry offers to eavesdrop on Hamlet and his mom while they discuss the prince's weird behavior. Hearing a rustle, Hamlet stabs Polonius through the curtain because he suspects it is his murderous uncle cowering behind there. Gertrude herself doesn't escape the play alive either. She drinks a cup of wine, poisoned by Claudius, who had intended it for Hamlet.

4. E (All of the above)

In this play, which T. S. Eliot called "the worst play written in the English language," all of the bloody doings above (and more) actually take place. Ultimately, Titus Andronicus hosts a feast at which Tamora is served her sons baked in a pie. For dessert, all the main participants kill one another.

LIT 101: A NOVEL APPROACH

Answers for pages 128–129.

1. E (Both B & C)
Anna runs off with Vronsky and they soon tire of each other. She has a daughter by him, then neglects her. In the end, she commits suicide by jumping in front of a train. Ironically, Karenin ends up raising her daughter.

2. E (Both A & D)
Moll returns to England where she has a number of escapades. She marries Jemy, a former highwayman, who turns out to be her favorite husband of all. Alas, the couple soon runs out of money, and he leaves her to return to his previous life as a thief. Impoverished and alone, Moll herself turns into a common thief and prostitute. Eventually, she is caught and imprisoned. She (falsely) pleads her belly and has her sentence reduced. Luckily for her, Jemy has also been imprisoned. The two reunite in jail and are eventually sent together to the United States.

3. C
Hester raises her daughter, Pearl, in a cottage bordering the woods. Pearl turns into quite a rebellious handful as she grows, but Hester never loses her dignity. She uses her sewing skills to earn money and do good works. She never betrays Pearl's father, who we learn is the town's minister.

4. B
Eliza flees with Harry. With Harry in her arms, she bravely crosses the Ohio River by jumping from one ice floe to another. With the help of the people of the Underground Railroad and a settlement of Quakers, she reaches Canada and is reunited

with her husband, mother, and sister-in-law. Eventually she and her family travel to Liberia to found a colony for ex-slaves.

SPOT THE MOM!

Answers for pages 232–234.

1. Indira had two sons. Her eldest son, Rajiv Gandhi (1944–1991), succeeded her as prime minister. The younger son, Sanjay (1946–1980), died in an air crash.
2. Margaret Thatcher was tough enough to raise twins—a boy and a girl.
3. Wilma Mankiller brought her two daughters with her when she moved back to Oklahoma. She also has a stepson by her second marriage.
4. Condoleezza Rice has no children.

MORE SPOT THE MOMS!

Answers for pages 250–252.

1. Beryl had a son who grew up with his father and rarely saw mom.
2. Jackie never had children.
3. Valentina's daughter Elena became a doctor. She was the first child to have had both parents who had been in space.
4. Dr. Ride has no children.

SPOT THOSE MOMS, AGAIN!

Answers from pages 272–274.

1. Frank and Annie had no children.
2. Jane Addams never married or had children.
3. Sandra Day O'Connor has three sons.
4. Whitman has two sons and the family has traded books, Beanie Babies, and Pokemon cards on eBay.

MAMA, YOU PUZZLE ME

C	A	P	P		O	H	A	R	A		E	L	S	A
O	T	R	O		R	E	G	A	L		N	O	R	M
S	P	E	E		E	R	U	P	T		T	O	T	E
M	A	Y	T	A	G	R	E	P	A	I	R	M	A	N
O	R	S	I	N	O		E	R	S	E				
		C	O	N	D	O	R		I	N	S	T	S
O	R	I		M	A	S		J	A	C	K	A	L
M	A	D	A	S	A	M	A	R	C	H	H	A	R	E
O	P	E	N	U	P		K	O	D			T	E	D
O	T	O	E	S		T	A	K	I	N	G			
		C	H	A	I		T	E	A	S	E	S
M	A	I	D	I	N	M	A	N	H	A	T	T	A	N
E	N	D	O		T	E	H	E	E		H	E	M	O
R	I	O	T		E	L	M	E	R		E	V	E	R
E	L	S	E		D	Y	E	R	S		R	E	S	T

Answers for page 53.

PUZZLED MOMS AND KIDS

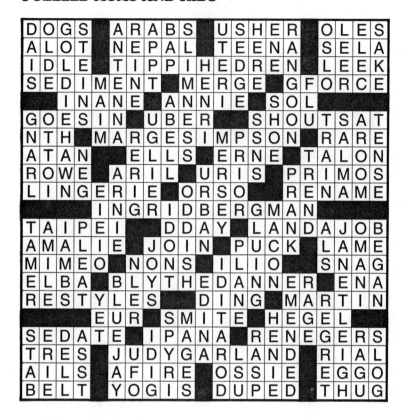

Answers for page 281.

The Last Page

Here at Portable Press, we feel that it is your right to always have the very best. So we've got a ton of books to inform, educate, and entertain you—all reading of the highest quality that can be proudly displayed in any room in the house!

Uncle John's new Readers are already in the works! Keep your eyes out for:

Big John #17—the original, now in its 17th year! (Nov 04)
Uncle John's Plunges into Texas (May 04)
Uncle John's Plunges into the Presidency (July 04)
Uncle John's Plunges into Michigan (Sept. 04)
Uncle John's Plunges into History Again! (Sept. 04)
Uncle John's Colossal Book of Quotes (Oct. 04)
Uncle John's Top Secret for Kids Only (May 04)
Uncle John's Book of Fun for Kids Only (Aug. 04)

Want more information on what's new with Uncle John? Then join the Bathroom Readers' Institute! Just send a self-addressed, stamped envelope to: Bathroom Readers' Institute, P.O. Box 1117, Ashland, Oregon 97520. Or just visit our website: **www.bathroomreader.com**. You'll receive an attractive membership card *and* issues of the BRI email newsletter, filled with useful information on special offers on our books and other merchandise.

As always, we thank you for your support and look forward to your thoughts and comments. Enjoy!